THE
COMPLETE BOOK OF
BATHROOMS

No. 2708
$24.95

THE
COMPLETE BOOK OF
BATHROOMS

JUDY AND DAN RAMSEY AND CHARLES R. SELF

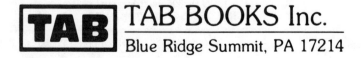

TAB BOOKS Inc.

Blue Ridge Summit, PA 17214

FIRST EDITION

SECOND PRINTING

Printed in the United States of America

Reproduction or publication of the content in any manner, without express
permission of the publisher, is prohibited. No liability is assumed with respect to
the use of the information herein.

Library of Congress Cataloging in Publication Data

Ramsey, Judy.
The complete book of bathrooms.

Includes index.
1. Bathrooms—Remodeling—Amateur's manuals.
2. Plumbing—Amateur's manuals. I. Ramsey, Dan,
   1945-   . II. Self, Charles R.   III. Title.
   TH6485.R36 1986   643'.52   86-3811
            ISBN 0-8306-0408-1
            ISBN 0-8306-2708-1 (pbk.)

Cover photographs courtesy of KOHLER COMPANY, Kohler, Wisconsin 53044.

Contents

Acknowledgments

THE FOLLOWING MUST BE ACKNOWLEDGED for their assistance in the production of this book:

Richard Day; Petersen Manufacturing Company, Inc.; Black & Decker Consumer Power Tools Division; Vaco Products Company; American Standard; Porter-Cable Corporation; Hyde Manufacturing Company; Resources Conservation, Inc.; Kohler Co.; The Tile Council of America; Nicholson; Thomas Strahan Co., Style-Tex; Benchmark; The Stanley Works; Scovill; U.S. Plumbing Products; Plumb; ThermaSol, Ltd.; Environmental Purification Systems, Inc.; Crescent; Sears, Roebuck, and Co.; NuTone; Italian Tile Center; Lufkin; Montgomery Ward; Delta Faucet Company; Masonite Corporation; Genova, Inc.; Paris-Wall; Celotex; and the Cooper Group.

A special thanks goes to these invaluable resources and the individuals who worked hard to make this book *complete*.

Introduction

THE BATHROOM HAS COME OF AGE. EARLY American homes were built with no plumbing and no indoor bathroom. Over the 200-year history of the United States, bathrooms have evolved to the point of being called a necessity. Few people have to follow the path out back to the outhouse. Nearly all homes are built with at least one bathroom.

Many homes contain two, three, or even more baths. While some baths are small and contain little beyond the basic fixtures, others are large and luxurious. Bathrooms now house saunas, whirlpool baths, and steam baths. They are stylishly decorated as an integral part of the home. The variety of bathroom fixtures available makes it possible to furnish a bathroom to your own taste.

Bathtubs are now round, square, sunken, or raised in addition to the traditional shape. They come in decorator colors matched to other fixtures to complement any color scheme. They come with or without showers and some have built-in whirlpool jets. And there are tubs designed to be installed outdoors. They can be located in their own setting or installed outside an existing bathroom, making a garden bath. Other bathroom fixtures come in just as many choices. You can mix or match colors and styles to create the look you want.

Bathrooms have been around in one form or another for many centuries, probably as long as people have inhabited any structure with a roof. The flush toilet has served humanity for quite some time, but effective flushing systems for our present in-home devices didn't come into wide use until the 1930s.

When Greek culture was dominant, bathing habits tended to be Spartan, with scrapers used to get rid of excessive moisture. Some years later the Romans turned to more luxurious bathing practices. Only a few of the very richest Romans had private baths, with most of the populace using the public baths. These public baths were usually heated by fires under the terra-cotta floors, and a few were built over natural hot springs. Roman baths often turned into what we would call a luxury spa, containing a game room or a library.

By the Middle Ages, the idea of frequent bathing had gone into eclipse and sanitation was nearly unknown. Turkish baths spread through the Christian countries but many had poor reputations. Only relatively recently has frequent bathing become popular again.

With the improvements over the ages, the modern bathroom is still often one of the most poorly designed rooms in a house. Many modern bathrooms are little more than utilitarian, even though adding a luxurious touch would not cost much more. Often a bathroom design reflects only an attempt to get as close as possible to the central plumbing. The problem is most evident in some older homes where the bathroom was added later, and the desire was to take up as little room as possible and to do the job inexpensively and quickly.

Beautiful yet functional bathrooms are possible. We might have to use water-saving appliances, but they can be installed in comfortable, well-lighted layouts.

The purpose of this book is to assist you in planning your bathroom project and in executing that plan. This book will help you to decide what needs to be done in your bathroom and to plan a design for the room. You will have to consider family needs as well as available space for a bathroom. Sample floor plans will be presented as well as guidelines for creating your own plan. This is all followed by a checklist to make sure nothing essential is being left out of the plan.

The tools that you will need for a bathroom remodeling or building project are fully discussed from the hammer to the pipe threader. Some are probably already in your tool box, but some are specialty tools that you may need to rent or purchase. Each tool is described and its uses listed. You will need some or all of the tools depending on your project. These subjects are covered in Chapter 2.

In order to plan and work on your bathroom plumbing, you will need to understand the home plumbing system, which consists of the water supply, drain-waste-vent, and septic systems. Each of these systems is described and illustrated in Chapter 3.

Once you have planned your new bathroom, you must organize your work so that the family routine is interrupted as little as possible. Chapter 4 contains some guidelines. It also tells how to remove old fixtures from a bathroom that is being prepared for new. Some principles of home construction, including simple framing, are included. In most areas of the country, local codes govern the requirements for residential plumbing. As a do-it-yourselfer on your bathroom project, you need to be familiar with plumbing codes. In some areas of the United States you can do nearly all the work yourself while in other areas certain parts of the job must be done by qualified plumbers and electricians.

Over the past few decades a number of materials have been used for plumbing pipe. The advantages and disadvantages of copper, cast iron, brass, and PVC pipe are discussed. The concentration is on PCV pipe as it is the most economical and easiest to install. Steps to installing pipe are described and illustrated in Chapter 5.

If the bathroom is being entirely remodeled it's likely that some wiring must be done to move lights, install a fan, or simply to upgrade the system. Chapter 6 discusses wiring for the bathroom, including lighting, heating, and ventilating the room.

Floors, walls, and ceilings must have attractive coverings, and Chapter 7 tells you how to install tile, linoleum, and carpeting. It also discusses plaster repair and has some hints on painting and wallpapering as well as window coverings.

For your new bathroom to be complete, you will need to install your new fixtures. Installation of tubs, sinks, showers, and toilets is presented in Chapter 8.

Once those basics are attended to, the last two chapters of the book offer some suggestions for decorating and keeping your bathroom in top shape. Simple bathroom repairs made promptly can prevent floor or wall damage. The steps for making many simple repairs are included in Chapter 10.

Whether you decide to redecorate, remodel, or add a new bathroom, you can do all, or nearly all, of the work yourself and save considerable expense as well as enjoying the satisfaction of creation. It is toward this independence that this book is written.

Chapter 1

Planning

Your Bathroom

NEW FAUCETS AND PAINT MIGHT BE ALL that is needed to make your bathroom bright, cheery, and functional for many more years. Or tearing everything from fixtures to walls to floors out and starting over might be necessary to achieve the look you want while fulfilling your needs. Or with your growing family you might be ready to add a second or even a third bathroom to your home (Figs. 1-1 and 1-2).

Redecorate, remodel, or add a bathroom?

Redecorating is the least expensive, easiest, and quickest way to make changes in your bathroom. Painting, wallpapering, changing faucets, adding towel racks, plants and clothes hampers can be done in just a few hours and give your bathroom a whole new look.

Remodeling will take longer and require a larger investment, but it is the only way to gain more room or change the function of your bathroom. Remodeling can be as simple as redecorating plus replacing old fixtures. Or it can be as complex as replacing all fixtures, adding new elements such as a jacuzzi or hot tub, and moving walls

(Fig. 1-3). It can take a few days or a few weeks. The cost will be determined by not only the extent of the remodeling, but by the quality of new materials being used.

The last option, adding an entirely new bathroom, is probably the most expensive and time consuming alternative. The task will be simplified if there is an existing room that can be converted to a bathroom, but you will still probably have to install new plumbing lines. If you have a room with some extra space, it could be divided into a bathroom by erecting interior walls. If your home offers no conversion possibilities, you will need to consider building an addition on to your home. The addition can be small and exclusively for the bathroom or it can be larger and include other rooms you might need, such as additional bedrooms or a new family room.

If you plan to add a bathroom to your home you need to carefully consider its location. It should be located where it is easily accessible to the people who will most often use the room. If you have a single bathroom upstairs you could find it handy to add

Fig. 1-1. A second bath can set new moods.

a bath or half bath downstairs for daytime use. If the family is growing you might wish to add a bath to the master bedroom for the exclusive use of mom and dad. If the new bathroom is for family use, it is best if it opens from a hall rather than from another room so that anyone can enter the bathroom without disturbing people in the other rooms. Also consider the visibility of the bathroom. Bathroom fixtures should not be visible from the living room when the door is open.

The location of existing water pipes plays an important part in determining the location of a new bathroom. Both manpower and money will be saved if the new bathroom can be installed either directly above already installed plumbing or on the back side of current plumbing, such as back-to-back with the kitchen or a bathroom.

The amount of space available and the amount of space needed for an efficient bathroom will help to determine the location and functions of a new bathroom. A full bathroom less than 64 square feet, or 8 feet on a wall, will be crowded, though a room no larger than about 5 feet × 7 feet can serve as a full bath, allowing a 60-inch tub, 20-inch wide basin, and a standard toilet. It's a tight squeeze but it can be done. With today's special baths and corner baths added to varied shapes and styles of basins and toilets, the small bathroom design isn't the problem it once was. It's nice, however, to step out of the tub or shower and not bang an elbow on a wall, towel rack, or mirror. Making sure there's at least an 8-×-8 room allows space for the addition

Fig. 1-2. Second bathrooms can use extra space behind a garage (Courtesy of Kohler Co.).

of special items and could be worked easily to provide room for two sinks.

A half bath, toilet, and sink can be fit into as little as 4 feet square. Fixtures must be placed carefully to ensure clearances. Building codes in most areas specify clearance requirements.

Your bathroom layout could be greatly influenced by the position of an existing soil stack. If that is the case, the toilet must be positioned first because it has to be near the stack. Face the toilet away from the door if possible, against a wall, and separate the toilet from the rest of the room with a partition.

Because a bathtub needs extra bracing to hold its weight, it is best positioned along a wall or in a corner with the foot of the tub against a wall that can be opened from the opposite side in order to make repairs.

Place the sink with care because it is the most frequently used fixture in the room. Leave plenty of space for towel racks and storage. Natural light from a nearby window aids in shaving or applying makeup.

Adequate storage and counter space seems to be a problem in every bathroom, whether new or old, large or small. To use space most efficiently, try some of the following suggestions: Install a vanity with counter and cabinet space (Fig. 1-4) in place of a pedestal or wall-mounted sink. Reverse the door so that it opens outward rather than into the bathroom, wasting valuable space. Construct shelves in the spaces between studs in the bathroom walls.

If room size is no problem, let your imagina-

Fig. 1-3. Moving walls for a new bathroom (Courtesy of American Standard Inc.).

tion go and plan the bathroom of your dreams. Bathrooms can include hot tubs, saunas, steam baths, suntanning benches, exercise equipment and most anything else the homeowner wishes.

FAMILY NEEDS

Each family is unique and has slightly different needs and wants in a bathroom. A person living alone in a small home might require only a basic bathroom in a small space. Or he or she might choose to reflect his/her personality in the design and decoration of a bathroom.

Families with small children have different needs from families with teenagers. And families with one or two children have different needs from families with six or seven children. Consider the fol-

lowing questions when planning and designing your bathroom.

- Who will be using the bathroom most? Adults? Children? Guests?
- What section of the home will the bathroom be serving?
- Is this a family bathroom or will it be located in the master suite?
- How much space is available for the bathroom?
- What do family members consider necessities in a bathroom?
- What extras do family members want in the bathroom?
- What is your budget for the project?

4

Fig. 1-4. Extra bathroom cabinets can be installed in an adjacent closet or room (Courtesy of Yorktowne Cabinets).

If there are elderly or handicapped members of your household you will have extra considerations in your planning. Non-skid shower and tub mats are available as well as sturdy rails for pulling oneself up from the tub (Fig. 1-5). Special fixtures and extra clearance space might be appreciated by someone in a wheelchair.

Infants and small children also need special consideration. An area for changing diapers and dressing a baby is handy in a bathroom. Extra storage space might be required for baby supplies. Small children need lower racks and step stools to reach some fixtures.

Large families have special needs. If there will be several people getting ready for work or school in the morning you will want to consider the convenience of additional fixtures—an extra sink or toi-

let and a stall shower in addition to the bathtub.

BATHROOM STYLES

Although bathroom styles can be as individual as you wish, there are a few basic bathroom styles that will fit most needs and dreams. Your bathroom plan can be identical to one of the basic styles, a combination of the best features of several styles, or a unique arrangement and setting. The illustrations in this chapter and throughout the book are intended to give you ideas that will lead to your individualized bathroom style.

The Family Bathroom. Bathrooms are usually found between two bedrooms and across from any additional bedrooms. It can have two doors, one leading into a bedroom and the other opening into the hallway. When two doors are used

Fig. 1-5. Angled grab bar for tub and shower.

Special compartments can also be used for other facilities such as a hot tub, sauna, exercise area, or even a photography darkroom.

A compartmented bathroom offers many possibilities but it also needs special consideration in heating, lighting and ventilating. Each compartmented area must have its own light and ventilation and might even need its own heat source.

Twin Sink Bathrooms. These bathrooms have all the features of a regular bathroom with the addition of an extra sink. In busy families, an extra sink can dramatically improve the morning bathroom rush hour.

Children's Baths. A children's bathroom should be located near their bedrooms. All surfaces should be easy to clean and resistant to water damage. Standard size fixtures can be used, with the addition of stools or steps to make access easy. Single control water faucets are easier for youngsters to mix water to the correct temperature.

Showers can include two shower heads, one at normal height which can be plugged until the children are tall enough to need it, and one at a lower height that the children can use while small and which can be plugged as they grow.

The Half Bath. This could be the answer when space is limited or only a toilet and basin are necessary in a particular area of the home. The half bath does not incorporate a tub or shower.

Half baths are convenient for homes with basement level family rooms. They can could also be useful if a bathroom is required on an upper floor with limited space. A half bath can be installed in a large closet.

The Garden Bathroom. This bathroom opens to a private garden or patio and gives the illusion of bathing outdoors. Privacy can be achieved through plants, screens, or fence. Some garden baths provide outdoor sunbathing areas and some include an outdoor shower on the outside wall of the bathroom. Most house plants grow well in the humid atmosphere of a garden bath.

Special Baths. These baths can make life easier for the elderly or the handicapped. Many elderly can maintain self sufficiency with a little extra planning. Durable, easy to clean materials

it is called a continental bath. This bath is meant for use by the entire family. It should measure at least 5- x -8 feet so that standard fixtures can be used.

The Compartmented Bath. This separates the tub, sink, and toilet areas by dividing the room with screens, dividers, or solid walls. The compartmented bath ensures privacy even when the bathroom is being used by more than one person at a time.

The compartmented bath can be divided in many ways. One popular method is to place a tub and toilet area at the back of the room, with a sink near the door. Installing two sinks in a compartmented bath can add to the usefulness of the room. If the bath is located between two bedrooms, the bathtub and toilet could be placed in the center in a separate compartment with a sink compartment on either side to serve each bedroom.

The compartmented bathroom also works well when the washer and dryer must be in the room.

should be used to eliminate the need for periodic replacement and heavy scrubbing. Ceramic tile, plastic-coated hardboard, and plastic laminates are effective and attractive.

Be sure that the doorway in a bath for the elderly or handicapped is wide enough for a wheelchair. Knobs and switches should be about 36 inches high to avoid the need for stooping, and flooring material should be nonskid. A seat in the tub or shower, as well as grab bars, add to safety. Grab bars should also be available for rising from the toilet seat. Single control shower, tub, and sink faucets will eliminate scalding accidents.

In addition, consider the individual limitations of any elderly or handicapped person who will be using the bathroom. The variety of fixtures and accessories for sale makes a convenient bath possible for most anyone.

There are three basic plumbing patterns that are commonly used and that serve most bathrooms well. The first, and simplest—designed for a limited space—arranges all of the fixtures in a row along one wall so that all of the plumbing is in that wall. This requires the least amount of cutting into the house and also uses the least fittings.

The second arrangement has plumbing on two adjoining walls. This requires more cutting into the structure for placement of pipes on two walls. However, it provides more moving space around the fixtures and additional storage.

The last plan, and the one with the most versatility, calls for plumbing in three walls. The room must be larger and fixtures will be separated further. The difficulty is that venting can become a problem. Local codes sometimes require that each fixture have a separate vent. Be sure to check codes in your area before settling on any bathroom design.

FEATURES OF A GOOD BATHROOM

The bathroom is different from any other room in the house so it has different requirements for making it an efficient, attractive room.

The first unusual necessity in a bathroom is that all surfaces be resistant to moisture. Many splashes occur in bathrooms and moisture condenses from showers and baths. Even bathroom ceilings must be able to withstand moisture damage.

A good bathroom must also have adequate heat, light, and ventilation. Bathroom heat should be separate from central house heating so that it can be used individually. Good light is necessary for applying makeup, shaving, and reading in the bathtub. Ventilation is needed to remove excess moisture as well as odors from the room.

Space to move around makes a good bathroom. The amount of space required must be determined on an individual family basis. A good bathroom offers plenty of storage space for towels, medicines, shaving equipment, and all the other items normally used in the bathroom.

Finally, the bathroom should meet all of the needs of each family member. A good bathroom will meet them all. Certainly compromises might have to be made if one member of the family wants a whirlpool bath, another wants a hot tub, another wants exercise equipment, and yet another thinks a sauna is necessary. But with some family give and take, you will be able to come up with a bathroom plan that has something for everyone in addition to meeting the traditional bathroom functions.

MAKE YOUR OWN FLOOR PLAN

Figures 1-6 through 1-13 present plans for a variety of practical bathrooms.

Once you have thoroughly surveyed your family needs, determined the square footage of your current or proposed bathroom site, and studied the bathroom floor plans in this book and elsewhere, it is time to make your own special floor plan. One good way for the amateur planner to design a bathroom is with a scale drawing of the bathroom parameters and cutouts of the fixtures you wish to install in the room, including cabinets and other furniture.

Another way is to make cut-outs of paper exactly the size of the fixtures you plan to use. Then arrange the cut-outs on the floor of the room you will use for a bathroom, or mark out the exact room dimensions and arrange the fixtures there.

Leave enough space between fixtures to move around them and to clean them easily. Allow at least

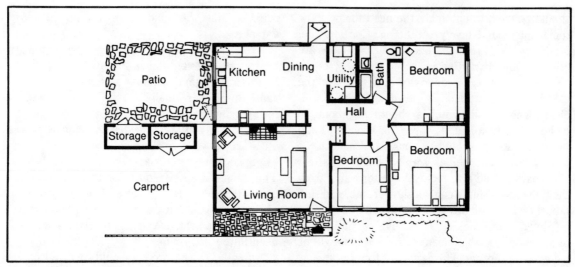

Fig. 1-6. Placing a single bath in a one-story house.

1 1/2 feet between the front of the toilet and 2 feet between the front of any fixture and the wall across from it. At the side of the fixtures allow at least 2 inches between the toilet tank and the sink, 3 inches between the toilet tank and the tub, 4 inches between the toilet tank and the wall at the side of it, and 6 inches between the sink and the wall. A minimum floor area for a person cleaning the tub is 30 inches along the side of the tub by 20 inches out from the tub.

Allow more than the minimum of space if you can. Be sure to plan space for cabinets, towel rods, and other necessities. Rearrange the cut-outs of the fixtures until you have them the way you think is best. Remember to work around any restrictions, such as an existing soil stack for the toilet and water lines that you do not wish to move.

CHECK YOUR PLANS

Have you planned your bathroom so that:

■ There is at least the suggested minimum space between fixtures and in front of them?

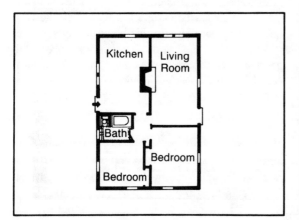

Fig. 1-7. Good location for a bathroom in a one-story house.

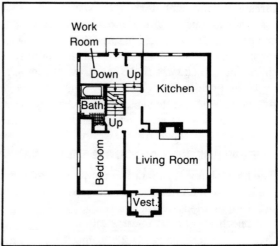

Fig. 1-8. Well-located first-floor bathroom in a two-story house.

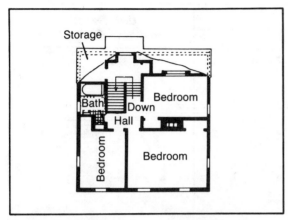

Fig. 1-9. A good location for an upstairs bathroom.

■ The fixtures will not keep the door from opening full width?

■ There is enough towel rod space for your family needs?

■ There is storage space for all supplies you want to keep in the bathroom (Figs. 1-14 and 1-15)?

Have you planned for safety in your bathroom in that:

■ The floors do not get slippery when wet?

■ The bathtub has a flat bottom?

■ There are grab bars at the tub and shower?

■ There is a mixer faucet combining hot and cold water at the sink and a mixer valve at the shower?

■ The heater is shielded and placed so there is no danger of fire or burns?

■ An electric heater is properly grounded?

■ The medicine cabinet is out of children's reach and can be locked?

Have you provided for light, air, and heat so that:

■ The room can be heated quickly?

■ There is a window or a ventilator in the room?

■ Light shines on the face of the person using the mirror?

Once you have worked your bathroom plan to fit your needs and wants, you are ready to think about decorating the room. Revisions in your plans might be necessary as you learn about plumbing codes for your area, think of new ideas, and discover idiosyncrasies in your house.

CHOOSING COLORS

Colors for modern bathrooms are practically un-

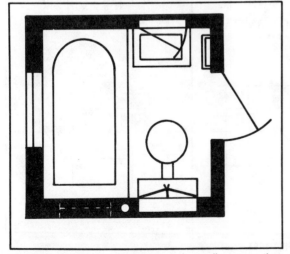

Fig. 1-10. A bathroom 5 feet square is smallest room that will take an average size tub.

Fig. 1-11 This bathroom, 5 × 7 feet, has space for door to open into room.

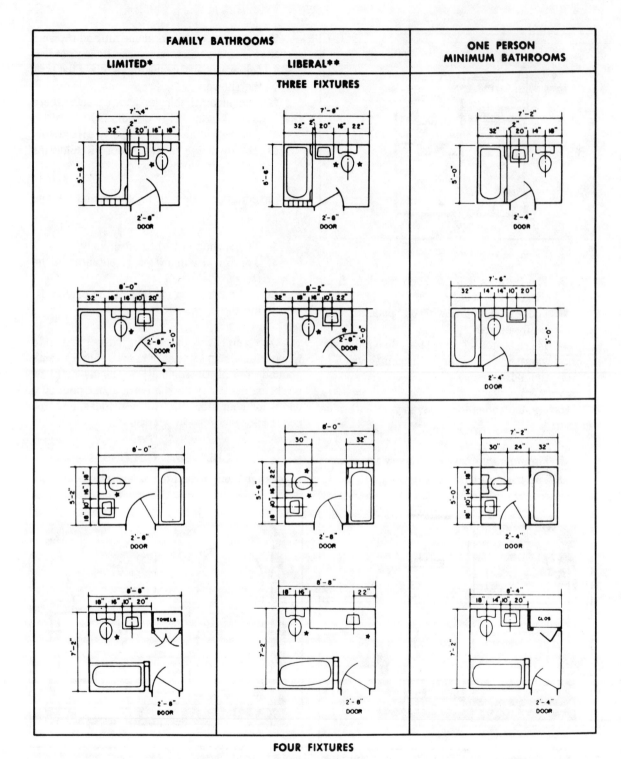

Fig. 1-12. Minimum and liberal bath sizes.

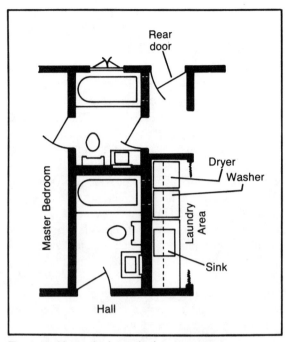

Fig. 1-13. Master bedroom bath arrangement.

limited. Your own taste is the most important consideration in choosing a color scheme. It is generally best to choose your fixture colors and build the rest of the room around them. Bright and bold colors are available, as are pastels and traditional white. You will probably want to have all of the fixtures in the same color. If it is important that your fixtures be exactly the same shade, consider purchasing all of them from the same manufacturer.

Color makes a statement about the personality of the individual or family that uses the room. Colors can be used to change the apparent configuration of the room. They can be warm and inviting or cool and sophisticated.

Because countertops, walls, and floors will be a part of the room for a long time, choose their colors carefully. Items such as towels or shower

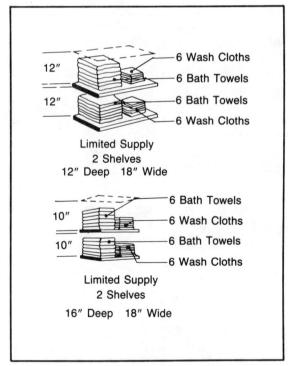

Fig. 1-14. Suggested shelf storage for limited supply of bath linens.

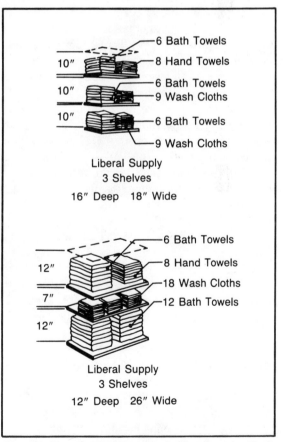

Fig. 1-15. Suggested shelf storage for liberal supply of bath linens.

curtains can alter the appearance of the room but are easily changed, so rely on them for appearance changes between major remodelings.

A color wheel is a useful tool when choosing any color scheme. You can purchase one at an art supply store or an art school. The color wheel will help you to learn which colors will successfully go together. Following are some attractive color combinations.

Complementary Colors. These colors appear opposite each other on the color wheel, such as red and green or blue and orange. If you choose a complementary color scheme use one color at full strength to dominate and a muted selection of the opposite color for accent.

Monochromatic Color Scheme. Such a scheme uses varying shades and intensities of one color. Fixtures can be in one shade of green, while countertops and shower curtains are another, with walls and floors yet another selection of green.

Analogous Colors. These colors are adjacent to each othr on the color wheel, such as violet, red-violet, and blue-violet. They usually result in bright and bold bathrooms.

Triads. Triads are made up of three colors that are equidistant from each other on the color wheel. The primary colors of red, blue, and yellow form a triad. These can also result in bright rooms.

Keep searching and trying different combinations of colors until you find the one that suits your personality as well as the room for which it is intended. Keep in mind that you will probably have to live with the finished product for several years, with color variations being provided only by the accessories. To be sure that the colors you like will look the same once they are placed in your bathroom, examine them under light that is similar to your bathroom, and on materials like those you will use in your bathroom.

Also remember that you will be seeing the room for many years, and choose patterns carefully. Consider limiting the use of patterns in the more permanent aspects of the bathroom and adding them in your accessories. When deciding on the color of the bathroom, check the amount of light, both natural and artificial, in the room. A dark ceiling cuts down on the amount of light in a room. A white ceiling will reflect more light into the room, reducing the need for artificial lighting.

CHOOSING FIXTURES

Possibly the most important part of planning your bathroom is choosing the fixtures that meet the needs of your family. Do you want a large bathtub for soaking? Do you want an efficient shower for the early morning rush hour? Will there be a whirlpool bath in your tub? One sink or two? Pedestal sink or cabinet model? A bidet? Chapter 8 gives detailed information about choosing and installing all bathroom fixtures. You might wish to read about the different types before making a decision. And it is certainly worthwhile to spend time browsing through your local stores to see what is available. Many retailers display fixtures in room settings so that you can get a much better idea of how they will look in actual use. Look through mail order catalogs for more ideas. Be sure to check prices on all items because you will find a wide variation in cost.

The largest item in your bathroom is the bathing fixture. You might wish to choose that fixture first and build your entire bathroom around its shape and functions. Bathtubs come in many shapes and sizes (Figs. 1-16 through 1-24), no longer limited to the standard 30- × -60-inch cast iron or steel. Many tubs are now made of fiberglass. There are sunken tubs, corner tubs, freestanding tubs, ex-

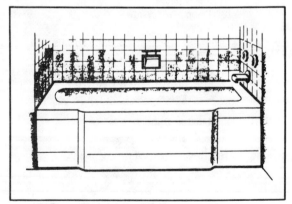

Fig. 1-16. Common recess tub.

Fig. 1-17. Recess tub with decorative mural (Courtesy of Kohler Co.).

tra large tubs, extra small tubs, tubs with built-in whirlpool baths, and tubs with special features for the elderly or handicapped.

Many bathrooms include a combination tub/shower to save space while providing a choice of bathing methods. Again, a great variety of styles and shapes are available. Shower stalls also come in a form to meet nearly every need. Shower materials include ceramic tile, cultured marble, plastic laminates, as well as fiberglass-reinforced plastic.

Several types of flushing mechanisms used in toilets are available. They vary greatly in efficiency and price. A number of styles are also available, including wall-hung toilets, corner toilets, water-saver toilets, and elongated bowl toilets (Figs. 1-25 through 1-29). See Table 1-1 for dimensions. The features of toilets will be fully explored in Chapter 8.

There is also a bathroom sink to fit your pur-poses. Sinks come in many shapes, colors, and sizes, ready to be placed in the appropriate bath-room (Figs. 1-30 through 1-37). See Table 1-2 for sizes. Be sure that the tub, toilet, and sink you choose are compatible in style. If possible, look at them together.

The bidet (Fig. 1-38) is a bathroom fixture that is gaining in popularity. A bidet is a sit-down wash basin with hot and cold water, and sometimes a spray, that is used primarily for washing the perineal area. Bidets come in as many colors as other bathroom fixtures. Installation is costly and complex because of the need for both hot and cold water as well as a drain system. A good location for a bidet is beside the toilet. A minimum of 3 feet × 3 feet along a wall is required for installation.

CHOOSING WALL COVERINGS

Common wall coverings for bathrooms include ce-

Fig. 1-18. Recess tub in old-fashion bathroom (Courtesy of Kohler Co.).

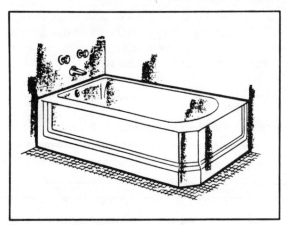

Fig. 1-19. Corner tub.

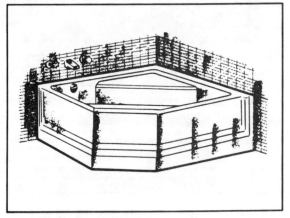

Fig. 1-20. Corner square tub.

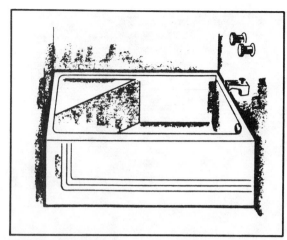

Fig. 1-21. Receptor tub.

ramic tile, plastic tile, paint, wallpaper, and wood paneling.

Ceramic tile is one of the most common as well as most durable and attractive wall coverings used in bathrooms. Ceramic tile won't scratch, warp, stain, or dent. It is made of fired clay, with the color baked in. Available in many colors and patterns, ceramic tile is among the most water resistant of wall coverings.

Plastic tile is a less expensive imitation of ceramic tile. It is not as durable, but is easy to install and comes in many colors.

Paint and wallpaper are inexpensive ways to brighten a bathroom. Walls must be in good condition. Be sure to use only semi-gloss or high-gloss

Fig. 1-22. Old-fashion free-standing claw foot tub (Courtesy of Kohler Co.).

Fig. 1-23. Sunken whirlpool tub (Courtesy of Kohler Co.).

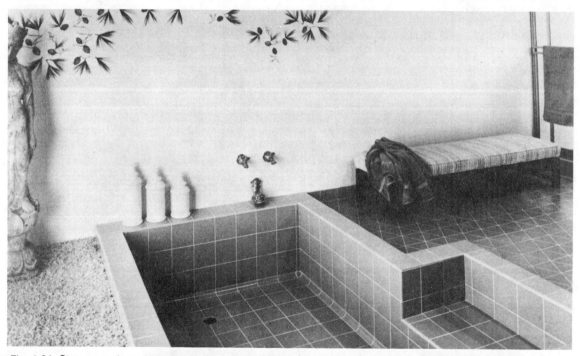

Fig. 1-24. Step-up sunken whirlpool tub (Courtesy of Kohler Co.).

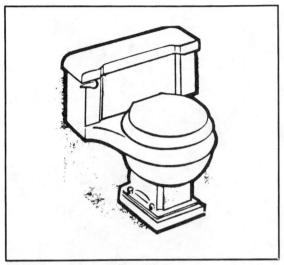

Fig. 1-25. One-piece toilet or water closet.

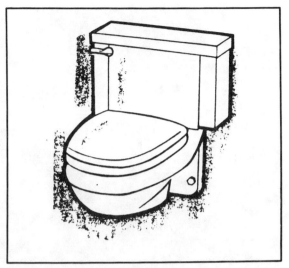

Fig. 1-27. Wall-hung toilet.

enamel paints, and vinyl or plastic-coated wall-papers with a special adhesive. Both are fully washable and attractive wall coverings.

Wood paneling with a warp-resistant finish can add beauty to a bathroom whether used alone, or in conjunction with paint or wallpaper.

Other materials occasionally used for wall coverings in bathrooms are mirrors or mirror tiles, fabrics, and sheet vinyl as is usually used on floors. Use your imagination and consider the many

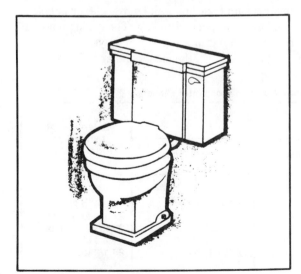

Fig. 1-26. Close-coupled tank and bowl.

choices before deciding on the wall covering for your bathroom. A later chapter will include instructions for installation of wall coverings.

CHOOSING FLOOR COVERINGS

The moisture factor and the high usage of a bathroom make the choice of a flooring especially important. Most commonly used floor coverings include ceramic tile, solid vinyl tile, cushioned vinyl, and wall-to-wall carpeting. All are good choices but some will serve better in some cases than others. For instance, wall-to-wall carpeting is attractive and warm, but is not best suited to a bathroom with small children where water is often splashed on the floor.

Ceramic tile is as good a choice for a floor covering as it is for a wall covering. Its water-resistant qualities plus its durability make it ideal for a high-moisture area such as a bathroom. The unglazed matte finishes are safer because they are more slip-resistant than glazed tile.

Solid vinyl tile is a strong material constructed of vinyl resins, plasticizers, pigments, and fillers that are formed under pressure while hot. Colors are clear and brilliant.

Wall-to-wall carpeting that is made especially for bathrooms is entirely machine washable and is an inexpensive way to renew an old floor without

Fig. 1-28. Water-conserving toilet uses only 3 1/2 gallons per flush (Courtesy of Kohler Co.).

removing the old one to install another. Carpeting made of nylon and acrylic piles with non-slip backings come in a wide range of colors. The ceiling in your bathroom is probably made of lath and plaster, gypsum board or wall board, tile, or panels if you have a suspended ceiling. The ceiling material can be covered in a variety of ways.

Paint is one of the most popular ceiling covers.

Table 1-1. Approximate Dimensions for Toilets or Water Closets.

	Tank		Extension of fixture into room (inches)
	Height (inches)	Width (inches)	
One-piece water closet............	18 1/2 to 25........	26 3/4 to 29 1/4.....	26 3/4 to 29 1/4.
Close coupled tank and bowl.......	28 1/2 to 30 7/8.....	20 5/8 to 22 1/4.....	27 1/2 to 31 3/8.
Wall-hung water closet............	27 to 29 1/2........	21 to 22 1/4........	26 to 27 1/2 (concealed tank 22).
Wall-hung tank...................	32 to 38............	17 3/4 to 22........	26 1/2 to 29 1/2.
Corner water closet...............	28 3/4..............	19 1/4..............	31.

Fig. 1-29. Old-style toilet (Courtesy of Kohler Co.).

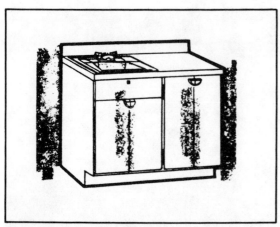

Fig. 1-30. Flat rim lavatory set into cabinet.

A semi-gloss or high-gloss enamel should be used to resist moisture and afford easy cleaning. White is a popular ceiling color because it reflects more light and bathrooms often need as much light as they can get. Paint is probably also the least expensive ceiling covering.

Wallpaper to match the walls of a bathroom is sometimes used as a ceiling covering. It also must be of the water resistant variety, vinyl or plastic coated, and hung with a special adhesive. Again, it is fully washable, making cleaning easy.

Either ceramic or plastic tile can be used on ceilings as well, matching that used on the walls. Acoustical tile is often used on a bathroom ceiling. Tile with a vinyl-acrylic finish is practical and wash-

Fig. 1-31. Oval lavatory (Courtesy of Kohler Co.),

Fig. 1-32. Self-rimmed china lavatory (Courtesy of Kohler Co.).

able. Do not use untreated ceiling tiles because they will not resist moisture adequately.

Fluorescent tubes installed above translucent ceiling panels diffuse soft light throughout the room. Such panels also can hide unsightly pipes and wiring, and can be lifted out for cleaning or for access to pipe and wiring for repair.

WINDOW TREATMENTS

Windows in a bathroom can open onto a private garden for a wonderfully relaxing bath. But windows in a bathroom can also pose a problem. What kind of window covering is most suitable for the needs of the room?

A window over the bathtub can be a nuisance. It can also be an attractive addition to the room. Clear window panes can be replaced with frosted glass to ensure privacy while letting in daylight. Or a second shower curtain can be hung over the window at little expense if installed on a spring pole hanger.

Other windows in the bathroom can be curtained, shuttered, or covered with full-size or mini-blinds. For an unusual and beautiful effect, try stained glass. To let in lots of sunlight and make the room seem larger, put in a skylight.

HEAT AND LIGHT FOR THE BATHROOM

When stepping out of the bathtub or shower it is comforting to find a warm, cozy atmosphere. Heat for the bathroom should be separate from heat for the rest of the home. There are times when only the bathroom will need to be heated; many people prefer it to be warmer than the rest of the house.

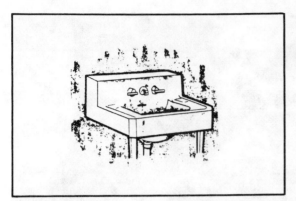

Fig. 1-33. Shelf back lavatory.

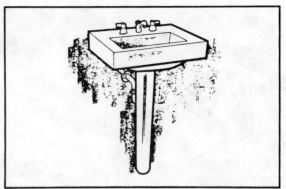

Fig. 1-34. Slab with china leg lavatory.

Fig. 1-35. Splash back lavatory.

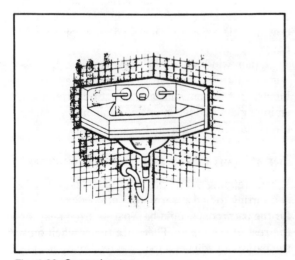

Fig. 1-36. Corner lavatory.

A ceiling unit that includes a heater, light, and ventilating fan is a good choice and provides warmth as well as light for reading in the tub. Local codes will usually require a ventilation system

Table 1-2. Typical Sizes of Lavatories.

	Width (*inches*)	Front to back (*inches*)
Wall-hung:		
Ledge back.........	19	17
	24	20
Splash back........	19	17
	20	18
	24	20
Slab..............	20	18
	24	20
	27	22
Shelf back..........	19	17
	20	14
	22	18 or 19
Set in or on cabinets:		
Rolled rim..........	20	18
	21	17
	27	20
Flat rim...........	20	18
	24	20
	19 1/2	15 1/4
Lavatory on cabinet..	27	21
	21 1/2	17 3/4
	36	18

Fig. 1-37. Slab with china leg lavatory (Courtesy of Kohler Co.).

Fig. 1-38. Bidet (Courtesy of Kohler Co.).

if there is no window in the bathroom. Each function of a good combination unit can be used separately, or all functions can be operated simultaneously.

A popular bathroom heater is the wall heater, which provides instant heat that is circulated through the room with a fan. Radiant-type wall or ceiling heaters are often used also. Infrared heat bulbs are used in some and provide light or radiant heat.

Light can be provided for a bathroom in many ways. Natural lighting is best and can be provided by windows and skylights. Next best is artificial light, that comes in many forms. Combination heater/light/ventilators and luminous ceilings have already been mentioned. Other types of lighting for the bathroom include direct ceiling light and area lighting, often installed over a medicine cabinet above the sink. It is also convenient to have strong light over the bathtub. Where lighting is limited and major work is not indicated, additional light can be obtained with lamps placed on counters, cabinets, and other bathroom furniture. Switches for both lighting and heating should not be accessible from the bathtub, especially if there are children in the home.

CALCULATING EXPENSES

Because most do-it-yourself home remodelers and redecorators are on a budget, the total you decide to spend on your bathroom project, whether redecorating, remodeling, or adding a new room, will be at least partially dictated by the bank account. Once you have set the total amount you can afford, careful shopping and perhaps some compromising can make a lovely new room possible.

When setting your budget, keep the following ideas in mind. Your home will be more valuable once the bathroom is finished. Is the bathroom an isolated project, or just one in a series of remodeling projects throughout the home? How long do you expect your remodeling project to last? In other words, when will you be willing to make major changes in your bathroom again? Consider other normal monthly payments you have to make and future expenditures. This might affect the amount you feel you can spend on your bathroom.

The next step in calculating expenses is to make a complete list of all materials you will need. In addition to plumbing fixtures, piping, paint, and so on, you might need to purchase tools for the job. If so, you can charge them entirely to the bathroom project, or you can charge only a part of that expense to your project if you will be using the tool for other applications later. If there are parts of the job you will not feel comfortable doing yourself, you will need to figure the cost of professional help into the budget. If your time is limited you could hire a general helper for a day or a few days. Don't forget to list this expense.

If you already know approximately how you want your bathroom to look, it will be easy to determine exact costs by visiting your local building and plumbing supply outlets and searching mail order catalogs. Before pricing piping, paint, wood, or other variable quantity materials, make an accurate estimate of the amount needed. It is inconvenient to experience shortages and can cause paints and other materials to not match exactly. Overestimating can leave you with unnecessary materials that might not be returnable.

Once you have made a detailed listing of costs for the project, add in the appropriate percentage of sales tax for your locality. It can be considerable and can push your budget into the red if not expected.

The ideal way to finance your improvement project is by depositing extra savings into a special account earmarked for your project. This will save a substantial amount in interest besides earning interest until it is used to purchase materials. The drawback is that it could take several years for the balance to equal the necessary budget. If you do not have savings already available and can-

not wait several years to begin your work, shop around at all local lending institutions for the best rate. Other alternatives for financing include borrowing against your mortgage or life insurance, or borrowing from a company credit union.

SAVING MONEY

Following are a few ways to save money on your bathroom project:

- Plan so that an upstairs bathroom is located directly above the lower bathroom, with the plumbing on the same wall to save on plumbing and carpentry.
- Place all fixtures on one wall to save on plumbing and installation.
- Position new fixtures at or near existing locations to save changing plumbing.
- Thoroughly examine any plumbing that you do not anticipate changing. It will be much easier and less expensive to make repairs or replacements now than after all the work is finished. It would be false economy to rely on questionable pipes and in a few months have to re-open a wall for repair of a leaky pipe.
- If your future plans call for more plumbing changes, rough them in while you have walls already open and avoid the time and expense of opening the walls again later.
- If possible, locate a new bathroom on a wall opposite existing bathroom or kitchen plumbing to save on plumbing expenses.

DO-IT-YOURSELF OR HIRE?

Your bathroom can be a do-it-yourself project entirely, it can be partly do-it-yourself, or it can be entirely professionally done by a contractor. Do as much of the job yourself as you feel comfortable doing. Don't let the fact that you've never done similar projects be the only factor preventing you from the satisfaction of completing your own project. You do not need to be a professional carpenter or plumber to do the job.

If you feel it necessary, by all means have an

architect draw up your plans, or draw your own and have them scrutinized by a professional. If you can connect pipes and place fixtures but cannot hang wallpaper straight, do the plumbing and hire someone to hang the wallpaper. Consider the investment of your time while you are deciding whether to do part or all of the job yourself. It could be worthwhile to you to hire someone for part of the job simply to save time.

FINALIZING YOUR PLANS

Now is the time to review your plans and your budget. Once more think about what you want from a bathroom. Is it all there in the plan? Will this bathroom be comfortable for the next several years? If your family is growing, did you allow for more family members sharing the room in the future? Does your complete expense list fit comfortably within your budget? Be sure to leave a little leeway for fluctuating prices, forgotten minor items, and changes of mind.

The plans are ready, the budget is set, and the materials list is complete. Your redecorating, remodeling, or adding a room will require the use of a variety of tools, from screwdrivers, to pipe wrenches, to paint brushes and tile-laying tools. Tools are discussed in the following chapter.

Chapter 2

Tools and Techniques

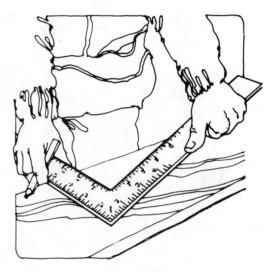

A NUMBER OF TOOLS WILL BE NEEDED TO complete any major bathroom project, including plumbing, carpentry, and finishing tools. Many of the tools are probably already in your toolbox (Fig. 2-1), but you might also need to purchase a few extra tools to make the job easier. This chapter is devoted to a discussion of most of the tools you will be working with as you complete your bathroom.

HAMMERS

The size and variety of hammers needed on any plumbing job will depend in large part on the jobs you must do. General framing work, as well as nailing of wallboard and molding, can be done with a 16- or 20-ounce carpenter's claw hammer (Fig. 2-2). If that's all there is to do, then no other hammers are needed. If you must install floor joists, ceiling joists, and other types of framing, consider investing in a 22-ounce framing hammer, as well as the lighter model you'll use for basic work.

Claw, or carpenter's, hammers come in a variety of styles and head weights. The most common is the 16-ounce head weight, and it's a good general use hammer, with either curved claw or the straight rip claw. Lighter styles, 13 ounces, come with curved claws and are useful for a variety of molding jobs, while heavier claw hammers range from 20 ounces to 32 ounces (Fig. 2-3). Very seldom will anyone need to go beyond a 22-ounce head weight in a claw hammer. Start with a 16-ounce hammer, with a handle material and shape that feels good to you, and use different ones according to your materials, up to and including sledge hammer handles. Steel-handled hammers can be either tubular or solid, and have the greatest strength. They don't absorb shock as well as wood or fiberglass, but are almost impossible to break, even under extreme mistreatment (Fig. 2-4).

Other hammers might be needed for work on bathrooms for jobs such as tapping tiles into place and tapping pipe along through walls. If you have to drill masonry, or drive hardened nails, a hand drilling hammer or an engineer's hammer will be needed, and these are most useful in 2-pound head

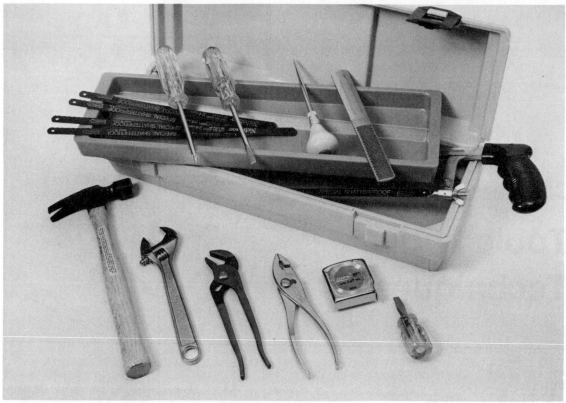

Fig. 2-1. Common tools in your toolbox (Courtesy of Cooper Group).

weights. The hand drilling hammer has a 10-inch handle and looks much like a stubby sledge. The engineer's hammer has a cross pein at one end with a regular striking face at the other, and a handle of about 15 inches in the 2-pound head weight.

Hardened nails, such as masonry nails, are not driven with a claw hammer. They'll certainly go in, but you'll quickly destroy the hammer because the face is not designed for such uses. It's also not meant for pulling nails. If you must pull a partially driven nail, insert a section of board under the hammer head to provide more leverage, and do the job as gently as possible to keep from pulling the handle out or snapping it off. Limit nail pulling to 12-penny nails and smaller nails if they're fully or almost fully driven; with larger nails pull only when they're partially driven. Otherwise use a nail puller.

Soft-face hammers come in many guises, but in most cases a rubber mallet serves for virtually all of the work you will need on plumbing systems.

These won't mar anything and the heads are light and bouncy enough to avoid damage to a pipe from a harder-than-needed whack. Deadblow soft-face hammers have very little bounce and all of the force stays where it is stopped or is transferred to the object to be moved. Deadblow soft-face hammer faces are changeable and can be replaced as they wear so that you can use a softer or harder substance to do the driving. These are also available in other styles, from ball pein, to engineer's, to sledge hammers.

HANDSAWS AND MITER BOX

You will find numerous handsaws on the market (Figs. 2-5 through 2-11), with one classified as the handsaw—it's really called a panel saw. Otherwise, you'll find compass and keyhole saws, coping saws and hacksaws, as well as backsaws that are generally used with miter boxes.

Panel saws come in two primary models, the

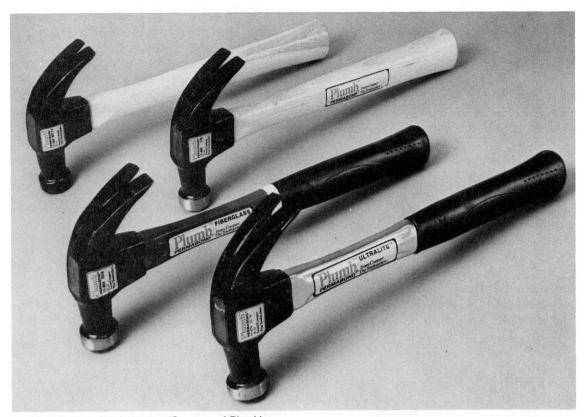

Fig. 2-2. Typical claw hammers (Courtesy of Plumb).

crosscut and rip saws. Rip saws are of little interest today and some companies no longer even make them as top-of-the-line models. The teeth have a wider set and are shaped differently than are the teeth of the crosscut saw. The more common crosscut saw is used to cut across the grain of a board as cleanly as possible and can generally be found with eight, ten, or a dozen teeth per inch. The more teeth per inch, the smoother the cut you'll get, but the slower your cutting will be. If you decide to work with handsaws extensively, be sure to purchase top quality.

On plywood panel, saws are used with the good side of the material facing up, as the cut is made on the down stroke so that any splintering is from the unseen back side of the board. If you decide to use Japanese saws, remember that the good side should face down, because they cut on the pull stroke, not the push stroke.

Compass and keyhole saws are used for cutting holes for such things as ceiling light outlets, and wall receptacles, and are handy in remodeling work. Both taper to a point and will have 8- or 9-point-per-inch blades, giving a fairly rough cut in wood, but also serving well in gypsum wallboard and other such materials. There is little expense involved and it's a good idea to have one or both in the toolbox. Some companies make what is known as nests of saws with several blades to fit a single handle. These can be exceptional buys and very useful.

Coping saws are not needed for bathroom work unless you plan on cutting molding or making coped joints. Then they're indispensable. The coping saw is inexpensive, with changeable blades, and is designed to cut very fine scrollwork and short radius curves that can't be handled with compass and keyhole saws.

Hacksaws are important tools for plumbers.

They cut pipe—whether plastic or metal—and other odd materials, and with the correct blade can be used to cut ceramic tiles. Blades come with 14 to 32 teeth per inch; the finer blades are meant for use in thin sheetmetal, and the rougher ones for heavy cast iron and wood. Get a good hacksaw frame and a selection of blades, with some emphasis on the 18-point-per-inch types. This is a general blade and will work with most materials, except for the lightest sheetmetals. You can also buy mini-hacksaws that allow only the last 2 or 3 inches of the blade to extend beyond the handle. These are meant for jobs where the hacksaw frame won't fit over the piece being cut. They're not expensive and are exceptionally handy.

Backsaws are generally used in conjunction with miter boxes to provide miter cuts of 45 degrees, or other angles, and to give definitive 90-degree cuts in light stock. The backsaw is a rectangular bladed saw similar to the panel saw, ex-cept that it seldom, if ever, has a taper from the teeth up, and has a rigid backbone of steel or brass at the top edge to make sure there is no twisting to throw the cut off. This limits the depth of the cut to the depth of the blade, but because most backsaws are used to cut molding for trim work, that's not often a problem. Generally a backsaw will have 12 teeth per inch, set for crosscutting so that cuts are as smooth as possible. Some backsaws are now on the market with hacksaw-like frames and blades, with the blades of very thin stock. This is supposed to give a tighter joint.

Miter boxes come in several forms, as do angle cutting guides. These vary greatly in price. Buy the quality that matches the amount of molding you expect to be cutting. With a cheap miter box you can get a decent fit on molding with a lot of care. With an expensive miter box and backsaw there will be no waste and you'll need to use only a little care to have accurate angle cuts and good fits. But

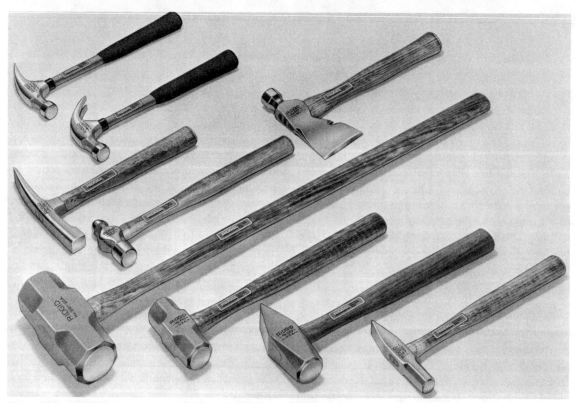

Fig. 2-3. Assorted hammers for assorted jobs (Courtesy of Ridge Tool Co.).

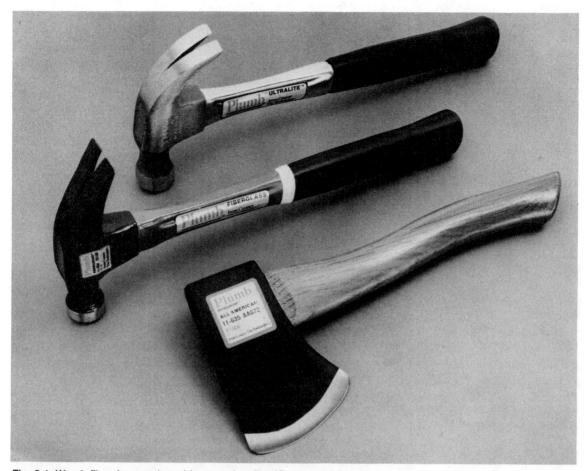

Fig. 2-4. Wood, fiberglass, and steel hammer handles (Courtesy of Plumb).

the difference in cost is great, so if you're doing a single room, figure on starting with no more than a mid-range miter box/backsaw combination that will cut to 4 inches deep. Professional boxes that will cut 6 inches thick and 10 inches wide are available, but are expensive and won't often be used.

SCREWDRIVERS

Screwdrivers come in many sizes, shapes, and forms (Figs. 2-12 through 2-14). A screwdriver is meant to do two jobs: it either drives screws in, or it extracts them. In its simplest form, the screwdriver is nothing more than a chunk of metal with a wedge shape on one end to fit into a screw slot. In more complex forms, that end can be made to fit a wide variety of shapes, though nearly all home workers will find a variety of slotted screwdrivers, standard and Phillips, sufficient for everything they need to do.

Look for good quality handles, tightly fitted to the screwdriver shanks. Tips should be ground to fit slots well, though it doesn't seem to make much difference in holding power if grind marks show or don't show on the tips. Most top quality drivers will show grind marks there, but nowhere else. The shanks can be plated and will extend well into the handle. Handles should be sturdy and shaped to fit the hand well.

Generally a top quality, 1/4-inch-tip standard screwdriver, with 3/16 inch for fine work, and the number 1 and 2 Phillips tips will be all that's needed around the home or for most plumbing jobs. Occasionally larger screwdrivers will be helpful, as will smaller ones, but you can buy these as the need arises. Offset screwdrivers will allow you to get into odd places. Ratcheting screwdrivers are exceptionally handy when you start working with a lot of screws.

Good quality metal and an accurately ground tip are essential to a good screwdriver, as is a good fitting handle. The handle should be as large as is practical within the limits of intended tool use so that the grip is comfortable and provides good leverage during use. While the number of screws driven and the number of screwdrivers needed during a plumbing job is limited, it is a good idea to purchase high quality screwdrivers. Screwdriver kits that claim to include one of just about every kind in a line do save you money; the problem is you'll probably never use several of the tools in the kit. Generally a kit made up of the six or seven most commonly used sizes is a better buy than a kit with 10 or 20 pieces.

WRENCHES

Several types of wrenches are essential when plumbing. Even when you're working with wrenchless installations you'll need wrenches to get the old material off before you can install the more easily worked modern materials. There are a few types

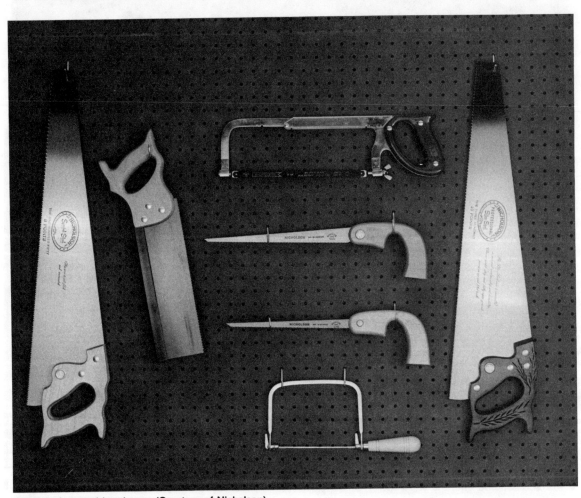

Fig. 2-5. Assorted hand saws (Courtesy of Nicholson).

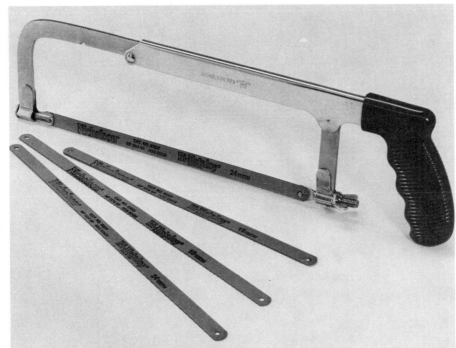

Fig. 2-6. Hacksaw frame and blades (Courtesy of Nicholson).

Fig. 2-7. A compass saw used to cut plastic pipe (Courtesy of Genova, Inc.).

Fig. 2-8. A coping saw.

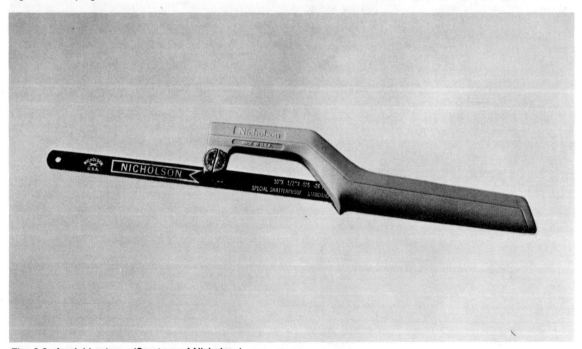

Fig. 2-9. A mini-hacksaw (Courtesy of Nicholson).

34

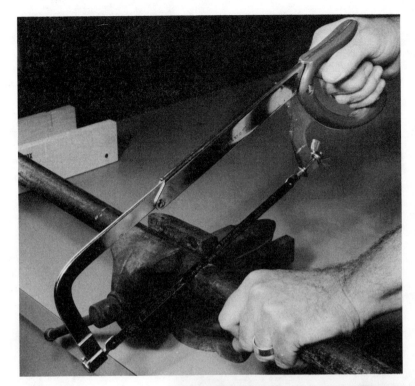

Fig. 2-10. Using a hacksaw to cut pipe (Courtesy of Nicholson).

Fig. 2-11. A grouping of saw blades (Courtesy of Nicholson).

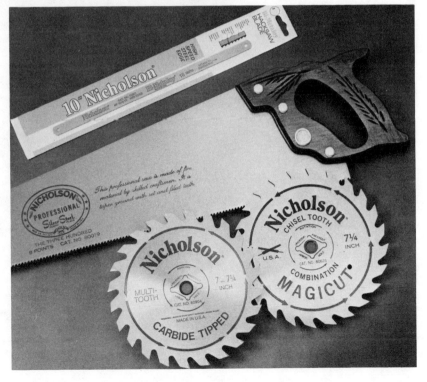

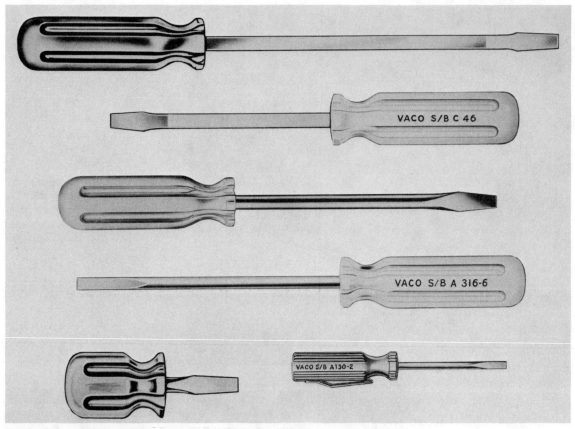

Fig. 2-12. Assortment of slotted screwdrivers (Courtesy of Vaco).

Fig. 2-13. Using a screwdriver to assemble bathroom cabinets (Courtesy of Yorktowne Cabinets).

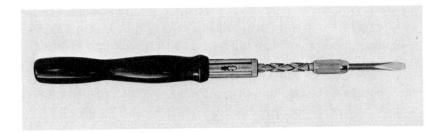

Fig. 2-14. The Yankee ratcheting screwdriver (Courtesy of Stanley Tools).

you must have and a few types handy for general uses.

Adjustable wrenches are essential to nearly any plumbing installation. Adjustable wrenches for most plumbing uses will fall in the 10- or 12-inch wrench length range, giving you a wide enough jaw opening to work with most plumbing fixtures in common use (Fig. 2-15). Good adjustable wrenches will have precisely ground faces on the jaws and well-knurled adjusters with cleanly cut gears. The adjustable portion of the jaw face, the gear, and the knurled adjuster all are replaceable as they wear. Adjustable wrenches are not a substitute for open end and box wrenches, because they will usually

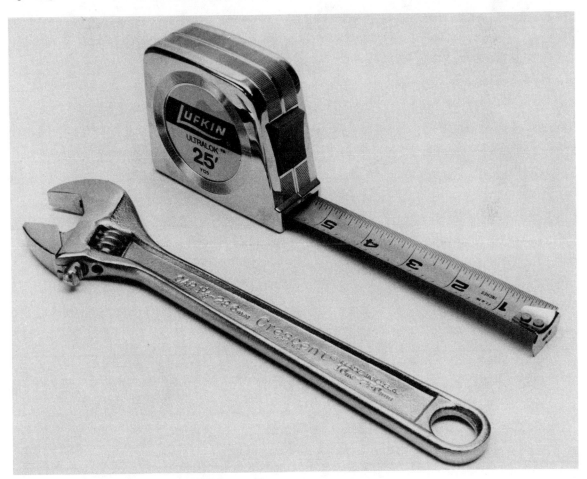

Fig. 2-15. Adjustable wrench (Courtesy of Crescent).

slip before the amount of pressure either of those can apply is used. Therefore, their suitability is fine for plumbing uses where fixtures are of softer metals, but they are less effective in other applications (Fig. 2-16).

Pipe wrenches are another need, but one that you might sometimes be able to forego. A pipe wrench is useful when it is necessary to turn a pipe instead of a connector. The jaw is pivoted, allowing the serrated jaws to firmly grip a rounded surface.

Chain pipe wrenches (Fig. 2-17) allow you to work in more limited spaces than do standard pipe wrenches. There is also a strap-style pipe wrench with the jaws made of heavy canvas or other material that can be used when you're working with easily marred materials, especially those that have been plated. In most cases, when the turning pressure, or torque, needed isn't extreme, you can wrap the fixture with a piece of old terry cloth towel and clamp down with your standard or chain pipe wrench.

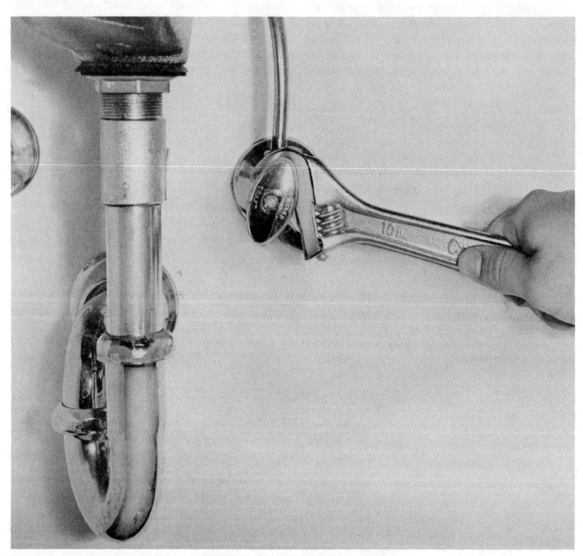

Fig. 2-16. An adjustable wrench in use on a sink valve (Courtesy of Crescent).

38

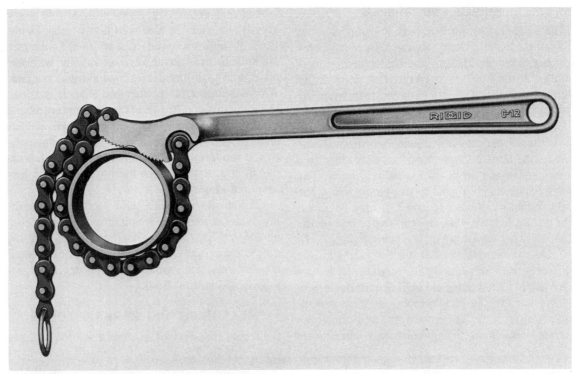

Fig. 2-17. Chain pipe wrench (Courtesy of Ridge Tools).

As always, look for a good finish and fit, and check the company reputation. Buying from a tool company known to you or to your local hardware store is the best bet in selecting any type of pipe wrench.

Open end and box wrenches are great for uses where sizes are moderate. Ratchet handles and sockets make some jobs easier. Any time you need to get into a tight place and turn a long bolt down, or run a nut in a long way, the ratchet and socket is the easiest method.

Basin wrenches (Fig. 2-18) can be hard to locate outside a plumbing supply store, but can be very useful. You simply cannot work without one if you have to remove or install a standard basin. The long barhandle allows you to get up behind the dip in the basin bowl to the point where the faucets are attached and the half-moon loose head, with teeth, lets you grip while the **T** bar at the other end allows a decent turn.

Inside pipe wrenches are strange looking and are seldom needed, but are sometimes essential. Basically, the inside pipe wrench slips inside a pipe where a twist expands it to grip the pipe's inside walls and lets you then turn the pipe. They're handy for removing flush mounted pipes or installing replacements in an already finished wall.

Pliers are wrenches without the grip. Most types of pliers are simply made for holding purposes, to increase the holding power available from your hand when a second wrench is not available or won't fit. They're suitable only for minimal tightening and loosening jobs.

Groove joint pliers usually have an angled head to allow an offset grip. The grooves steady and strengthen your grip without danger of slipping to a larger size, as is possible with slip joint pliers. Groove joint pliers are often called Channellock pliers, but many other companies also produce them. Lineman's or sidecutting pliers are handy for heavy wiring jobs as are long nose and needle nose pliers (Fig. 2-19).

KNIVES AND CHISELS

Knives are important items in any remodeler's or builder's toolkit. Utility knives (Fig. 2-20) come with retractable blades. The blades are replaceable and should be changed often. A sharp utility knife blade makes many jobs easier, from trimming sheet materials such as gypsum wallboard to scoring metals such as aluminum for breaking.

Electrician's knives commonly come with one leaf-style blade and one screwdriver blade with a sharp edge and an insulation pulling notch. The screwdriver blade should lock open. As a tool, the electrician's knife is misnamed. It may be an aid to wiring but it's also, if kept sharp, one of the handiest pocket knives on the market (Fig. 2-21).

Putty knives (Fig. 2-22) and joint taping knives are necessary for finishing any room. Putty knives are useful for removing old glazing material in windows, installing new and scraping old paint or wallpaper from walls and woodwork, and numerous other tasks. Joint taping knives are often over-looked and people try to substitute wide putty knives with flexible blades to do the jobs. Don't. Blade flexibility and the extra width of a joint taping knife helps to do the job more rapidly, with less mess, and with less need for sanding at the end. A corner joint knife is also available. It is aimed at producing as near perfect inside corners as can be achieved with joint compounds and tape, and has an angle of a bit more than 45 degrees on the blade so you can force it to 45 degrees and draw the corner tightly. It works beautifully, with much less time and effort.

A flat cold chisel is a helpful tool when plumbing. It can be used for forcing threading into a connector to help prevent leaks. It can also be used to notch connectors and to shear or cut away rusted connectors. Chisels are made of tool steel and have a hardened cutting head.

MEASURING AND MARKING TOOLS

Some marking devices, such as a scratch awl, are

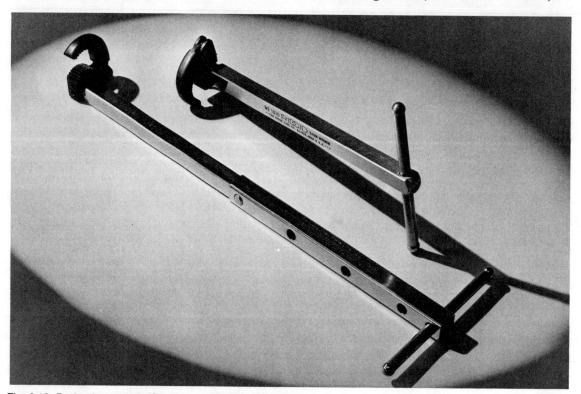

Fig. 2-18. Basin pipe wrench (Courtesy of Ridge Tools).

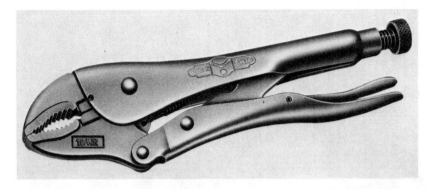

Fig. 2-19. Locking pliers (Courtesy of Petersen Manufacturing Co.).

among the simplest of all tools, and those are the ones you're most likely to need while working around a bathroom. Items such as a carpenter's pencil and a chalk line will also prove handy. The scratch awl takes the place of the pencil, making a scratch or gouge on the surface to be cut. The scratch awl offers the advantage of not leaving behind traces of graphite as a pencil does. With care, the mark will disappear in cutting and there will be no trace left at all.

The carpenter's pencil is a simple soft lead pencil except that it is rectangular in shape so it can't roll easily. The lead, or graphite, is also rectangular and is sharpened with a knife or piece of sandpaper to give a wide, clean edge.

The chalk line is encased in a plastic or metal housing and will be 50 or 100 feet long, with the housing filled with chalk powder. The line is drawn out of the housing, placed on the marks, and is then lifted and snapped to allow the chalk to form a line for your cut or for aligning items. The line is rather broad and isn't suitable for close work, but the chalk line is the most efficient device for marking items of more than 8 feet for cuts or installation. The line will have a loop, or metal end, to allow attachment to a nail so one person can make the

needed marks, and most cases today are designed to be used as plumb bobs as well as chalk lines. However, it is not as accurate as a good plumb bob.

Chalk comes in several colors, most commonly blue and dark red, and in powder form that lasts for quite some time. It is a good idea, however, to have about an 8-ounce container on hand.

Get the best chalk line you can find. If you do any amount of work around your home you'll soon find it nearly indispensable after you get used to snapping lines straight. Make sure you get the line as taut as you can and then lift it straight up 6 to 10 inches before letting it snap back. Assuming there's plenty of chalk on the line it will give you a fine mark.

Measurements for marking with the tools above can be made in several ways, whether with tape measures, folding rules, or yardsticks. In most cases a folding rule will be used for shorter measurements and a tape for longer. A 25- or 30-foot measuring tape is good for most work around a house and it's probably the longest you'll need for remodeling or building bathrooms. Select the best measuring tape and the best folding rule that you can find.

Look for an epoxy-coated blade in a tape mea-

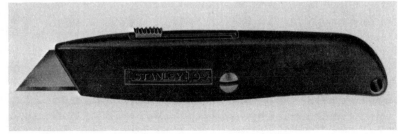

Fig. 2-20. Utility knife (Courtesy of Stanley Tools).

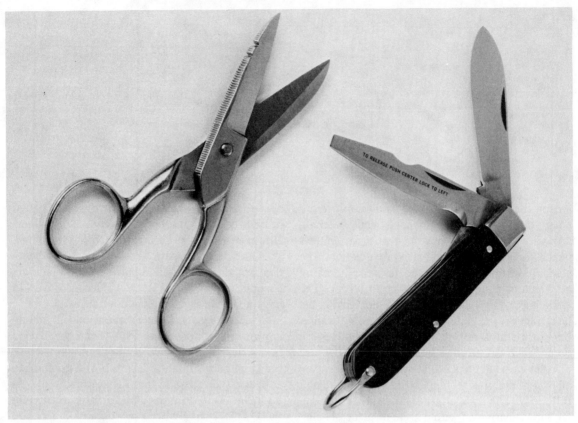

Fig. 2-21. Electrician's knife and scissors (Courtesy of Wiss & Boker Tree).

sure and a wider blade over a narrower one unless the tape is exceptionally long. A wide blade adds too much weight when a tape passes about 30 feet. It should retract on demand with no winding, unless it's over 30 feet long, and should have a positive lock to keep it out once you get it out (Fig. 2-23). The lock should retract easily and the case needs to be sturdy. A belt clip is optional. Some carpenter's aprons have enough space that the clip is allowable even there, while others don't. If the tape is used mostly with an apron on, then you might have to remove the belt clip or use a smaller tape with the apron.

Folding rules should have easy-to-read markings and brass joints. You might or might not want brass extensions, and some come with a single 6-inch extension, while others come with none or with one on each end. The wood should allow flex,

but not too much, and the rule should fold and unfold easily.

Marking gauges probably won't be vital in bath work, but if you do need to make any long cuts of shallow width or need to mark laminates for trimming near the edge, nothing will beat a good wood and brass marking gauge. Select one with care and check marks for accuracy on at least three settings before buying the gauge. Make sure the gauge can be easily and rapidly set to the distance you require (Fig. 2-24).

For the most accurate squares look to try squares (Figs. 2-25 through 2-28). These are fixed at 90 degrees, blade and handle, usually with three rivets. The handle can be wood or metal while the blade is of metal, usually steel. The blade will often be marked in inches, which can be very handy. The blade length will vary from 8 inches to about

Fig. 2-22. Wide blade putty knife (Courtesy of Stanley Tools).

Fig. 2-23. Three styles of tape measures (Courtesy of Lufkin).

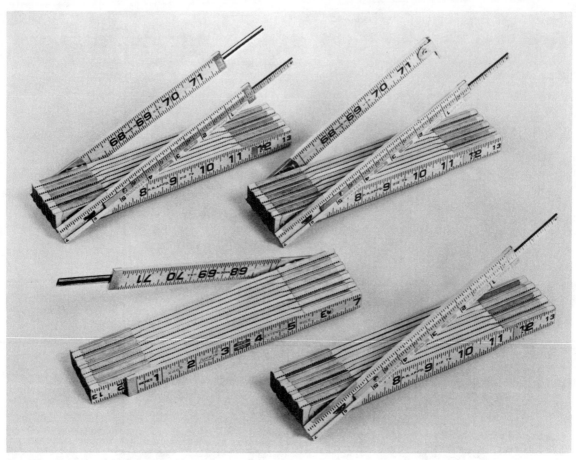

Fig. 2-24. Folding rules (Courtesy of Lufkin).

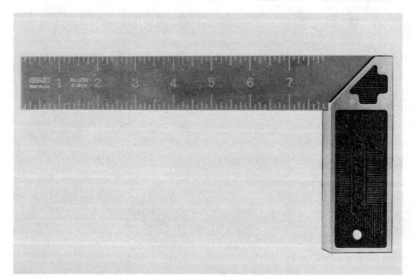

Fig. 2-25. Try square (Courtesy of Stanley Tools).

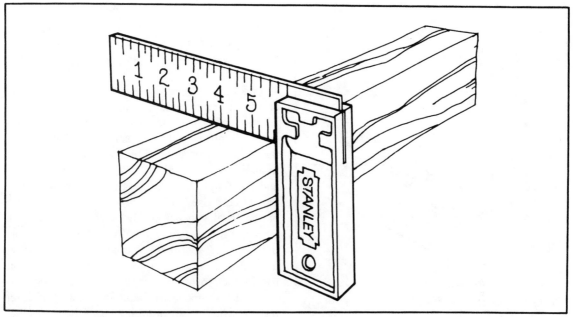

Fig. 2-26. Using a try square (Courtesy of Stanley Tools).

1 foot and some handles are shaped to give a fairly accurate miter because they're attached with a 45-degree cut. For 90-degree cuts done freehand there is no more accurate marking device then a try square, assuming the square is well made.

The combination square offers a slightly wider variety of uses than does the try square. It serves to square boards at 90 degrees, but also allows a

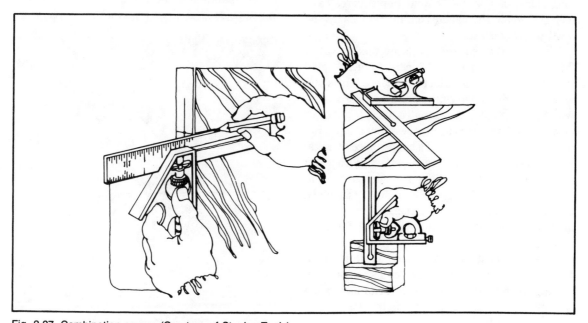

Fig. 2-27. Combination square (Courtesy of Stanley Tools).

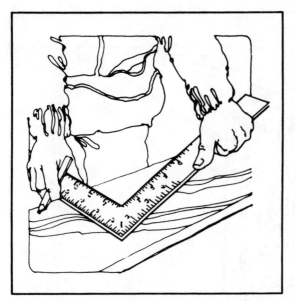

Fig. 2-28. Framing square (Courtesy of Stanley Tools).

better miter job, with its sliding handle cut also at a 45-degree angle. The foot-long blade is always marked, whether in inches or metric, allowing its use as a ruler. Many come with scribes slipped into the handle. You can set the sliding blade at its proper inch marking and use the scribe to make long marks on boards. Combination squares have a spirit level in the handle, but in many cases the level is not accurate.

The framing square is a large model with a 2-foot handle and a 16- or 18-inch tongue. A good framing square is essential to any large job as you will soon find it is worth the extra cost associated with stainless steel. A framing square is good for checking room corners for trueness, but that's a minor use. The tool is made of a single piece of metal with markings on its blade and tongue. With it you can determine the length of any common, hip valley, or jack rafter for any roof pitch, and then use the square to check cuts for the rafters. They're also used for laying out stair stringers and for many other jobs.

You will most likely only need a rafter square for checking corner trueness and as a straight edge. Buying the best rafter square you can locate is a worthwhile investment if you plan to do any more remodeling or building jobs.

A level (Fig.2-29) is an essential tool for most types of carpentry and for many kinds of plumbing. Start with a 2-foot aluminum- or mahogany-bodied level of the best quality available. Levels must have a set of plumb vials as well as vials to show a level. When you're setting a door, vanity, or a vertical pipe run, knowing whether or not the job is plumb can be vital to a proper function. Doors out of plumb and pipes not on a true vertical do not serve their purposes well. In many cases you'll need to allow for a drop or rise in a horizontal pipe run and the simplest way to do this is to cut a wedge equal to the rise per foot and tape it to the bottom of the level you use to check the run. In other words, if the pipe run must drop 1/8 inch per foot, then with a 2-foot level, you want a wedge tapering from zero to 1/4 inch over its full length. If you use a 9-inch torpedo level to measure or check the line, cut a shim one foot long and center the level on that (Figs. 2-30 through 2-32).

Figures 2-33 and 2-34 illustrate two additional measuring and marking instruments.

ELECTRIC SAWS

Circular saws are needed for almost any kind of work done around a house (Fig. 2-35). The most common blade diameter is 7 1/4 inches, which gives

Fig. 2-29. Common levels (Courtesy of Stanley Tools).

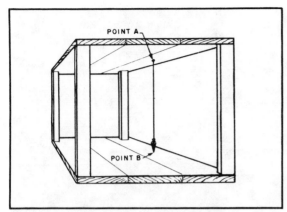

Fig. 2-30. Locating a point with a plumb bob.

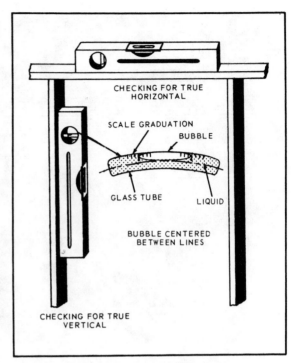

Fig. 2-32. Horizontal and vertical use of level.

a cut deep enough to slice through a 2-×-4 at a 45-degree angle. In 7 1/4-inch diameter saws look for one that weighs at least 10 pounds and draws at least 10 amperes of current (for heavy duty models). Don't buy any portable power tool that draws much more than 13 amperes or you'll have problems when the starting surge on the motor pops your circuit breaker. Most common circuits used to run power tools will handle 15 amperes safely, but no more.

Check the saw for freedom of baseplate movement when you're adjusting for depth of cut and cut angles and make sure the controls fall easily to hand. Grips should be large and comfortable. Pass

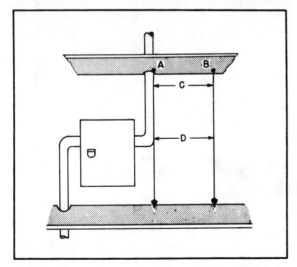

Fig. 2-31. Plumbing a structural member with a plumb bob.

by saws with smaller than 7 1/4-inch diameter blade capacities because eventually the cut depth won't be great enough for your uses. By the same token, you're not likely to need a saw with an 8 1/4-inch blade because the cut depth gain is moderate and the price of the saw goes up. If you expect really heavy duty work to crop up, consider a gear driven saw.

Reciprocating saws (Fig. 2-36) work with the saw blade being stroked back and forth about 1 inch at a time, usually at several thousand rpm. Two-speed saws and saws with variable speeds over the complete range are available. Considered a utility tool for making rough cuts, the reciprocating saw is exceptionally handy for opening up walls, roof decking, ceilings, and other points where you might need to run pipe or wiring and don't wish to tear entire sections of wall or other structure out. The blade styles available allow you to cut metal, plastics, wood, and other materials to add to saw versatility.

Saber, or jig, saws (Fig. 2-37) are small saws with blades moving back and forth just as they do

Fig. 2-33. Fifty-foot tape (Courtesy of Lufkin).

in a reciprocating saw. The primary differences are in size, power, and position. A jigsaw is used mainly to make cuts on a horizontal plane and is handy for making cut-outs in countertops and other such areas as well as in general scrolling. It also has a wide blade selection to allow you to cut metals, plastics, and other materials, but lacks the powerful motor of the reciprocating saw, so the extent of the jobs

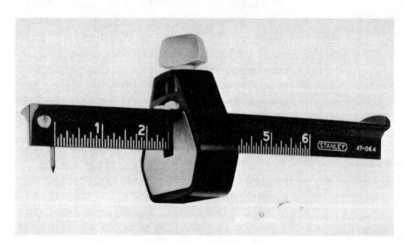

Fig. 2-34. Marking gauge (Courtesy of Stanley Tools).

Fig. 2-35. Circular saw (Courtesy of Sears, Roebuck & Co.).

is smaller, as is the entire saw.

The table saw (Fig. 2-38) is the most common of the stationary power tools that can be used in constructing or remodeling a bathroom. Stationary power tools provide greater power and precision than do portable power tools. It is not possible to hand hold a board and make as accurate a cut with a moving saw as it is to feed that board, using guides, through a saw that is stationary.

Check the table saw well for quality. Blade diameters start at about 8 inches. The best all-around choice is a good 10-inch diameter blade. The larger arbor, the center post, and nut that hold the blade on the turning motor shaft, do on stationary saws reduce the depth of cut available from a particular size blade, so 10 inches is a good compromise.

The radial arm saw (Fig. 2-39) is a version of the table saw with the blade and motor suspended from an arm above the cutting table. It has advantages and disadvantages when compared to a table saw. Both are excellent tools.

ELECTRIC DRILLS

Electric drills are present in nearly every home. If you're going to buy just a single electric drill, consider an industrial rated model in 3/8-inch size. The cost is higher than for a consumer model, but the tool has enough bulk and power to substitute for a 1/2-inch drill occasionally, while still being light enough for general work and some cabinet work. Virtually all available accessories will fit on a 3/8-inch drill (Figs. 2-40 and 2-41).

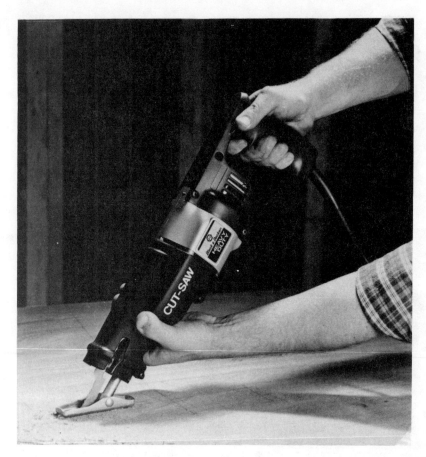

Fig. 2-36. Reciprocating saw (Courtesy of Black & Decker).

FASTENERS

The world of fasteners is a complex one and getting more so each day. Previously you had a choice of flour paste, hide glue, nails, screws, or pegs, with the odd nut and bolt tossed in. Not so now.

Adhesives alone come in a wide array with each doing one or two specific jobs effectively. Most work around the bathroom will involve contact cements and thin set tile setting adhesives. Both are relatively easy to work with. Select the adhesive recommended by the company making the item to be glued and then follow the instructions on the adhesive package.

Contact cements (Figs. 2-42 and 2-43) come in non-flammable styles and it makes sense to use one of those. Contact cements are applied to both surfaces to be attached and allowed to dry. Once they're dry to the touch, 15 to 45 minutes, place the surfaces in contact. That's it; no movement is possible from that point on. If you think you might have to adjust things, for example as you lower a sheet of formica onto a vanity top, use either butcher's brown paper or short sections of lath to keep the cemented surfaces from touching. Then, with lath, slip out end piece after adjustments have been made and allow that end to make contact. Go up the sheet and do the same. Butcher's brown paper can also be slipped out in sections. Make sure the surfaces don't move as you're doing this. A rubber roller run over the surface using heavy pressure will assure a tight fit for years to come.

Wallpaper adhesives have changed a great deal, as have those used for setting ceramic tiles. Both will be covered more extensively in their respective chapters.

Nails are the primary form of fastening anything when building a home. Sized in pennies (abbreviated d), standard, or common, nails are used for framing and general work, with specific and special designs taking care of other work. Casing nails are used for moldings and have a countersunk style head that's left level with the molding in most cases. Finish nails are driven below the surface with a nail set and are then usually puttied over.

Wallboard nails are designed to be driven with a dimple around the head so that joint compound can cover the nail head for a finished look. Use ring shank nails only when installing wallboard. You can also buy a selection of nail/screws for wallboard. These are driven with a special Phillips driver chucked into an electric drill. Such wallboard screws are best used during ceiling installation; driving nails overhead is difficult work.

Woodscrews are used for installing items such

Fig. 2-37. Jig saw (Courtesy of Porter-Cable).

Fig. 2-38. Table saw (Courtesy of Black & Decker).

as door hardware. A pilot hole makes screws easier to drive as does a touch of soap on the threads. Beeswax also works well. Flathead screws can be left flush with the surface of the wood, countersunk to allow for puttying over, or counterbored to allow installation of pegs to cover the screwhead. Oval and round head screws are generally run in until the bottom part of the head meets the wood surface, and left to show.

Machine screws and nuts can be used to hold most parts, no matter the material, together. Lag screws or bolts are generally seen holding wood parts to masonry or other heavy wood parts. When used with masonry, a lag shield is installed. This lead shield expands and grips the masonry, but will require some drilling for installation.

DRAIN PIPE CLEANING TOOLS

One of the most effective drain cleaning tools, the auger, consists of galvanized spring wire with a spiral gimlet head. For cleaning a pipe, the auger head is put into the drain pipe and rotated with a handle or wheel at the other end of the tool. The gimlet head is forced through the clog, picking up some

Fig. 2-39. Radial arm saw (Courtesy of Black & Decker).

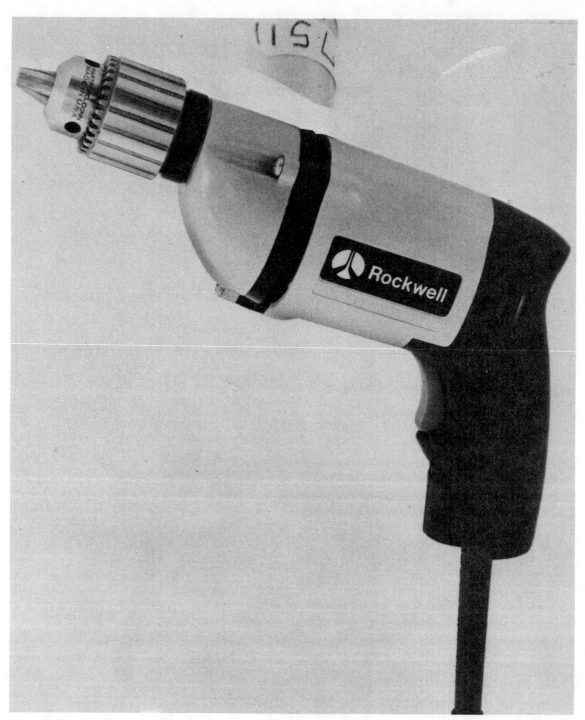

Fig. 2-40. Three-eighths-inch electric drill (Courtesy of Porter-Cable).

Fig. 2-41. Using an electric drill for plumbing prep (Courtesy of Genova, Inc.).

of the blockage on its head. The tool is then removed and cleaned, and the progress repeated until the drain is cleared. Gear driven augers are available, as are other types, including power augers. Other drain cleaning tools include wire brushes, clean-out screws, and various cutters, including root cutters. Specially designed toilet bowl augers are made for cleaning out clogged toilets. Power augers are not used on toilets.

PIPE CUTTERS, PIPE THREADERS, AND THREAD CUTTERS

Because it is not always possible to purchase pipe in the exact length and diameter that you need, with threads at both ends, you may need to use a pipe cutter to tailor your own. Pipe cutters are used on steel, brass, copper, wrought iron, or lead. A pipe cutter produces a clean, correctly angled cut that is difficult to achieve with a hacksaw. Directions for using a pipe cutter will be included in a later chapter.

If you must cut your own pipe you will proba-

bly also need a thread cutting tool. It consists of the die and the die holder. A guide will ensure a correct angle.

FLARING TOOL

Flaring copper tubing is simple with a flaring tool. The flaring tool will push into the tubing, forcing the end to assume a bent-out shape with an outward bent lip.

PAINTING TOOLS

For speed and convenience, homeowners usually prefer to use a roller on walls, ceilings, and other large surfaces, and then use a brush at corners, along edges, and in other places a roller cannot reach. Proper depth of the pile or nap on the roller cover is important and varies from one surface to another. Follow the manufacturer's recommendations.

Rectangular applicators are available that offer the speed and convenience of rollers. They, too, are desirable to use on large surfaces. These applicators are available through most retailers.

Fig. 2-42. Solvent-weld kit (Courtesy of Genova, Inc.).

Fig. 2-43. Cements for plastic plumbing (Courtesy of Genova, Inc.).

56

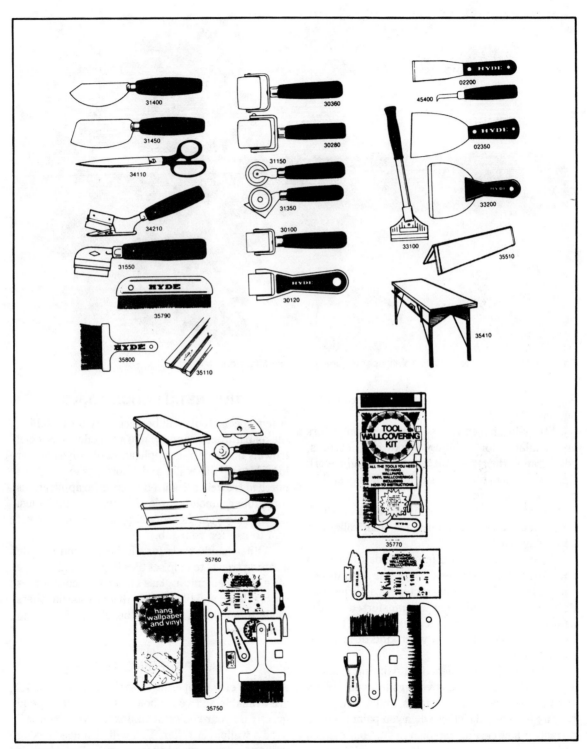

Fig. 2-44. Wallpapering tools (Courtesy of Hyde Mfg. Co.).

Fig. 2-45. Paste brush for installing wallpaper (Courtesy of Hyde Mfg. Co.).

Again, follow the manufacturer's recommendations.

Specially shaped rollers and other applicators are available for painting woodwork, corners, edges, and other close places. Some might work fine, others not so well. A small brush may still be best for such work.

Woodwork is usually painted with a brush. A brush penetrates better on wood than rollers or spray painting can.

Keep in mind that different kinds of brushes and rollers are recommended for use with different kinds of paint. The characteristics of the bristle affect how well paint is transferred to the painting surface. Your paint dealer should be able to furnish sound advice on what kind of brush or roller to buy.

Other equipment needed for painting includes a stepladder, protective coverings to avoid splash or spillage on the wrong surfaces, and wiping rags. Be sure to wear old clothes when you paint because no matter how careful you plan to be, your clothes will end up with at least a few paint splatters.

TILE INSTALLATION TOOLS

A few special tools will be necessary for installing tile on bathroom floors, walls, and ceilings. Special trowels make correct application of adhesives for long lasting tile walls and floors easier. Various notched trowels are suited to specific applications for rubber, linoleum plastic, and ceramic tiles. Check with your flooring supplier for the correct tool to use for your job.

Other handy tools for tile installation include a setting trowel to help set tiles in place and to wipe off excess cement; a glass cutter for scoring tiles for breaking; and tile nippers that are special pliers made to notch out openings on tiles to fit around water pipes.

WALLPAPERING TOOLS

A variety of wallpapering tools (Figs. 2-44 and 2-45) are available and your choice of tools will depend greatly on your choice of wallpaper type. You will need a wallpaper roller. You will also need casing knives for trimming wallpaper on walls while it is still wet before the paper dries around windows, door frames, and baseboards. Wallpaper knives may be used to trim paper on a paste table with a straight edge as a guide or on walls at ceiling and baseboard.

Shears are used to trim paper around light switches and ceiling fixtures. Forged steel shears with 12-inch blades would be a good choice for wallpaper shears. A razor knife with a replaceable single edge razor blade is an all-purpose trimming tool for wallpaper. Special vinyl wallcovering trimming knives are available that hold a disposable single edge industrial razor blade. Sometimes called a "seam buster," the tool cuts overlapped seams for a perfect butt seam. These as well as other wallpapering tools are available at your local wallpaper dealer. Ask his advice about the most practical tools for installing wallpaper in your bathroom.

Chapter 3

Your Home's Plumbing and Septic Systems

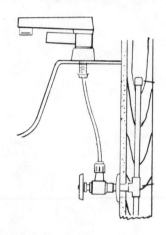

IN ORDER TO PLAN AND REMODEL OR BUILD A new bathroom, you must understand how your home's plumbing and septic systems work. Each adult in a typical home will use from 50 to 100 gallons of water each day, and a child under two will need the top end of that estimate. Therefore a family of five could easily use 400 gallons of water per day. That's a lot of washes and flushes moving through the pipes. If well designed and executed a plumbing system can easily handle such a load. A poorly designed, installed, or maintained system, however, can be expected to let the family down somehow, whether in low pressure, leaks, clogs, or even broken pipes. Understand your plumbing system before you attempt to modify it. Learn its limitations and its capabilities and respect them.

Your home's plumbing system (Fig. 3-1) can be broken down into two separate systems that function together. They are the water supply system and the drain-waste-vent system. One cannot function without the other and the two must be designed to be totally compatible.

SOME PLUMBING TERMS

Learning some common plumbing terms will help when you check your local plumbing codes and will help in planning your bathroom.

A drain pipe is any pipe in a building's drainage system carrying water or water-borne waste, while a fixture drain is the portion of a drain line between the trap of a fixture and the point at which the drain line joins any other drain pipe. A waste pipe is applied only when a pipe receives the discharges from fixtures other than water closets, urinals, and other appliances receiving human waste products directly. You'll find waste pipes only on sinks, bathtubs, laundry trays, washing machines, showers, and similar fixtures (Fig. 3-2).

A soil pipe or a soil stack is the largest pipe in diameter in the drain-waste-vent installation, with its lower end connected to the building or house drain (Fig. 3-3). The house drain is the pipe leading outside to the house sewer, that then leads to the street sewer or your septic tank and field.

A main is any major pipe to which other drains

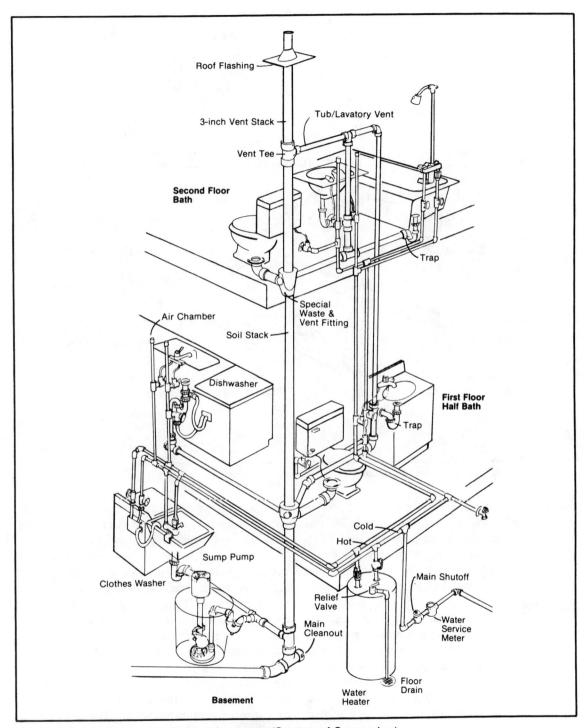

Fig. 3-1. A look inside your home's plumbing system (Courtesy of Genova, Inc.).

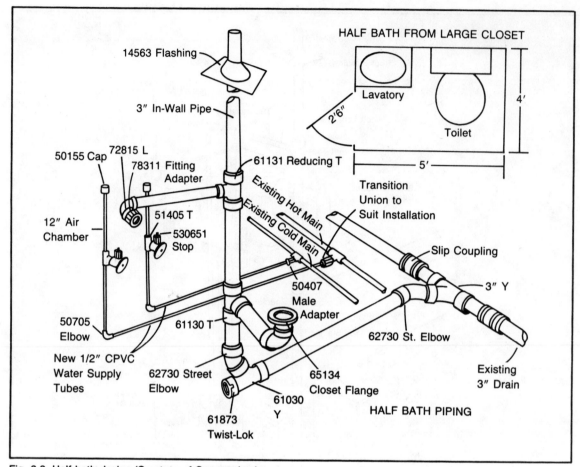

Fig. 3-2. Half bath design (Courtesy of Genova, Inc.).

or waste pipes are connected and the connection can be indirect, through branches. Vertical mains are called stacks, which can carry any form of effluent, while waste stacks carry only liquids received from lavatories, bathtubs, and the like, and not from toilets and urinals. Vent stacks are vertical mains in the venting system (Fig. 3-4).

Branch vents are vent pipes connecting the vent stack to branches in the drainage system. A dual vent connects at the point where two fixture drains meet, while a continuous waste and vent is a vent pipe and a waste pipe in a straight line.

A relief vent runs from a branch of the vent stack to the soil stack or the waste stack so that air can circulate between the two connected stacks. A back vent is any vent connected so that air will enter a waste pipe and water cannot be siphoned out, while a wet vent is the part of a waste pipe that acts as a vent for other fixtures on the same line.

A horizontal, or lateral, branch is a drain pipe extending from the soil stack, waste stack, or building drain, and it receives the discharge from one or more fixtures. It can include some vertical sections as well as horizontals. An offset is a combination of fittings to carry a line off to one side and then continue that line parallel with the original line. A double-offset (jumpover) is two offsets, one of which reconnects the offset with its original line. A dry vent is a vent that at no point carries water or water-borne effluent, and a continuous vent is a waste pipe running from one or more fixtures into a single trap (Fig. 3-5).

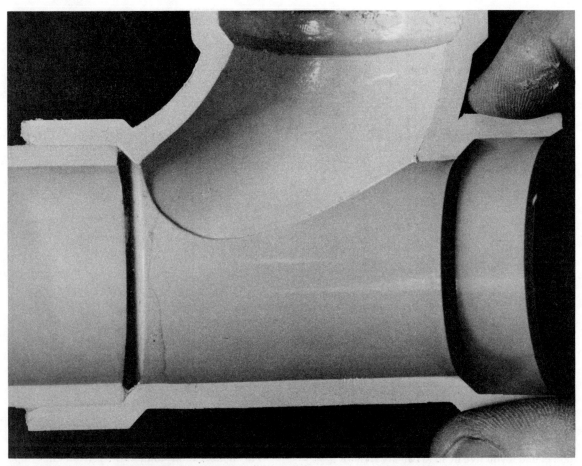

Fig. 3-3. Cutaway of plastic DWP pipe (Courtesy of Genova, Inc.).

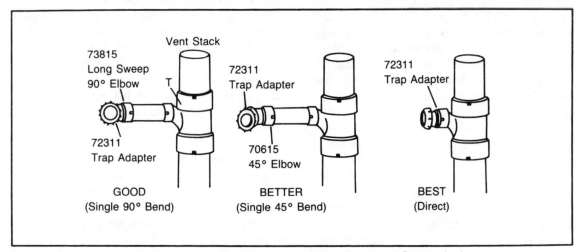

Fig. 3-4. Three methods of installing above-the-floor lavatory wastes (Courtesy of Genova, Inc.).

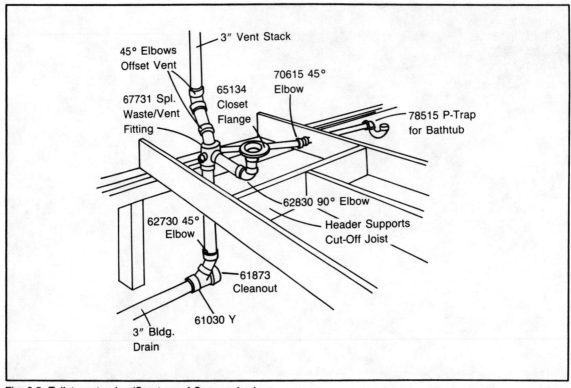

Fig. 3-5. Toilet waste pipe (Courtesy of Genova, Inc.).

WATER SUPPLY SYSTEM

The water supply to the home is of great importance, and if you live in an urban area, there's very little you can do to change things outside your front door. If you live in the country, or in certain suburban areas, you'll have your own well. Now is the time to consider changes that might be needed in that area, whether for inlet supply lines, a deeper well, more powerful pump motor, new storage tank, or other upgrading. An adequate flow of water must be available to the home for the internal plumbing to function optimally.

Near the low point of your main water supply should be a shut-off valve for the entire system, whether you're on a well or a city water system. The system may be supplied with what is called a stop-and-waste valve, that allows you to back drain the entire system after shutting off the water flow totally. This valve should be labeled in case of emergency and it should also be marked with a reminder that any time it's used, the hot water

heater *must* be shut down as well. Heating an empty hot water tank will rapidly ruin it.

The house main comes away from the stop valve and will stop first at the water softener if there is one in the house line. Water for outdoor use, and often general cold water use, will bypass the water softener. The main runs in near the hot water heater, where it splits so that you have two water supplies, hot and cold. From this point, the water is routed on to the various fixtures throughout your home, from the hot and cold mains. Branches lead to the fixtures and risers come up through the floors or walls to the fixtures themselves.

When attaching a home to a municipal water supply, the first step is to determine the position of the water main under the street and make a street cut to remove a section of pavement. From that cut a trench is made all the way back to the house. The trench must be well below the maximum frost line.

A water service line is attached to the main by bolting a saddle around the water main. The hole on the top of the saddle must be positioned correctly, with a valve threaded into the hole and tightened. The valve can be opened with a drill bit and a hole bored into the water main. Little water will escape. After the bit is removed the valve is closed and the tool removed.

Pipe or tubing are attached to the valve and run to another valve, probably positioned near the sidewalk. This curb valve may also be where your water meter will be installed for accurate reading of water consumption. The line is finally extended into the house.

Pipe sizing is important for correct water flow. You might find air chambers behind the wall where fixtures are located; this indicates top quality plumbing. You can easily install air chambers if they are missing from your system. They are nothing more than extensions of the supply pipes, about a foot long, capped on one end. What they do is prevent water hammer that can damage the fittings. When the system is pressurized, the water rises in the chambers but leaves an air pocket compressed at the top. That air pocket cushions the shock of fast water running through the system as it stops suddenly when you shut off the tap. Really rapid

shut-downs can create water pressures up in the 500-pounds-per-square-inch area, causing the action called water hammer that can damage the system over time.

Each fixture must have a shut-off valve in its riser tube. In most cases the shut-off valves will be directly under the fixture near the floor, but in some cases the shut-offs will be found under the floor. Their purpose is simple: you can't make a repair to the faucet or any upper part of the system while there's still water pressure on it, and the shut-off valve allows you to cut the supply to either the hot or cold water side of any fixture.

Too often, sinks and bathtubs are overlooked when shut-off valves are installed, yet these heavily-used fixtures are among the first to need minor repairs. Install the shut-offs the first time you have to work on the fixture (Fig. 3-6).

DRAIN-WASTE-VENT SYSTEM

The purpose of the drain-waste-vent (DWV) system is to carry away wastes and excreta that contain disease producing micro-organisms. The DWV system, therefore, is a very important part of the overall system and must be well understood before you attempt any plumbing work, including simple repairs (Figs 3-7 through 3-9).

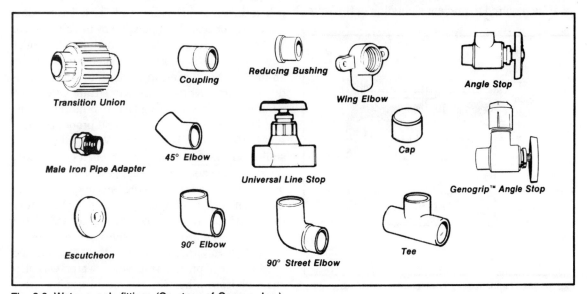

Fig. 3-6. Water supply fittings (Courtesy of Genova, Inc.).

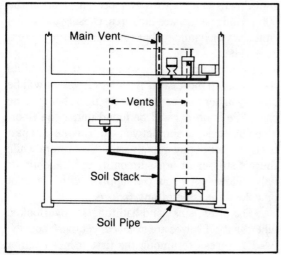

Fig. 3-7. Diagram of economical waste and vent piping.

Of the two main portions of a drainage system, one part is designed to carry liquids and water-carried waste, and the parts of the system involved are the drain pipes, waste pipes, and the lower portion of the soil stack. Included in this section are the traps at the various fixtures. The second part of the DWV system is the vent system. A vent is any pipe allowing flow of air to or from the drainage pipes. It can also be any pipe providing for circulation of air within the DWV system. This flow of air is required to prevent siphoning of the water

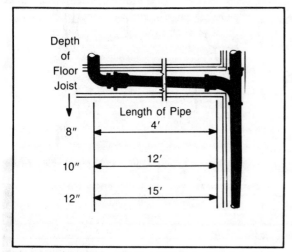

Fig. 3-8. Joist depth needed for different length of waste pipe sloping 1/4 inch per foot.

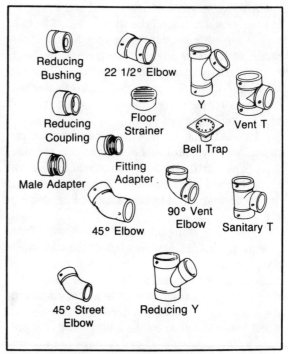

Fig. 3-9. Drain-waste-vent fittings (Courtesy of Genova, Inc.).

from the traps, or just as bad, a build-up of back pressure that would blow the water back out into the room and leave the traps open.

As a general rule, each fixture must have its own trap, but occasionally you'll see a fixture without a trap or one that appears not to have a trap. In the case of toilets, traps are built into the toilet bowl and there is no need to install a second one on the fixture exterior. In some cases several laundry trays drain through the same trap. Otherwise a fixture requires a trap and a trap requires a vent.

Vents are very important, and proper connection in the system is essential. Vents must be installed so there is a continuous open connection, through the vents, to the upper part of the soil stack or vent stack and through the tops of the stacks to the open air. Vent pipes equalize air pressure through these connections, so that trap seals have the same pressure on both sides and are not siphoned off in either direction. Without vents the suction effect on the trap when water was discharged from other fixtures could readily draw enough water from the trap to break the seal, allowing sewer gas to enter the house. Too, without venting the sewer side of the traps might eventually build enough pressure to force the sewer gases through the trap and into the building (Fig. 3-10).

When drainage pipes are carrying no discharges, the system allows free travel of air from the building drain through the soil or vent stack, the waste lines, and on to the roof terminal. Air circulation in this manner helps cut down on the slime formed in drainage pipes and can help reduce corrosion in systems using metal pipe (Figs. 3-11 through 3-14).

Stack venting is commonly used these days, with the connections to the stack providing the vents as long as the fixtures are not placed great distances from the stack itself. The upper end of

the stack forms the vent pipe and projects through the roof of the house so that the stack vent is essentially an extension of the soil or waste stack, going on above the highest horizontal branch or highest fixture branch connected to that stack. The stack vent should be the same diameter as the soil or waste stack if the stack has two or more floor levels. If the vent off the stack is for only a single floor level, it need not be any larger than would be required for a separate vent, unless the soil stack is carrying its full allowable load (Figs. 3-15 through 3-23).

Fixture vents are required when the fixture is far from a soil stack, with the vent placed between the stack and the fixture, but usually closer to the fixture. In some cases, the vent is placed closer to

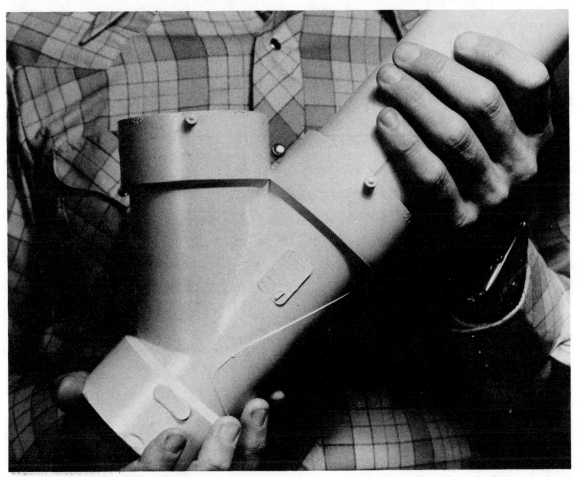

Fig. 3-10. Y fitting (Courtesy of Genova, Inc.).

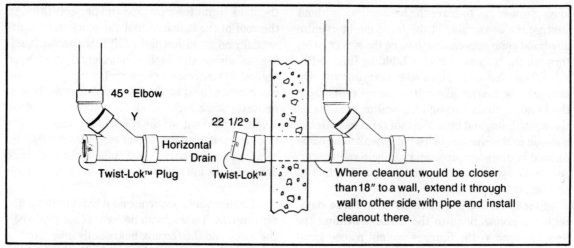

Fig. 3-11. Installing cleanouts (Courtesy of Genova, Inc.).

the stack to allow easier placement of walls. Toilets require their own vents using a special fitting attached to the closet bend, and the vent extending upwards from the fitting.

Venting for several grouped fixtures may be used with a single vent. This method may be used with a single or double story stack, with fixtures above and below, but the most usual use is when the toilet is on the lower floor with a sink and there are bathrooms above as well. For a complete bathroom vent when no other fixtures are above, the vent is run between the fixtures, off the waste line,

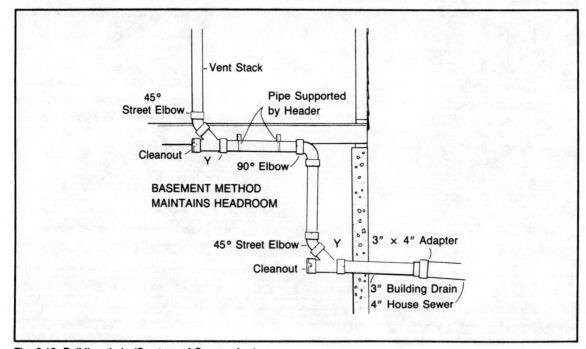

Fig. 3-12. Building drain (Courtesy of Genova, Inc.).

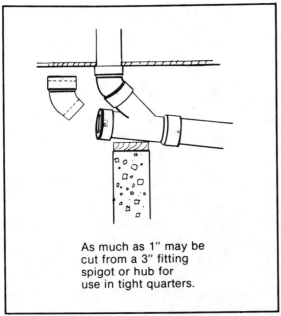

As much as 1″ may be
cut from a 3″ fitting
spigot or hub for
use in tight quarters.

Fig. 3-13. Alternate building drain (Courtesy of Genova, Inc.).

and then run back to the soil stack above the fixture height. This sounds more complex than it actually is (Fig. 3-24).

Back-to-back, or duplex, venting is a bit different but still can use a single soil stack and vent, simply backing them up to each other and making sure the common (top) vents are well above fixture height when they hit the stack.

There are several other types of venting, but most arc far more involved than necessary and unlikely to be used in modern residential plumbing, so there's little point in covering them here. Adding complexity of vent design adds complexity throughout the system and uses more materials.

The stack vent is the venting system normally chosen today and it would be helpful for you to recognize the names of the parts of the stack vent. A branch vent connects from a branch of the drainage system to the stack and forms parts of almost all venting systems. A back vent is any branch vent installed mainly for the purpose of protecting fixture traps against siphoning. Back vents include most vents not installed just to allow circulation of air between vent stacks and soil or waste stacks.

A continuous waste and vent is a vent pipe that lies in a straight line with a waste pipe to which it is connected, and forms a continuation of that waste pipe. A side vent connects to the drain through a 45-degree Y fitting. A dry vent is one that doesn't carry liquids but acts just like a vent, carrying only air all the time. A group vent is a branch vent that provides vent air for two or more traps and must be at least 1 1/2 inches in diameter to be effective. A dual vent is a type of group vent but is connected to the point where two fixture drains join, acting as a back vent for both drains. If the drains are on different levels, the separation between the connections cannot be more than five times the drain pipe diameter and the waste pipe must be large enough for both fixtures all the way to the top connection.

A circuit vent is a form of group vent that connects from a vent stack to a point on a horizontal branch in front of the last fixture connection on that branch, and a loop vent is much the same except that the vent is brought back to the soil or waste stack instead of connecting to the waste drain line. A relief vent is a vent pipe coming from a vent stack and connected to a horizontal branch at a point between the first fixture connection on that branch and the soil or waste stack. The main use of a relief vent is to allow air circulation between the vent stack and the soil or waste stack. It is unlikely you'll need these. Yoke vents are a form of relief vent but are carried into a Y fitting in the soil stack leading to the relief connection and the horizontal branch (Fig. 3-25).

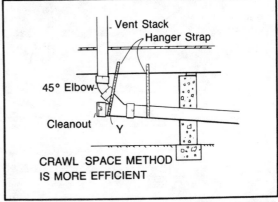

Fig. 3-14. Crawl space building drain (Courtesy of Genova, Inc.).

Fig. 3-15. A vent pipe being installed (Courtesy of Genova, Inc.).

Fig. 3-16. The base must be plumb, and the plumb line must hold all the way up (Courtesy of Genova, Inc.).

Vent pipes are connected so that liquid that happens to collect in the vent will drain into the soil stack, a waste or a drain with no help from anything but gravity. A horizontal vent pipe, then, must be pitched toward either the soil stack, the waste stack, or a drain. There should be no dips in horizontal vents; water from rain and condensation might remain at those dips. Vents on fixtures other than toilets should have their openings no lower than the dip of the trap protected by the vent.

When a vent pipe is connected to a horizontal waste pipe or to a horizontal soil pipe, the vent must be taken off the other pipe at a point above the pipe's center line. From that point of connection the vent must run straight up, or at an angle of not less than 45 degrees from the horizontal, to a point at least 6 inches higher than the fixture being vented before the vent can turn to the horizontal, or before it can connect to the main vent or soil stack. If such connections are made too low, the vent pipe might eventually load up with solids, rendering the system unvented.

Traps are essential to a safe plumbing system and are one of the first things the building inspector will check out. Traps are classified according to their shapes as **P** or **S** traps. They're really not

Fig. 3-17. Drive a nail through from underneath to mark the edge of the roof sheathing cut (Courtesy of Genova, Inc.).

Fig. 3-18. Making an elbow in the vent pipe (Courtesy of Genova, Inc.).

much more than downward loops in the undersink pipe that allow the flow of water through the drain without allowing sewer gas to discharge back into the house. Traps need to be of the proper size and design for a particular fixture and for the overall system. As long as a fixture is used occasionally there is little problem with trap leaking. The evaporation of water in a trap can allow sewer gas seepage, as can sudden high winds hitting the vent tops and causing air pressure that sucks the traps dry. The latter happens only infrequently and the seal is replaced as soon as the fixture is used. The

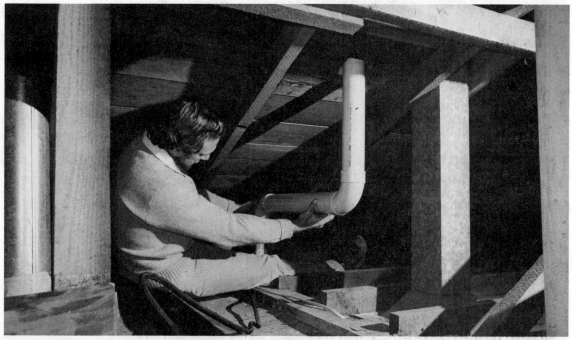

Fig. 3-19. Elbow can improve location of vent pipe (Courtesy of Genova, Inc.).

Fig. 3-20. Removing the shingle for the vent pipe (Courtesy of Genova, Inc.).

Fig. 3-21. Cutting sheathing (Courtesy of Genova, Inc.).

evaporation problem is readily solved by using the fixture for a flush or so every couple of weeks, or even monthly (Fig. 3-26).

Traps at one time were almost entirely made of cast iron, but recently lighter metals have come into use, and now plastic is also used. Drain line traps are of heavier material than are fixture traps and it is always wise to have traps with cleanout plugs at their bases, regardless of the materials they're made of. It is far simpler to remove a clog through a cleanout plug than it is to disassemble the entire trap. Toilet traps won't have cleanout plugs.

All traps must be vented, usually with a back vent connection to a waste or drain pipe on the sewer side of the trap.

Traps are required between each fixture and the drain pipe or stack. You can use a single trap for no more than three laundry trays or basins, but this could allow waste water flowing from one fix-

Fig. 3-22. Install flashing (Courtesy of Genova, Inc.).

Fig. 3-23. Paint the vent pipe to match or contrast (Courtesy of Genova, Inc.).

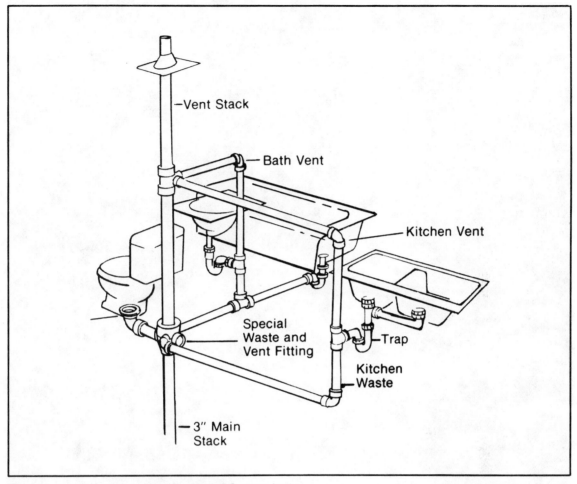

Vent Stack

Bath Vent

Kitchen Vent

Special
Waste and
Vent Fitting

Trap

Kitchen
Waste

3" Main
Stack

Fig. 3-24. A typical stack system (Courtesy of Genova, Inc.).

ture to rise into the bowl of another. This is not a good idea even where it's allowed. The savings in materials cost and installation time is minimal. No fixture is double trapped so that its discharge has to flow through one trap and then another before reaching the stack or house drain. No toilet trap may be used for any other fixture. Traps are placed as close to the fixture as is practical. In most instances in the bathroom this will be directly underneath the fixture drain (Fig. 3-27).

PIPE FOR PLUMBING

Local plumbing codes will require specific interior pipe diameters for specific uses. If your local codes do not agree with the figures here, follow local codes. The needed size for drain pipes depends, in part, on the kinds of fixtures drained. The toilet drain must run directly to the stack. See Table 3-1 for drain pipe diameters.

Pipes are sized to allow good waste flow so the pipe doesn't overfill and add to self-siphoning action, but the pipe diameter is kept small enough to allow good velocity through the pipe of the wastes. If several fixtures use a single drain, the single drain has to be so large that there's a severe drop in effluent velocity as it enters the larger pipe. This drop in velocity causes the effluent to drop in temperature and the two combine to cause greater sludge build-up at that point and for a distance beyond (Fig. 3-28).

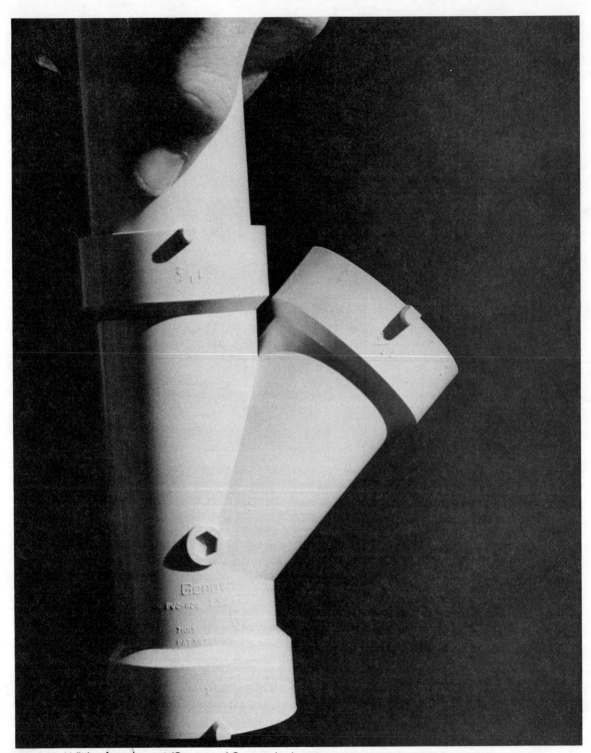

Fig. 3-25. Y fitting for yoke vent (Courtesy of Genova, Inc.).

78

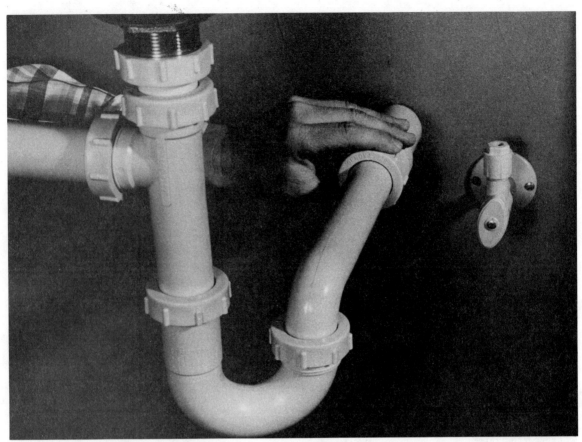

Fig. 3-26. P trap (Courtesy of Genova, Inc.).

Drain pipes are pitched to lessen velocity problems, and the pitch will vary from as little as 1/16 inch to as much as 1/2 inch, with 1/4 inch per foot the most commonly used. Pitch must never be so great that the outlet from an unvented portion of the pipe is lower than the dip of the trap on the fixture, or you'll have siphoning problems. While it may not seem important over a long drain pipe run, the horizontal drop at 1/2 inch per foot can be considerable and must be considered. If the result is as above, use less pitch.

The more likely problem is a long run of relatively small diameter drain from a single fixture not having enough pitch. Over time, this allows the build-up of sludge, restricting the pipe size and allowing the pipe to completely fill during heavy discharges that will siphon the traps.

To determine the slope of horizontal fixture drains, figure the total distance from the trap dam (plug) under the fixture to the fitting attached to the vent pipe. This should be no more than a single pipe diameter in total drop. In other words, use no more than a 1 1/2-inch drop over the run for a pipe 1 1/2 inches in diameter and 2 inches for a pipe 2 inches in diameter.

The length along the center lines of the pipe from the trap dam to the vent fitting should be at least two pipe diameters but no more than 48 pipe diameters. Thus, a 1 1/2-inch fixture drain should be no shorter—on the horizontal run—than 3 inches, and no longer than 6 feet. Keep the slope of pipe from 2 inches in diameter down no less than 1/4 inch per foot. Larger pipe can use a slope of only 1/8 inch per foot, up to 5 inches, and 1/16 inch per foot, from 5 to 8 inches. You won't be working with anything larger in residential plumbing and in fact

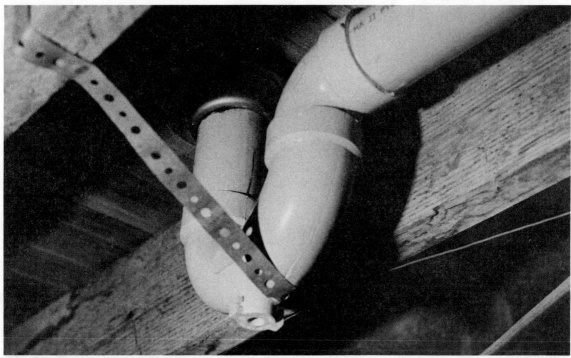

Fig. 3-27. Plumber's strap support for P trap (Courtesy of Genova, Inc.).

Fig. 3-28. Pipe size; Schedule 30 on right (Courtesy of Genova, Inc.).

80

Table 3-1. Minimum Drainpipe Diameters.

Fixture	Diameter
Bathtub, Bidet	1 1/2 inches
Shower (single)	1 1/2 inches
Basin (single)	1 1/4 inches (1 1/2 is better)
Basin (double)	1 1/2 inches
Toilet	3 inches

will seldom be getting to 6 inches.

Table 3-2 indicates the drain pipe length and slope for sizes from 1 1/2 to 6 inches in diameter, omitting intermediate sizes seldom used today. All sizes are in inches.

Drainage fittings present a few problems as any sudden enlargement or recess becomes a sludge collector, so the fittings are typically quite different from those used in water supply systems. Flow must be as even and clear as possible, with the inside diameter of the drainage fitting matching the inside diameter of the pipe that fits into it, so the bore remains continuous through the length. Water supply fittings vary considerably in bore size from line to fitting and back, but the velocity of the incoming water tends to even things out in such places, while the velocity in waste fittings is often far lower. Directional changes tend to be less sudden too, with more smooth lines designed into even 90-degree elbows so that velocity is maintained as much as possible and there is no sharp corner for sludge build-up.

Vent pipe sizes, in diameter, are important to proper system protection and no vent pipe should be under 1 1/4 inches in diameter. This is the ab-

solute minimum diameter to accommodate waste pipes of the same size. A vent connecting to a waste pipe 1 1/2 inches in diameter must also be 1 1/2 inches in diameter, and the same size can be used for waste pipes up to 2 inches in diameter, with vent pipe size rising to 2 inches after waste pipe size increases to 2 1/2 inches or larger. Vents 1 1/2 inches in diameter normally can serve two or three small fixtures, while 2-inch diameter vent pipe can serve as many as six small fixtures. Vents must never be less than half the diameter of the waste or drain pipe they protect.

Vent pipe lengths become important when they must change diameters, because the change in diameters restricts air flow: each piece of 2-inch pipe will have interior air flow resistance equal to 8.7 feet of 3-inch pipe. Every elbow or T fitting in the vent system has an air flow equivalent, usually several feet of straight pipe of the same size, and the tables here will help determine the overall length of your system for air flow purposes.

Though the figures used are for iron pipe, plastic pipe with its smoother interior surface allows better air flow. But such a better air flow is seldom allowed for in codes, so the maximum vent lengths remain the same. You might be able to get a variance.

The allowable limits for most codes, in vent stack length, must consist of all vents and fittings in the system, and of course vary with the diameter of the soil or waste stack and the diameter of the vent stack, as well as the number of fixtures connected. See Table 3-3 for guidelines.

Things can become much more complex with stacks running to 8 inches in diameter and various

Table 3-2. Drainpipe Fall.

Pipe Size (inches)	Length Minimum	Length Maximum	Fall Minimum	Fall Maximum
1 1/2	3	72	1 1/2	1 1/2
2	4	96	2	2
3	6	144	1 1/2	3
4	8	192	2	4
5	10	240	1 1/4	5
6	12	288	1 1/2	6

Table 3-3. Vent Fixtures.

Soil or waste Stack dia. (in.)	Fixtures Connected	Vent Diameter (inches) 1 1/2	2	2 1/2
1 1/2	8	150		
1 1/2	10	100		
2	12	75	200	
2	20	50	150	
2 1/2	42	30	100	300

fixtures rated at equivalent numbers of fixtures (and with different classifications for public fixtures in gyms and such places), but if you rate the fixtures as follows you should have no loading problems on your system. A bathtub equals 2-3 fixture units, depending on size; a bidet rates 2; a showerhead rates 2; a toilet rates 2 or 3 (2 for water saver models); and a sink rates 1. A bathroom group, including a sink, toilet, and a bathtub with or without a showerhead, rates from 6 to 8.

If we assume a more or less standard bathroom being added to a house and the soil and vent stacks are already 2 inches in diameter or larger, the added capacity will mean little, with a total of only 6 or 8 units for fixtures, assuming the stack is not fully loaded already. If it is fully loaded, you have two choices: add a stack or replace the current stack with a larger one. It is generally easier to add a stack, especially if the new bathroom unit will not be opening up walls enclosing the old stacks.

If you are simply replacing an old bathroom, there's little problem. Or should be little problem. If the current plumbing meets the codes, the new plumbing should too, because it is only connecting with what is already in place as a base. Make sure all new traps are installed correctly and you've almost got it made. Most houses are built with drain and waste stacks from 4 to 6 inches in diameter, so there's seldom any real problem, as a 4-inch diameter stack would allow a maximum of 384 fixture units, and a maximum of 300 feet of venting, while a 6-inch stack would allow far more fixture units than you'll ever need (over 2000), and over 500 feet of venting. Using sanitary T instead of Y fittings would reduce those figures to 256 fixture units for the 4-inch stack and not quite 1400 for the 6-inch stack. That's still far more than adequate for any residence (Fig. 3-29). Figures 3-31 through 3-35 illustrate the relationships between fixtures, lines, and vent stack.

THE SEPTIC SYSTEM

If your home is not hooked into a city sewer system you will have a private sewage disposal facility. Septic tanks and fields are the most common method of dealing with rural wastes, and they consist of a sewer pipe line from the house, a septic tank, and the seepage field. The line brings all household effluent to the tank where solids settle out, or float, while being decomposed by bacterial action (aerobic action). The resultant liquid, which is really what is defined as effluent, flows out into the seepage field where it is absorbed by the ground.

This system is built below the ground, with piping sloping from the house to the far end of the seepage field so gravity flow will help keep down clogging problems. The system must be situated according to local codes, and only after percolation tests can it be determined how large both tank and field need to be to meet the intended uses of the house or other structure. In no case can the seepage field be located closer than 100 feet to a well, and all other parts of the septic system must be at least 50 feet from a well.

Most codes require the tank be at least 5 feet from the house and 10 feet from the lot line, while other portions of the system may be no closer than 8 feet to the house and the same 10 feet from lot lines. These are general rules and should only be followed if your local codes are not more restrictive. A check with local health authorities or building inspectors is essential before placing a septic tank and field.

The septic tank must be sized to handle expected waste flow and it should not be under 750 gallons for a two-bedroom home. The tank will need to be at least 900 gallons for a three-bedroom house and each additional bedroom will require an additional 250 gallons of tank capacity. Such sizes are minimums and soil and other local conditions might require increases in these sizes.

Two-compartment septic tanks are best because they work more efficiently and will need less frequent cleaning. Tanks may be built of concrete block or they can be ordered in cast concrete in the appropriate size. If you're building your own septic tank from block or other materials, figure each cubic foot of capacity as holding 7 1/2 gallons. No matter how much of the rest of the system you plan to build, you should hire out the digging portions once you decide on tank location and field layout.

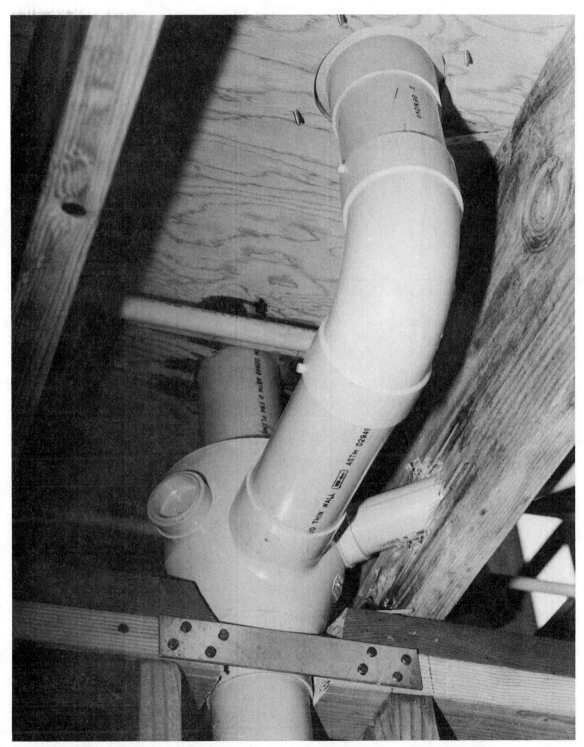

Fig. 3-29. Special waste-vent fitting (Courtesy of Genova, Inc.).

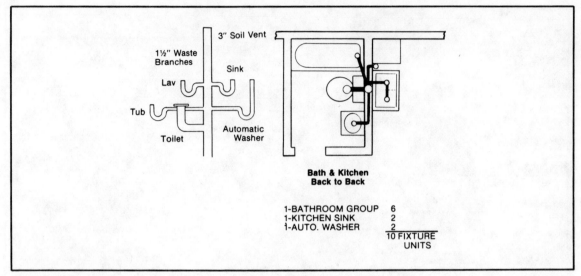

Fig. 3-30. Plumbing for back-to-back bath and kitchen (Courtesy of Genova, Inc.).

The excavation is an enormous job.

Percolation, or perk, testing presents another side to the question of size, particularly of the seepage field. Too small a field will overload the soil with effluent and probably turn the surface into a marsh at least part of the time. Too large a spread of seepage pipe simply eats up money you could use for other things. Thus, to size the seepage field properly a percolation test is required. In some areas you might be allowed to perform the test yourself, while in others you'll have to pay for the test, and in still others the test will be done for you at little or no cost by the local health department.

Seepage field size is going to depend on the amount of water it's likely to get from the house. The perk test determines the ability of the soil to

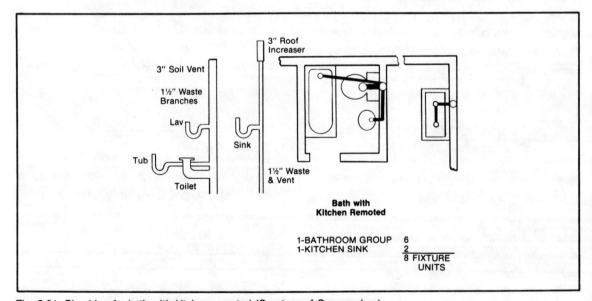

Fig. 3-31. Plumbing for bath with kitchen remoted (Courtesy of Genova, Inc.).

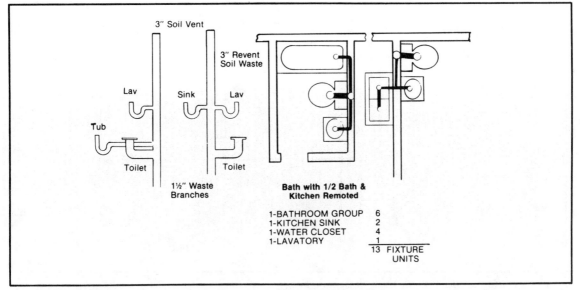

Fig. 3-32. Plumbing with half bath and kitchen remoted (Courtesy of Genova, Inc.).

handle the effluent. Tight clay fields absorb very little effluent, while loose sandy soils absorb the most; so a smaller drain field is required in sandy soil areas.

To do your own perk test, dig at least six holes around the area you plan to use for a seepage field. Make sure the field area is downslope from your house if possible, so there will be good gravity flow into the field. If the ground itself doesn't slope, a slope will have to be created as the field is trenched.

Make the test holes 4 to 12 inches in diameter and dig them the same depth your seepage bed must be, as much as 3 feet in cold areas, less in others (check local codes). Space the holes uni-

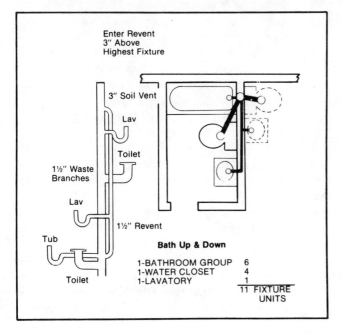

Fig. 3-33. Plumbing for bath up and down (Courtesy of Genova, Inc.).

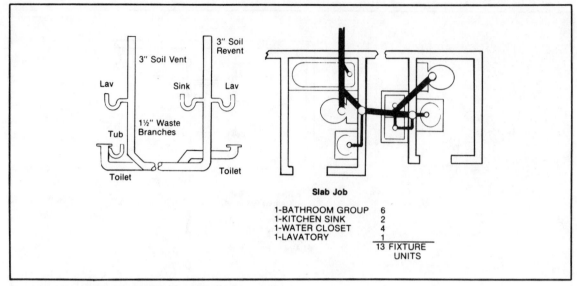

Fig. 3-34. Plumbing with slab job (Courtesy of Genova, Inc.).

formly over the entire bed area and roughen their sides to help absorption. Remove loose dirt and add 2 inches of sand or gravel to the bottom of each hole.

Now put at least a foot of water in each hole, adding more water as needed to keep the water level above the hole bottom for at least four hours. Finally, adjust the water level in each hole to 6 inches from the bottom. Wait 30 minutes and measure the water drop. Multiplying that figure by two will give you the inches of fall per hour, which is your soil's perk rate. Use an average for all the holes as a final figure.

If water seeps into the holes as they're being dug, the water table is too high to allow for a successful septic field and system.

If water won't stand in your perk test holes overnight, you're in good shape, lucky in fact. To check the water absorption rate there, add water to a 6-inch depth and keep adding more to hold that level for 3 1/2 hours. Then measure the water drop over the next 30 minutes and double that to get your perk rate. If the soil is very sandy, simply hold the water level at 6 inches for 50 minutes, bring it back to 6 inches and measure the drop in 10 minutes. Multiply that figure by six to get your perk rate.

If your soil gives a perk rate of under 1 inch per hour it's unsuitable for any type of soil absorption system. You will have to change locations or check with local health officials for an alternative plan.

The chart in Fig. 3-35 shows the seepage rate requirements, in square feet per bedroom, required for different soil absorption rates, and shows where seepage pits or trenches can be used instead of seepage beds. Such pits and trenches are generally used only where the surface soil presents major seepage problems, while the substrata will allow a decent perk rate. Trenches are considered better than pits because the sides of the trenches as well as the bottoms absorb effluent. Seepage pits are deep holes in the ground, with an exterior lining of porous masonry or concrete.

Should you require, for example, 200 square feet of seepage field for each bedroom, a three-bedroom house will require 600 square feet, or an area of 20 × 30 feet.

Once the system is planned, you can move on to the digging and installation of the tank and the seepage field lines. Most modern codes will allow you to continue the Schedule 30 In-wall outside the exterior house wall and the septic tank if you're using three-inch, in-house DWV, or continue with a 4-inch line if that's the case. Such codes simplify

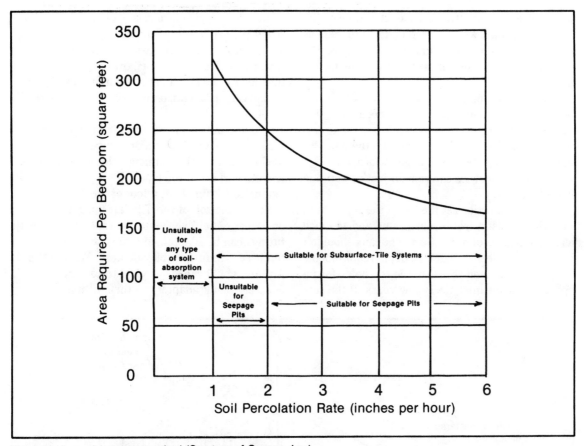

Fig. 3-35. Area of seepage required (Courtesy of Genova, Inc.).

things because you don't have to make a connection to a larger sewer line. Make sure you keep the slope to the septic tank at least 1/4 inch per foot so drainage will be good (Fig. 3-36).

If local codes require that you tie your 3- or 4-inch house line in with larger sewer pipe, you can get suitable solvent-weld PVC adapters for the job. Usually a 4-inch line is the largest required for any residence.

You'll want to install—and will probably have to in order to meet codes—a cleanout for the horizontal house-to-septic tank sewer line. This is situated at a point in the basement, crawlspace, or just outside the foundation wall, and should be reasonably easy to get to in case of future clogging problems. You can use a Y fitting with a twist-lock closure for an outside ground-level cleanout fitting. No cleanouts are required for the effluent lines.

Dig your sewer trench a few inches lower than required for the pipe and replace the dirt taken out with pea gravel or other coarse, absorptive dirt. Check the fill to go under the lines to make sure it's free of large rocks and lumps of frozen dirt. Dampen and tamp it down, making sure all fill has a uniform slope before any sewer line is laid on it. Dig extra depressions for fittings so that the lines rest only on the pipes. If fittings are the only support, you'll soon get line sag and clogging problems. No pipe should need to form a bridge over a depression in the trench bottom, nor should the pipe cross large bumps that haven't been properly dug out.

You'll probably find it easiest to assemble the sewer pipe lines on top of the ground rather than fumbling around in narrow trenches. If you do, wait at least 12 hours after solvent welding is complete before you lower the lines into the trenches. The joints cure and gain strength over that time so the leverage as you lower them won't damage them as they might if they were uncured. You save the 12-hour wait by solvent welding on the trench bottom.

Backfill around the sewer pipe with pea gravel or selected earth fill. Earth backfill should be lightly tamped down around the pipe while you make certain no rocks have made contact with the pipe. Final backfill should be free of large rocks and foreign matter, but otherwise can remain just as you dug it up (Fig. 3-37).

Tank connections at the top of the septic tank must be at least a foot below ground and as much as 3 feet in areas of heavy frost. The tank shouldn't be placed any deeper than frost depth requirements because you'll need access to the top holes for inspection and cleaning every few years. If the sep-

tic tank has no pipe fittings at its inlet, run the PVC sewer pipe right into it and use mortar to seal the space between a concrete or masonry tank and the sewer pipe. Don't use an elbow or T on the end of the pipe for the tank inlet as such fittings plug easily and can make horizontal drain cleaning more difficult.

At the outlet end of a septic tank without fittings, use a PVC T with a drop pipe into the tank, having the drop pipe running at least 18 inches below the surface of the liquid. This pipe can safely extend to within about a foot of the bottom of the tank and the top of the T is left open as a septic, or seepage, field vent into the tank. A tank with fittings can be adapted, and the clay pipe most often used will fit suitable adapters. With cast iron fittings you'll need a vinyl-to-cast-iron spigot adapter. Caulk adapters to their fittings.

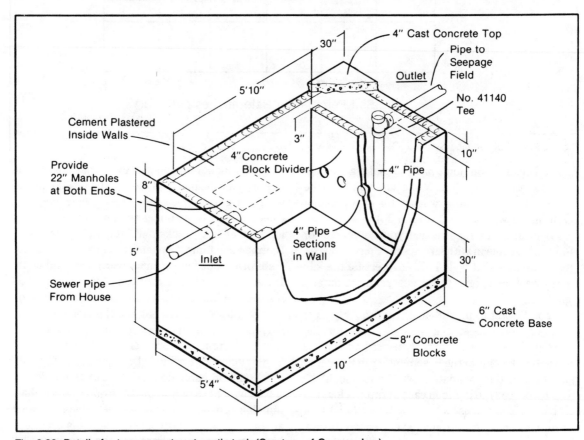

Fig. 3-36. Detail of a two-compartment septic tank (Courtesy of Genova, Inc.).

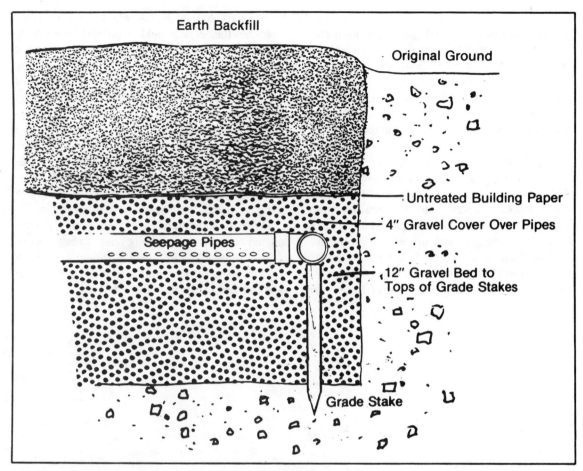

Fig. 3-37. A typical seepage bed (Courtesy of Genova, Inc.).

Seepage fields joint at outlet Ts through the septic tank wall and you should use a 6-foot length of PVC solid wall sewer pipe for this job, fitting its field end into a bull-nose T to start a grid system seepage bed. The bull-nose T, perforated pipe, and solid pipe are then used to construct the seepage field grid. The grid should be large enough to cover your required seepage field area.

Place perforations in pipe on the bottom when laying out the seepage field. Seepage pipe and fittings do not need to be solvent welded, though they may be if you wish, but a push fit is considered adequate.

To keep effluent from backing up in the field lines, make sure the slope is from 2 to 4 inches per 100 feet, which isn't a great deal (some codes might even require that they be level). When the land slopes, the seepage field lines should follow the land contours.

When the area for the seepage field has been excavated, put in about a foot of gravel and rake it out evenly, checking that the smallest gravel pieces are about 1/2 inch in size, while the largest are no greater than 2 1/2 inches. Build your seepage grid on the gravel and backfill the grid around the pipes with more gravel until you're at least 4 inches above the pipes. Using untreated building paper or straw, cover the gravel to prevent the soil from infiltrating. Then backfill the grid area with soil. If the seepage field and tank and other lines are to be inspected by local officials, do *not* backfill until after the inspection.

Seepage trenches, if you must use them, should be from 1 to 3 feet wide and spaced no closer than 6 feet apart (sidewall to sidewall), with 10 feet preferred. Usually seepage trenches are 3 feet deep and no trench should be any more than 100 feet long. If the length needed exceeds that, use several trenches. Calculate the seepage area of a trench by figuring the width times the length in feet. Pipe laying and backfill are the same as for a seepage bed.

If properly designed and laid, a septic field will last for a number of years, and if the seepage bed and tank are sized properly and installed with the correct slope, cleanout won't be required often. Some systems can function for more than 15 years without cleaning, and still present no problems.

The cleaning of a septic field becomes necessary when solid waste builds up too deeply on the bottom of the septic tank so that the effluent is not being swarmed over by bacteria to treat it before it reaches the seepage field. A properly sized tank, with a properly designed field, can make aerobic treatment more effective, meaning less sludge moves into the seepage field, and to the bottom of the tank, and problems are put off. Eventually any septic system require clean-out, while septic seepage fields eventually also become filled with sludge or the pipe will collapse. Old styles of pipe, such as Orangeburg and clay pipes, presented greater problems and were more likely than plastic pipe, particularly PVC, to collapse under the weight of heavy vehicles, frost heave, and other abuse.

With an understanding of your home's plumbing and septic systems you're ready to begin work on your remodeling or building project. Chapter 4 will guide you through preparation of the room for new finishes or for new fixtures.

Chapter 4

Preparing
Your Bathroom

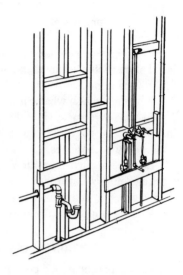

THE FIRST STEP IN PREPARING YOUR BATH-room for redecorating or remodeling or to build a new bathroom, is planning. You know what you want your bathroom to look like when you're finished, you know your budget, you have priced materials. Now is the time to plan the work schedule. This will be critical in a home with one bathroom in need of major alterations. It will be inconvenient at best. Bathroom work should be done as quickly as possible because it is a room used by every household member several times each day.

If your project consists mostly of decorative changes you might decide to work for a few hours each evening after other commitments are completed and finish the job in a few days or a week. Painting could be done in one or two evenings; a new sink cabinet another evening and floor tile laid on a third evening. The results could be beautiful with little disruption to anyone's schedule.

If your plans are a little more complex you will have to plan your schedule more carefully. Perhaps an intensive weekend's work with a helper or two

will see the completion of the job. If you're lucky enough to have another bathroom available for use, you will not be as pressured to finish the project, allowing plenty of time to perfect each stage of the project before moving on.

Your work will progress smoothly if you have all tools and materials on hand before starting. Valuable work time will be lost with each trip to the building supply or hardware store. Having everything on hand will also eliminate the frustration of not being able to locate the exact size of pipe you need or the type of tile knife you prefer to use. Beginning with enough of the correct color paint and sufficient adhesive for affixing tile will avoid stopping in the middle of the job to run to the store and will also ensure proper color matching.

There are five basic tasks in remodeling a bathroom: demolition, rough-in, installation, trim-out, and finishing.

Demolition is just what it implies. Old fixtures are removed, walls opened for access to plumbing and wiring, all the unwanted is eliminated.

Rough-in is the preparation for the new fix-

91

tures, repair of walls, relocation or addition of new pipes or wires, framing for closets, cabinets, or partitions.

Installation is the installation of all pieces except the toilet, because it is set on top of the finished floor. It is also the replacement of flexible supply lines and broken shut-off valves, and repair or change of pipes and wires.

Trim-out consists of hooking up plumbing for fixtures, connecting outlets, switches, and lights, installation of shower doors, medicine cabinets, and other such items.

Finishing is also what it implies. It includes applying wall coverings, smoothing subflooring and installing floor coverings, installing the toilet and adding any accessories.

Be sure to turn off your water supply before working on any bathroom fixture. Depending on your tasks, you can usually shut off individual fixtures or the supply to the entire house.

REMOVING FIXTURES

Turn off both the hot and cold water supply valves usually located under the sink. Using a basin wrench or an adjustable wrench, unscrew the top coupling nuts. Unscrew the coupling nuts above the shutoff valves if there are shutoff valves on the lines. This will free the lines. If there are no shutoff valves the supply lines can be removed after the sink has been moved.

Before disconnecting the trap to drain the pipe, place a bucket directly below the trap. Unscrew the cleanout plug then unscrew the slip nut to remove the trap from the tailpiece. Disconnect the pop-up drain by unscrewing the retainer nut.

To remove a countertop sink, place a 2- x -4 across the sink top and connect a wire around the 2- x -4 and through the drain hole to a wood block below the sink. Twist the block until it rests against the tailpiece and unscrew the lug bolts. You can then untwist the block and the basin will lower.

To remove the faucets, lay the sink face down and unscrew the lock nuts from the faucet stems. Lift out the washers and turn the sink upright. If the faucet assembly will not lift out easily, tap it lightly to break the putty seal.

Carefully clean all fittings and other parts that will be reused. Discard any fixtures and parts that will not be used again.

To remove a toilet, first turn off the supply valve tightly and flush the toilet to empty the bowl. Sponge out any remaining water from both the tank and the bowl. Remove the tank cover and toilet seat. Disconnect the supply line at the tank. Unscrew any bolts and washers holding the tank to the bowl and lift the tank out of the way. Now pry the caps off the flange bolts that attach the toilet to the floor and unscrew the nuts. Gently rock the bowl to loosen the putty seal and lift the toilet off. Clean old setting compound from the gasket with a putty knife. The flange may be reused if it is in good shape, but should be replaced if there are cracks or other signs of wear. Plug the hole with rags to prevent the escape of sewer gas into the room.

To remove a wall-mounted toilet, turn off the water supply, flush the toilet, and sponge away any water left in the tank or bowl. Remove the toilet seat and tank cover. Disconnect the water supply line at the tank. After removing bolts, nuts, and washers holding the tank to the bowl, lift the tank away. Remove the spud washer from the tank.

With a helper to hold the bowl, remove the caps, nuts, and washers from the bowl mounting bolts. The bowl can now be lifted off and set aside. Old setting compound should be removed from the toilet flanges and wall.

The first step to removing a bathtub is to turn off the water and drain both hot and cold water supply lines. If there is an access panel opposite the head of the tub, open it and loosen the slip nut connecting the waste and overflow pipes to the drain outlet. If there is no access panel you might choose to create one in the wall opposite the head of the tub. A 14- x -14-inch hole from floor level opposite the head of the tub will be useful if repairs are needed or a leak develops.

If there is no access panel and you choose not to make one, there is an alternative method to remove the drains. You can remove the overflow plate, lift-linkage, and strainer.

You will have to remove some of the wall covering above the tub to free the tub flanges. Cut away at least 4 inches above the tub if the wall covering is plaster, wallboard, or laminate panels. If tiled, use a cold chisel and hammer to chip away the molding and the first row of tile. With a fiberglass or steel tub there might also be screws or nails that must be removed to free the flange from the studs.

A steel or fiberglass tub should now pry away from the wall. A cast iron tub may require help for prying. In some cases, if the tub is enclosed on three sides, you might have to cut a hole through one wall to push the tub through and carry it out from another room.

Once the fixtures in your bathroom are removed, you will need to seal all of the exposed pipes. Supply lines with shutoff valves simply need a tape over the valve outlet hole. Supply lines without shutoff valves as well as drain outlets must be capped. Threaded pipe can easily be capped with a screw-on cap of the same material. Plugs will be needed for short pipe extenders with female threads and elbows. Cement on a plastic cap for unthreaded plastic pipes and solder on a copper head for unthreaded copper pipe.

NEW WALLS

If you are replacing walls and floors in your bathroom or are creating a bathroom out of another space, you will need to remove old wall and floor coverings and perhaps even pull down the walls and subflooring.

Know what is inside the wall and what you can do with it before beginning destruction. Plumbing pipes, wiring, and air ducts will have to be elsewhere accommodated if they are in a wall that is to be eliminated. If you are simply rebuilding the wall, you will need to be careful to not disturb such internal structures. Be sure to turn off electrical power to any wiring within a wall being torn down. Most non-load bearing walls can be easily changed or eliminated.

To begin removal, smash up a plaster or wallboard wall between the studs, using a heavy hammer. Wearing heavy gloves, pull out sections of wall by hand. A pry bar can be used to loosen any stubborn pieces. A circular saw can also be used to re-move walls of plaster, wallboard or paneling. Set the saw to the depth of the wall covering and saw out sections between studs. Tile walls must be broken up with a heavy hammer and torn free by hand and pry bar. Always wear protective gloves and goggles when tearing down a wall.

If you are taking out the entire wall, it is an easy task to remove the second side of wallboard, or other wall surface. From the back, simply loosen the wall panels and push them into the next room.

If the wall is to be eliminated, you can now cut the studs in half and pull them away from the top and sole plates. To remove end studs and the sole plate, make two cuts about 2 inches apart, halfway down the stud or plate. Work out the wood between the cuts and use your pry bar to loosen half of the piece you are removing. Then pry up the other half.

The top plate can be removed by using a keyhole saw to cut the ceiling along the inside edges of the two joists that flank the top plate. Cut in this manner between each block of wood that the top plate is attached to. Score the gaps in the cut with a utility knife and then use a hammer to break up the plaster and wood lath or wallboard between the ceiling cuts. Pull away the ceiling material with your hands. The top plate can now be pried away from the blocks.

The ceiling can then be patched with lengths of 1-×-2 nailing strips that are cut to fit between the blocks along the two joists. Plasterboard can be cut to fit the opening and nailed to the nailing strips and blocks. The floor can be repaired with a piece of wood the same thickness as the floor. It can be finished with the floor covering of your choice.

BASIC HOME CONSTRUCTION

Understanding basic home construction will be helpful as you rebuild your bathroom. After excavating for the basement, trenches are dug for the footings and piers. Footings, foundation walls, bearing post footings, chimney footings, and porch piers are put in. Cellar window frames are set into place as the foundation wall is built. Girders and posts are moved into position and fastened, then the sills are laid out. Floor joists go in, and openings through the floor for cellar stairs and chimney are framed. Bridging pieces are nailed into place between joists. Rough stairs to the basement are fastened into place.

During the second stage of construction studs and top plates for the first floor bearing partitions are cut and nailed together, and door openings are framed into the partitions before they are raised and braced in place. The top and bottom plates and ribbon boards for the outside walls are cut to length and position of outside wall studs marked on each. Window and door openings are also marked. Studs are notched to receive the ribbon board. Corner studs are framed, raised, and braced in place. The ribbon board and remaining studs are attached and second story floor joists are nailed into place, creating a base for the upper story.

During the third stage of construction, openings for chimney and stairs are framed, and joists are doubled under partitions running parallel beneath them. Outside wall studs are capped with double top plates and temporary bracing is put in. Cutting, doubling, and trussing in the outside wall for first floor windows and doors are put in. Sheathing is nailed into place up to the second floor. Outside walls are straightened and bridging is put in between the second floor joists. Headers are also put in. The subfloor for the second story is laid, diagonally, but in a direction opposite to the first floor subfloor. Interior second floor partitions are built in the same manner as those on the first floor.

Openings for second story windows are cut and framed in during the fourth stage of home construction. Attic floor joists, with stair and chimney framing are cut and fastened. The attic floor is laid. Outside wall sheathing is extended up to the attic floor line. The ridge board or rafter and roof rafters are laid out, cut to length and nailed into place. Gable end studs at each end of the structure are fitted into place and the balance of the rafters are put up and the chimney opening is cut. At this point the roof structure is nearly complete. Rough framing for the porches is done next.

During the fifth stage of construction the roof structure is completed, roof boards are nailed into place, and the shingles laid. Piping and ducts for

the plumbing and heating systems are installed. Window and outside door frames are set in and outside finish—such as base, corner boards and siding—are put on. Interior walls are ready to receive plaster or wallboard, with insulation. Porches are completed. Finish floors are laid, trim hardware installed, and finish coats of paint applied inside and out.

FRAMING FOR THE BATHROOM

Special framing needs for plumbing aren't great, but they are essential. It is necessary to give some thought to the framing of interior partition walls so they are able to accept larger-than-usual stacks and other plumbing runs. Special bracing is needed only under bathtubs, and then only when the bathtub is inserted so that its length runs the length of joists under it. An extra joist needs to be installed to support the loaded weight.

Special care must be taken when drilling or notching joists for pipe runs. Never notch the center 50 percent of any joist. Such notching and hole boring must be kept to a minimum to keep from weakening the joists a great deal. Bored holes (check your local codes) may be no greater than 2 inches in diameter, with the edge of the hole no nearer than 3 inches to the top or bottom of the joist (which means you must be starting with at least a 2-×-10 joist, since 2-×-8s will not leave the required 3 inches per side. Hole size in 2-×-8s is limited to 1 1/2 inches (Fig. 4-1).

Notches require joist reinforcement after you make the cuts. Notches can only be made in the end quarters of the span (while it's best to bore only in the end quarters as well, most codes will allow boring closer to the center). Notches may be only 1/6 the depth of the material, with any greater notching requiring bracing and sometimes headers and a tail beam. Scabs for reinforcement can be made with 3/4-inch plywood and should be attached with eight-penny screw nails on both sides of the notch (Fig. 4-2).

Bathtub support is best achieved using a doubled outer joist under or close to the outside edge of the bathtub and scab nailers are supports on the wall edge. These nailers are cut from the same ma-

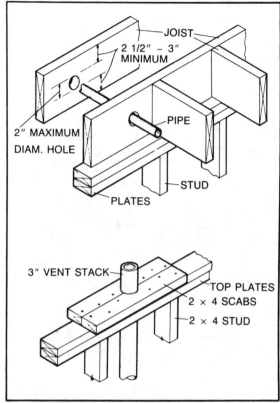

Fig. 4-1. Running pipes through joists.

terial as the wall studs and hold the bathtub lip before the interior wall is to be installed. Running an extra joist down the center of the bathtub is also a good idea, but make sure it's offset enough to allow clearance for the tub drain and trap. For the type of bathtub fitting into the wall, insulation—if that's an exterior wall—should be brought right to the tub side instead of just filling the spaces between the studs. If the tub is cast iron or steel, using foamed insulation from pressurized cans will assist in retaining heat. Before closing things up entirely, empty three or four cans as needed to fill the cavities around the bathtub (Fig. 4-3).

Wall framing for bathtubs generally involves the use of scabs where drain, waste, or vent pipe runs through sole and top plates (Fig. 4-4).

Basic wall framing is similar no matter what size lumber you use. Non-load bearing interior partitions are almost always legal on 2-foot centers. Using 2- × -6 studs, you can readily open up the centers of non-load bearing partitions to 30 inches, but then you will run into other problems. Almost all wall covering materials are designed to fit in foot multiples: 4- × -8 feet, 4- × -10 feet, 4- × -12 feet and so on. There are no 30-inch breaks, and all joints must have a nailing support on these materials. So you're

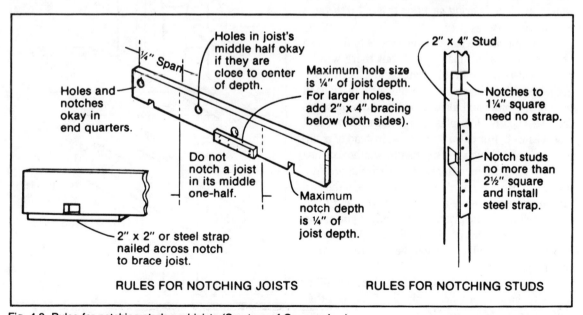

Fig. 4-2. Rules for notching studs and joists (Courtesy of Genova, Inc.).

95

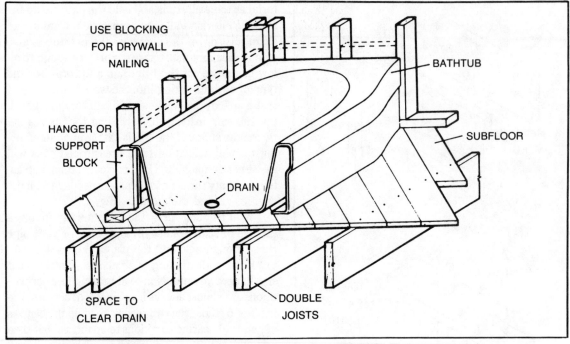

Fig. 4-3. Installing the bathtub.

pretty much held to 2 feet on center in your walls. There's no reason for going to 2-×-6 partition walls unless you want to retain 24 inches on center distances in a load bearing partition (Figs. 4-5 through 4-10).

You can cut the paneling materials to fit or use other materials to finish a wall, but there will be a lot of waste in the first instance and a lot of work in the second. Gypsum wallboard is most often used with taped joints and filled-in nailhead dimples. It's fast, less costly than plastering, not as dirty, and it serves well. For extra sturdiness, instead of a single layer of 1/2-inch thick gypsum wallboard, use two layers of 3/8-inch thick wallboard. Stagger the joints and use construction cement between the two layers and you'll have a finished wall that's difficult to tell from true plaster, especially if you spend a bit of time over the finish (Figs. 4-11 through 4-13). Interior wall finish will be covered later in this book.

A fast wood check is needed when installing a new bathroom, or when replacing floors or other components. Moisture is a constant in most

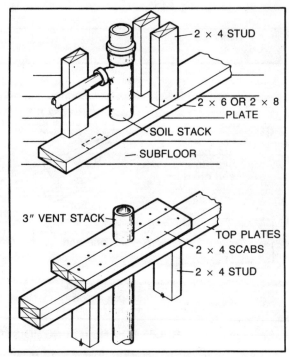

Fig. 4-4. How to frame walls for plumbing.

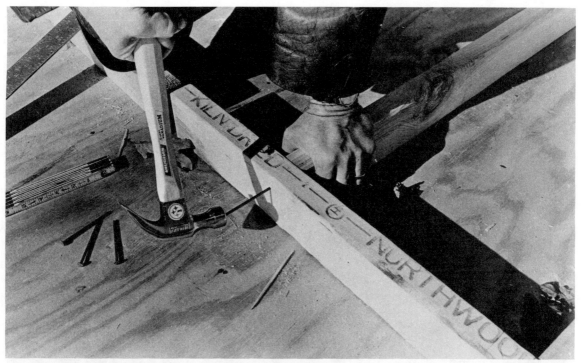
Fig. 4-5. How studs are nailed into sole plates (Courtesy of Vaughan).

Fig. 4-6. Notched 2-×-6 studs (Courtesy of Genova, Inc.).

Fig. 4-8. Furring is used to thicken walls and hide DWV runs (Courtesy of Genova, Inc.).

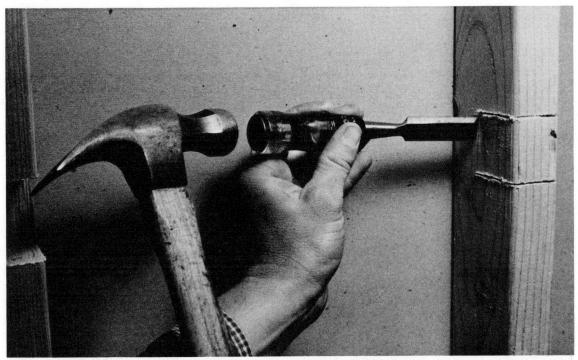
Fig. 4-9. Notches this size will require either plates or scabs (Courtesy of Genova, Inc.).

Fig. 4-10. Cutting through a header (Courtesy of Genova, Inc.).

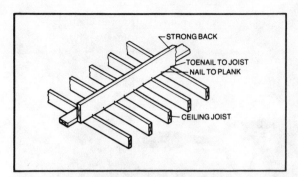

Fig. 4-11. Backing for installing wallboard.

bathrooms, no matter how carefully the building and ventilating is done. Special materials are required for floor underlayment, subfloors for walls around showers and bathtubs, and for finish coverings.

Consider the following story. A bathroom floor had to be replaced after only a dozen years because the plywood subfloor had peeled up in layers. Of course, the subsurface peeling also lifted the finish resilient tile from the floor and forced removal of the tub, toilet, and basin. A sheathing grade subflooring had been used, which is generally considered sufficient for occasionally moist conditions, such as might be found in a bathroom. But the builder didn't consider that the home was in a humid climate which made the toilet tank sweat. Because the floor was carpeted it stayed damp for

months on end. The result was rot and ply separation.

The simple solution is to use exterior grade plywood. The wood might rot after years of exposure to moisture but the plies will not separate. With a light coating of some good shellac, the plies are unlikely to ever separate because of wood rot either.

However, there is the possibility of rot in the lower portions of studs framing the walls around a shower stall or bathtub. Leaks can stay hidden for many years in such locations and by the time of discovery there will be little to do but rip the wall out and start from scratch. If you're starting from scratch, consider using pressure-treated lumber in those areas. For the few extra cents the treatment costs, you could find house life extended significantly. Inexpensive treating chemicals are sufficient for any wood not exposed to the ground.

The actual framing of any room depends on the overall design of the room, but some basic design details remain the same. Once subflooring is down, the sole plate is laid, and if the wall is an exterior one you'll want to check local building codes to see if you must work on 16-inch centers or if you can open up 2-foot centers. It never hurts to go to 2- × -6 use in exterior wall construction anyway, because this allows you to add a great deal more insulation in the wall (Figs. 4-14 and 4-15).

Once the exterior walls are framed and the in-

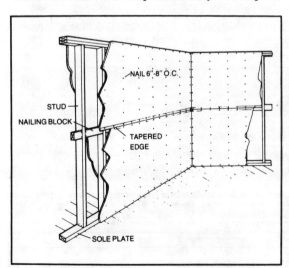

Fig. 4-12. Installing gypsum wallboard horizontally.

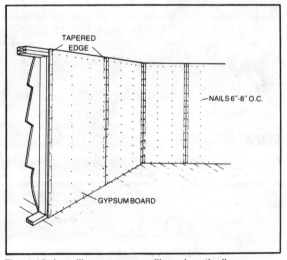

Fig. 4-13. Installing gypsum wallboard vertically.

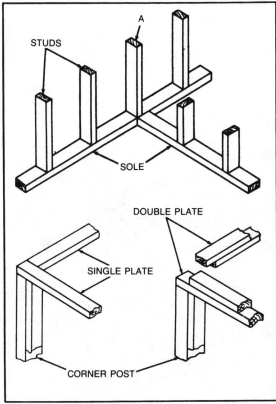

Fig. 4-14. Sole plate and top plate designs.

been nailed with 16-penny nails), and cut top plates to length using only a single top plate if you wish. Top plates are effective even on non-load bearing walls; they help to tie the overall structure together. Assemble the top plates using 12-penny nails if you're doubling them. Mark stud layout on them and nail the studs to them. If you're using doubled top plates, cut studs to length before adding the top plate second layer and nail through the top plate into the stud, using two 16-penny nails per stud. Then nail on the final top plate using 12-penny nails. This is tilted into place a section at a time, on the sole plate, and the toenailing is done using 12-penny nails. You might wish to use framing anchors instead of toenailing. It's easier and faster and you don't have to worry about water damage because the framing anchors and the special nails for them are all galvanized.

Corner posts are doubled and tripled as needed to form nailing anchors for interior finish materials, and to make sure there is no wobble to the framed walls (Fig. 4-16). Make sure all studs are plumb using at least a 2-foot level and checking each stud as it goes into place. Sole plates should be level. In old construction you'll almost certainly have to shim the sole plates to get them level. If this is needed, use shims, thick or thin as needed, about every 6 inches or even closer.

Framing doors isn't much of a challenge if the rest of the work is done neatly. The door you se-

sulation is in place, interior sole plates are laid and nailed in place to form the room shape. Next, mark the stud layout on the sole plates (which will have

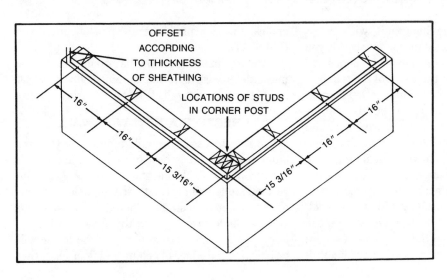

Fig. 4-15. Studs laid out in this manner will save a lot of work in wall assembly.

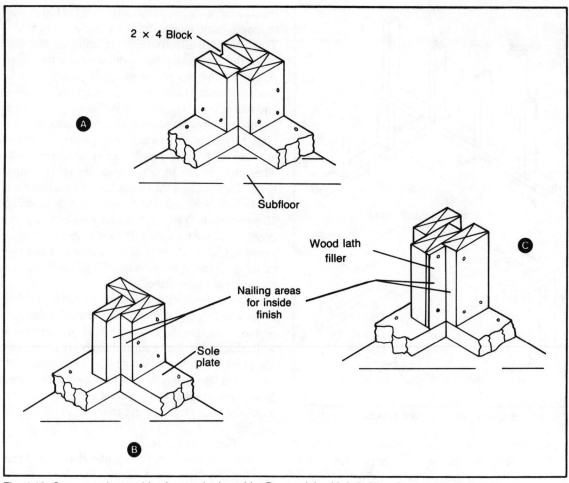

Fig. 4-16. Corner stud assembly: A—standard outside; B—special, with lath filler; C—special, without filler.

lect will probably be a prehung unit, with everything installed but the molding for finish. All you need to do is find the center line of the door location and measure out half the width of the required rough opening for your unit. Frame with trimmers and a doubled header to fit and install the door as the manufacturer advises, making sure it is plumb in both directions, so it will open cleanly and well. Nail on the molding, which will probably also already be mitered for the upper corner fit, after the finish wall is in place. There can be some difference in needs if you are finishing with wood paneling or gypsum wallboard and even more if you use ceramic tile. Cut out the section of sole plate where the door fits (a reciprocating saw is very helpful)

and nail the sill in place after the finish floor is down (Fig. 4-17).

Before finishing off the bathroom walls there may still be work to do on plumbing and wiring that is run through the walls (Figs. 4-18 through 4-26).

ERECTING A NEW WET WALL

When it is necessary to build a new wall to carry plumbing pipes, it is best to make a 6-inch thick wall using 2- × -6s. Using staggered 2- × -4s for the vertical studs will eliminate drilling holes for running pipe between studs. When the new wall is to be at a 90-degree angle to the floor and ceiling joists, the top and bottom plates of the frame will be nailed to the edges of ceiling and floor joists that it intersects. If the new wall will run parallel to floor and ceiling joists, simply place the frame beneath a ceiling joist and nail the top plate through the ceiling to that joist.

Because your new wet wall is non-load bearing, you have more latitude in the placement of studs. Studs are usually placed at 24-inch intervals, but can be moved in this case if they interfere with fixture placement.

Once you have determined the position of the new wall, remove the ceiling and floor molding from the two walls that the new wall will intersect with. Cut a 2-×-6 the length of the new wall to use as a sole plate. Lay the new sole plate in position and mark where the soil stack will need an opening. Cut on either side of the stack position, allowing about an inch extra on each side of the hole. The two

pieces of sole plate can now be nailed into position with 16-penny nails.

With the sole plate now in position, place another 2-×-6 the length of the wall alongside the sole plate. On the sole plate and the extra piece of 2-×-6, mark the position of the end studs and measure and mark for studs on each side of the sole plate and top plate at 24-inch intervals, staggered on either side of the sole plate and top plate.

Cut two end studs of 2-×-6 stock and the necessary number of 2-×-4 studs to fill in the wall at 24-inch intervals on each side. Attach the end studs to the top plate, nailing through the top plate into the stud. Then position and nail onto the top plate the remainder of the studs. The studs should be 1 1/2 inches less than the distance from the ceiling to the floor where the wall will be erected. This will

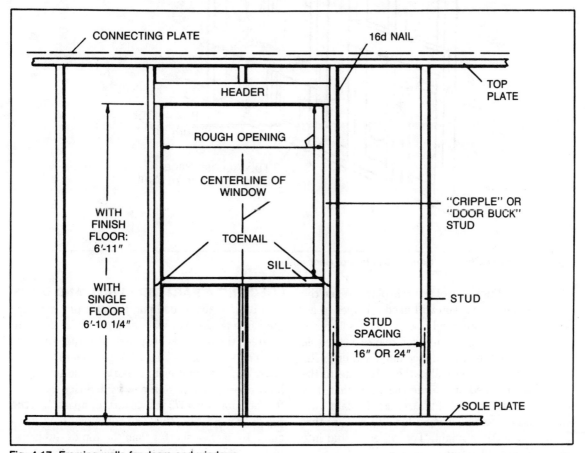

Fig. 4-17. Framing walls for doors and windows.

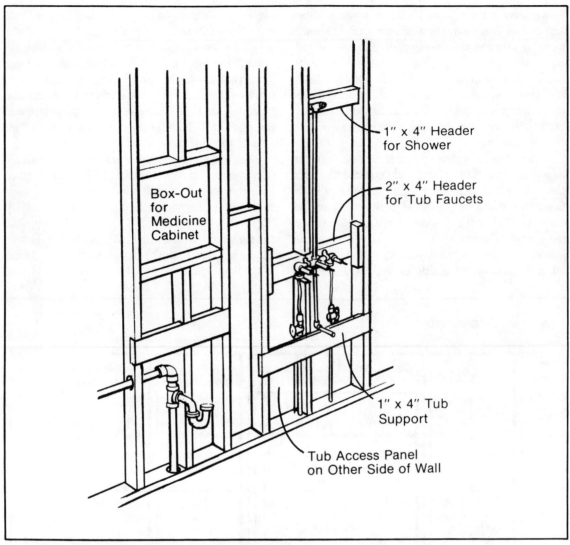

Fig. 4-18. Framing a bath for fixtures (Courtesy of Genova, Inc.).

allow for the thickness of the sole plate. When the frame is completed, you will need a helper to assist in lifting the frame and placing on the sole plate. When the end studs rest on their marks on the sole plate, nail the top plate to a ceiling joist, or joists, in the same way you nailed the sole plate to the floor. Nail the end studs into the walls that they touch. Toenail the end studs to the sole plate. Nail each stud into place, using a level to be sure that each is perfectly straight. Toenail each stud into place. Your wall frame is in place.

ERECTING A PARTITION WALL AND DOOR

The basic steps to building the partition wall are the same as the wet wall, except that 2-x-4s are used for the top and sole plates, and the studs are set across the plates instead of parallel to them. It is also an easy matter to make a frame for a pre-hung door to go into your new wall. Space the studs for the doorway 3 1/2 inches farther apart than the top door jamb. Nail two jack studs that have been cut 1 1/4 inches shorter than the top of the jamb, to the outer studs, flush with the bottoms of the

Fig. 4-19. Plumbing must often run up from the crawl space and through an inside wall (Courtesy of Genova, Inc.).

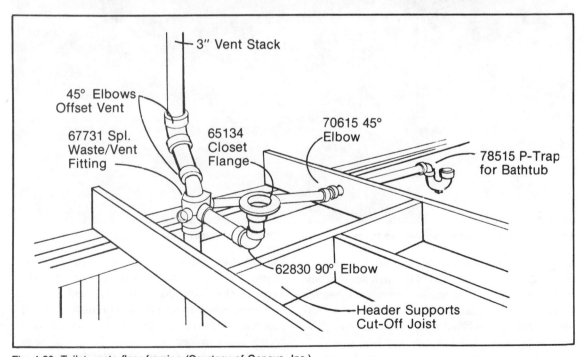

Fig. 4-20. Toilet waste floor framing (Courtesy of Genova, Inc.).

Fig. 4-21. How the toilet waste lines are framed into the wall (Courtesy of Genova, Inc.).

studs. A 2-×-4 header should be nailed between the outer studs, across the tops of the jack studs. Then nail two 2-×-4 cripple studs between the header and the top plate. Erect the wall frame as directed for the wet wall. When the wall is up, cut away the part of the sole plate between the jack studs.

To install the door, slide the half jamb contain-

ing the door into the frame. With the door supported on wood scraps, insert a 1/8-inch shim between the strike side of the door and the jamb, and two shims between the top of the door and the top jamb. The casing can now be nailed to the frame. From the opposite side of the wall, place two 1/4-inch shims between the frame and the top jamb,

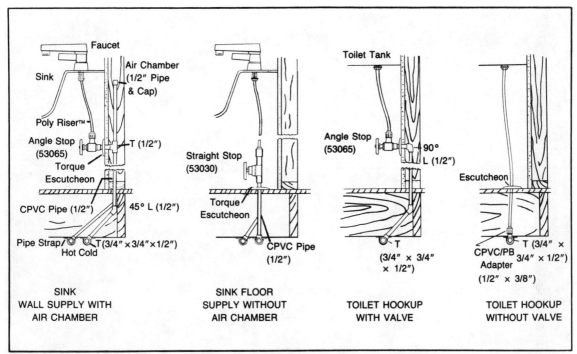

Fig. 4-22. Framing and installing lavatory and sink water supplies (Courtesy of Genova, Inc.).

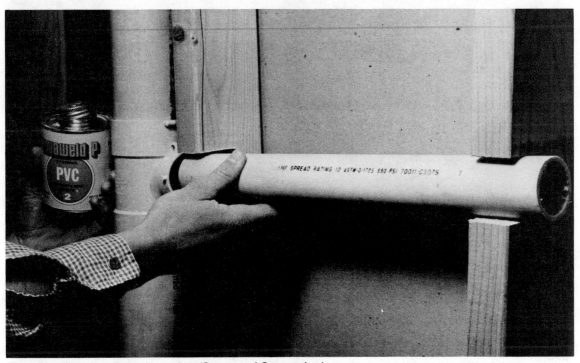

Fig. 4-23. Waste installation in notches (Courtesy of Genova, Inc.).

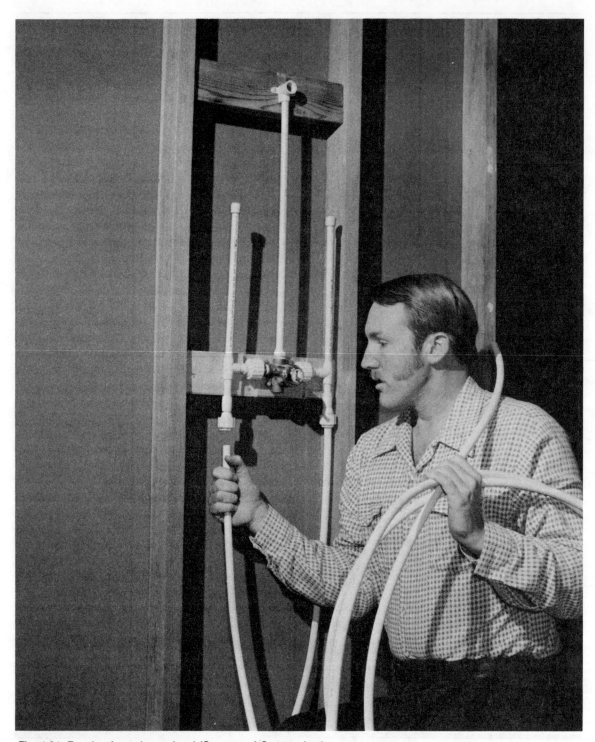

Fig. 4-24. Framing for a shower head (Courtesy of Genova, Inc.).

Fig. 4-25. Cutting the sole plate for a pipe run (Courtesy of Genova, Inc.).

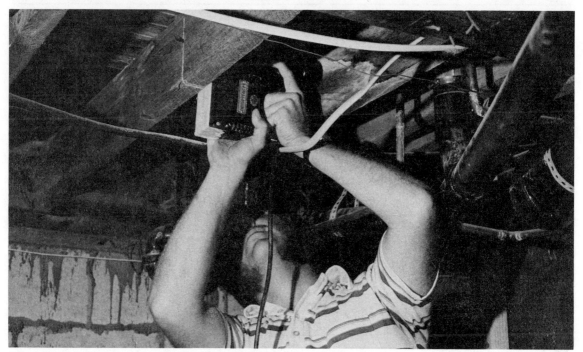

Fig. 4-26. Larger framing cuts will require support (Courtesy of Genova, Inc.).

109

and three more shims between the frame and each side jamb. Break off the shims at the edge of the jambs and nail the jambs to the frame through the shims. Put the other half jamb snugly into place and nail the casing to the wall. The jamb should be nailed to the frame at 1-foot intervals. The shims holding the door closed can now be removed.

FRAMING A BATHTUB

When you know exactly where you plan to position the bathtub, cut a 1-foot square hole in the floor, centered on the mark for the drain hole. It should extend to the sole plate. Cut headers to fit between the floor joists and nail to the uncut joists. Your rough-in markings should show the position of faucets and shower head. At the appropriate heights, mark the end stud and the front or back stud that lies closest to the horizontal position. A horizontal support of a 2-×-4 should be nailed at each pair of marks. If necessary, use blocks of wood nailed to the studs to position the supports at the correct depth. The faucet assembly and shower head can

be screwed onto the supports.

The weight of a filled bathtub requires extra support. Cut three 2-×-4 flange supports to the height called for in the tub installation instructions. Nail those supports to the studs nearest the ends and center of the bathtub.

SUBFLOORING

If you are building an addition to your home for your bathroom or if your bathroom floor has dry rot or other ills, you may have to install subflooring. Subflooring is used over floor joists to form a working platform and base for finish flooring. It usually consists of either square-edge or tongue-and-grooved boards no wider than 8 inches and not less the 3/4 inches thick—or plywood 1/2 to 3/4 inches thick, depending on species, type of finish floor, and spacing of joists. As mentioned earlier, exterior grade plywood is a good choice for bathroom subflooring because of its water-resistant qualities.

Subflooring can be applied either diagonally

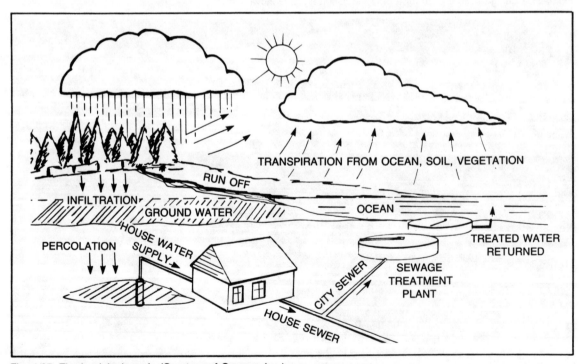

Fig. 4-27. The hyrdologic cycle (Courtesy of Genova, Inc.).

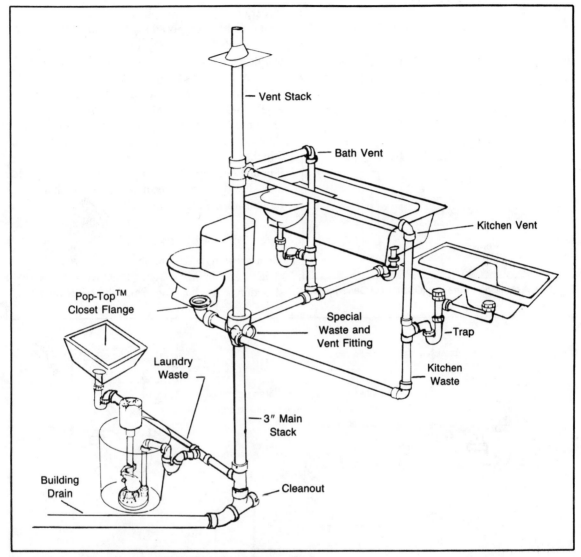

Fig. 4-28. A drain-waste-vent system (Courtesy of Genova, Inc.).

(most common) or at right angles to the joists. When subflooring is placed at right angles to the joists, the finish floor should be laid at right angles to the subflooring. Diagonal subflooring permits finish flooring to be laid either parallel or at right angles (most common) to the joists. End joists of the boards should always be made directly over the joists. Subfloor is nailed to each joist with two 8-penny nails for widths under 8 inches and three 8-penny nails for 8-inch widths.

The joist spacing should not exceed 16 inches on center when finish flooring is laid parallel to the joists. Markings on plywood indicate the allowable spacing of rafters and floor joists for the various thicknesses when the wood is used as roof sheathing or subfloor. For example, an index mark of 32/16 indicates that the plywood panel is suitable for a maximum spacing of 32 inches for rafters and 16 inches for floor joists.

Plywood should be installed with the grain

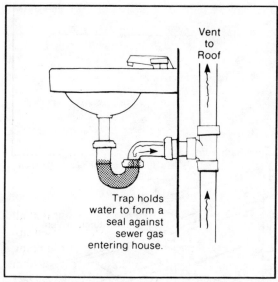

Fig. 4-29. A plumbing fixture trap (Courtesy of Genova, Inc.).

Vent
to
Roof

Trap holds
water to form a
seal against
sewer gas
entering house.

direction of the outer plies at right angles to the joists, and be staggered so that end joints in adjacent panels break over different joists. Plywood should be nailed to the joist at each bearing with 8-penny common or 7-penny threaded nails for plywood 1/2 to 3/4 inch thick. Space nails 6 inches apart along all edges and 10 inches along intermediate members. When plywood serves as both subfloor and underlayment, nails may be spaced 6 to 7 inches apart at all joists and blocking. Use 8- or 9-penny common nails, or 7- or 8-penny threaded nails. For the best performance, plywood should not be laid up with tight joints.

PLUMBING CODES

Most areas have zoning laws that govern the use of land and building codes that oversee the construction of any building. Plumbing codes are a part

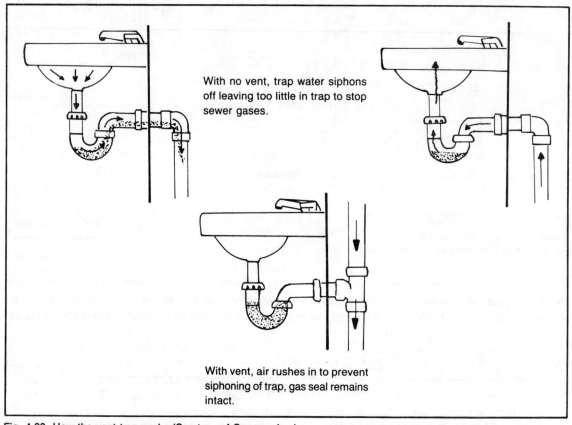

With no vent, trap water siphons off leaving too little in trap to stop sewer gases.

With vent, air rushes in to prevent siphoning of trap, gas seal remains intact.

Fig. 4-30. How the vent trap works (Courtesy of Genova, Inc.).

of that general building code. Check with your local city hall or county courthouse for requirements in your area. Before you begin any home remodeling you will want to be sure that your plans meet all regulations.

The idea of plumbing codes is to ensure sufficient water supply pressure to reach all outlets and to have sufficient drainage, with traps to prevent entry of sewer gas, to allow waste water and products to be gotten rid of with no health problems cropping up. In some areas you will have to hire a plumber and an electrician to stay within code, while in others you can do the entire job yourself, with inspection requirements depending on the area. Most places, except a few rural areas, now

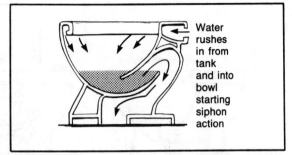

Fig. 4-32. Toilets have built-in traps (Courtesy of Genova, Inc.).

require at least a building inspector's word that all is well assembled before the walls are closed up.

In general, a universal meeting of plumbing codes is possible simply by making sure all system pipe sizes and distances from fixtures are correct and that all drainage outlets are trapped and vented as required, in the distances required. Materials are usually acceptable across the board. If you plan to use plastic piping, make sure it is allowed. If plastic is not specifically denied or approved and you wish to use it, request a written variance permitting plastic plumbing.

Plumbing codes tighten up on drainage systems. Without modern sewage facilities, we'd still be suffering many of the plagues of the Middle Ages. In rural areas, a percolation test as described earlier in this book, will be needed to learn how large a septic field needs to be installed for specific sewage system use, usually based on family size (Fig. 4-27). Urban drainage sewers are usually standard in size for residences, and all of your last stage DWV (drain-waste-vent) pipe must be designed to fit that size (Fig. 4-28). Air must be prevented from entering the system, so that makes venting important in conforming to code (Fig. 4-29). Without using stacks, siphoning is possible, and will empty the water traps located under sinks and other bathroom fixtures, allowing sewer gas back into the house (Figs. 4-30 and 4-31). Venting also allows built-up sewer gas to escape, so that it cannot build pressure and force its way past the traps. Fresh air flows through the system, cutting down on corrosion in metal pipes and slowing the build-up of sludges.

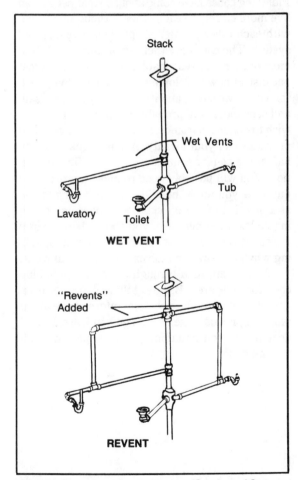

Fig. 4-31. Wet vent and revent system (Courtesy of Genova, Inc.).

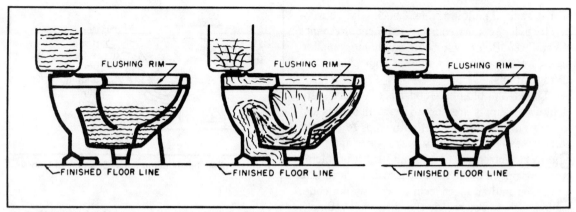

Fig. 4-33. How the toilet works (Courtesy of Montgomery Ward).

Codes call for each trap to be vented and each fixture to have a trap. Traps are visible on all fixtures except toilets and bidet, which have built-in traps (Figs. 4-32 and 4-33). The trap holds a water plug to prevent the backwards passage of sewer gases and the vent allows the sewer gases to pass off into the atmosphere. All this means a series of measurement needs, with specific spacing designed to allow various vent pipe sizes to handle the needs of its system. Follow local codes.

In general, plumbing codes will tell you how long a pipe run can be for a particular size pipe and what sort of venting is needed for waste pipes, and how far from the fixture that venting might be. Trap styles and placement will also be specified and almost all this is worked out on the basis of engineering facts and figures. Traps placed in a certain way and vented at a specific distance, with a certain diameter and height vent, will not be siphoned, so are safe. Perk tests, drainage rates, septic field sizes, and all the other addenda you'll see in your local plumbing code are there for sanitation. Sanitation is a requirement for good public health.

Plumbing codes have come about so that people can live more closely to each other without interfering with each other's water supply or waste disposal system. The codes are there to protect people and most of them are reasonable. Where reason is lost because of new developments, you can always ask for a code variance, and if the variance seems safe and sensible, it will probably be granted. If you do wish to obtain a variance, there will be a prescribed procedure for your locality. Again, check with city hall or the county courthouse for specific information. You will possibly need to make a written request, or you might need to present your request at a meeting of the official body governing building codes. In either case, you should be prepared to defend your request with expert information telling why and how you alternate method will work.

If you can, read through the entire plumbing code for your area. Besides telling you what is legal, it will provide valuable information about plumbing needs in general. You can learn a great deal about good plumbing practices just by reading the code.

Chapter 5

Plumbing Your Bathroom

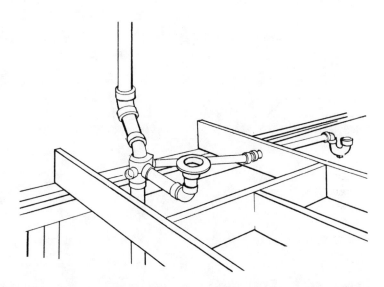

I F YOU ARE BUILDING A NEW BATHROOM OR making a complete change in your plumbing system, you will have to make a choice from the several types of plumbing materials available. If you are doing repairs or simple additions to your current system, you will need to work with the existing material. Following is a discussion of the advantages and disadvantages of the various types of piping used for residential plumbing.

PLASTIC PIPE
ADVANTAGES AND DISADVANTAGES

Plastic plumbing is becoming increasingly popular. It is the easiest pipe material to install (Fig. 5-1). It cuts easily and joints fit together quickly (Fig. 5-2). One of the factors making plastic pipe easy to use is its weight. Plastic pipes and fittings often weigh as little as one-tenth the weight of the same items made of galvanized steel. In addition to making it easier to handle, the low weight of plastic means it requires less support.

The flexibility of the plastic also aids in making it easy to install. Polyethylene (PE) water supply pipe comes in a roll and is flexible enough to run around corners fairly easily. Rigid plastic pipe is also more flexible, making it more easily worked than any metal pipe. Polybutylene tubing can be pulled through holes or fished through walls in the same manner as electrical wiring is installed. This flexibility of plastic pipe eliminates the need for many of the fittings that would be required if the same work were done in metal.

Plastic pipe is durable. It will not dent or squash like metal pipe. It resists corrosion and will not rust. It can be buried or left exposed without adverse effects. Plastic does not conduct electricity and the smooth plastic resists any build-up inside the pipe, so the flow rate should remain constant over the years. The flexibility of plastic also means that the pipes will not burst as easily from frozen water inside the lines.

Plastic pipe insulates the hot and cold water supply lines between than metal because the plas-

Fig. 5-1. Plastic pipe easily feeds through walls for retrofit plumbing (Courtesy of Genova, Inc.).

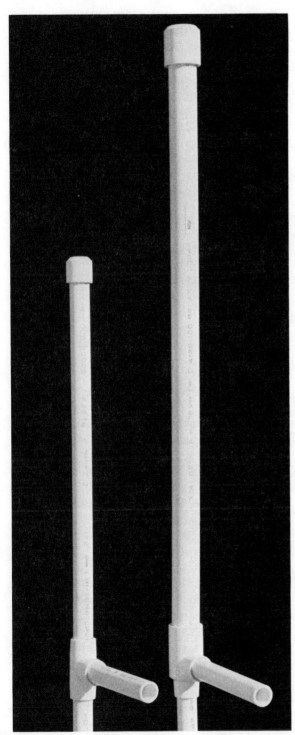

Fig. 5-2. T joint and caps (Courtesy of Genova, Inc.).

tic does not transfer the heat or cold as well. You will not burn yourself on exposed plastic hot water supply lines and they save on water heating bills because the water arrives at its destination without losing as much heat. Plastic water lines do not sweat as badly as metal pipes either.

A final advantage of plastic pipe and fittings is the price. Plastic costs considerably less than any metal; an entire plumbing system can be installed with plastic materials much more quickly, easily, and less expensively than with any other material.

Using plastic for plumbing has a few disadvantages, including local codes in many areas still not allowing its use. In some areas plastic may not be used at all, while in others it can be used for some specific purposes. In still other areas plastic materials can be used for the entire system. If you wish to use plastic piping and fittings and they are not allowed by local plumbing codes, you have the option of applying for a variance to the code.

Another potential disadvantage of plastic is that once the system is in place, it is permanent. That is, plastic plumbing systems cannot easily be modified as can metal systems. Plastic systems often use welded joints making the fittings not reusable. This is a disadvantage that can be overcome, however.

Plastic pipe cannot be wrapped with common heat tape. Although there is a heat tape that can be used on plastic, it is expensive and difficult to locate. And plastic pipe can be difficult to thaw if it does freeze because any open-flame heat would melt or deform the pipe. Because heat tape cannot usually be used and plastic pipes are hard to thaw, special care must be taken to position plastic pipes away from areas where they could be frozen easily.

Care must also be taken to use the proper plastic pipe for carrying hot water. CPVC or PB are meant to carry water up to a maximum of 180 degrees Fahrenheit, which is more than adequate for domestic use. Using pipe not meant for hot water could lead to pipe failure.

As with most any product, it is best to stay with one manufacturer as much as possible throughout a project to ensure proper matching. Be sure to use the proper fittings and the correct welding solvents and cleaners for the particular job.

ADVANTAGES AND DISADVANTAGES OF COPPER PIPE

Plumbing systems in most newer homes are made of copper. Copper piping has a number of advantages. It is relatively easy to work with, resists corrosion, and is longer lasting than brass or steel. It is also lighter weight than other metal plumbing materials. Copper is not as susceptible to a build-up on the interior of the pipe as other metals. Because it is smoother than the other metals, water flow is better. And copper pipe can be soldered.

Copper can be used in the water supply system and the drainage system. It is used to carry both hot and cold water in the supply lines, as well as branch pipes to individual fixtures. Copper can be used for the soil stack, vent pipes, and for soil pipes from fixtures.

Copper pipe comes in both rigid and flexible tempers. Hard temper pipe is straight, like iron pipe, and is rigid. Soft-temper pipe made of copper is flexible. Copper pipe comes in several degrees of thickness and a large variety of fittings are available for different applications.

A major disadvantage of copper plumbing materials is the cost. A copper plumbing system will be the most costly of any available. Another potential disadvantage is the softness of copper as compared to other metals. While the flexibility makes the piping easier to work with, it also makes it more susceptible to damage. Copper may be nicked or dented if dropped, and too much pressure on copper while working with it can deform the pipe.

OTHER METAL PIPES

This book will focus on the use of plastic and copper pipe because they are the choices of most homeowners today. Methods of working with cast iron and steel pipe will also be discussed for those who are updating plumbing systems in older homes.

Cast iron pipe can be used in the home drainage system for the main soil stack and the house drain. Because of its durability, cast iron works well for underground plumbing. The two types of cast iron pipe available are hub and hubless. Cast iron pipe takes extra time and extra work to install. It

is very heavy. Cast iron also allows more of a build-up inside the pipes than do either plastic or copper.

Brass and steel pipes are also sometimes found in older plumbing systems. Both are used for water supply as well as drainage systems. Steel is often used for hot and cold supply lines as well as for branch pipes to individual fixtures. Steel can also be used for the drainage system, but cannot be put underground. It is fairly easy to work with and fairly inexpensive.

PLUMBING WITH PLASTIC

Three types of plastic are used in plumbing a house, starting with polyvinyl chloride (PVC), chlorinated polyvinyl chloride (CPVC) and polybutylene (PB). PVC is the oldest in terms of use and has been pretty much replaced by the tougher CPVC, which is better for supply systems and PB, which is heat resistant and flexible, and the newest plastic in the plumbing field (Fig. 5-3). PB is nearly ideal when you have to run new lines and don't want to rip off much finished wall, as it can be fed through walls in much the same manner as you might fish a wire in replacing an electrical circuit (Fig. 5-4).

CPVC comes as a light beige, rigid plastic pipe and a wide range of fittings are available to use with both hot and cold water supplies. Generally, you'll find it in 1/2- and 3/4-inch diameters in 10-foot lengths. CPVC is easily cut with a handsaw, and joins by solvent welding.

PB comes as a flexible beige plastic pipe, also for hot and cold water supplies, and is available in 1-inch, 3/4-inch, 1/2-inch and 1/4-inch inside diameters in 100-foot coils. All but the largest also comes in 25-foot coils. It can be cut with a sharp utility knife and is joined to CPVC with special PB/CPVC adapters plus CPVC solvent weld materials.

Both materials are accepted by the Federal Housing Administration. The materials are sized to regular copper water tubing sizes and measured by inside diameter (ID), so that the inside diameters of 1/2-inch CPVC and PB measure about 1/2 inch, while the outside diameter (OD) is about 5/8 inch. CPVC in 3/4-inch ID is about 7/8-inch OD, while the 3/8-inch PB scales about 1/4-inch ID and

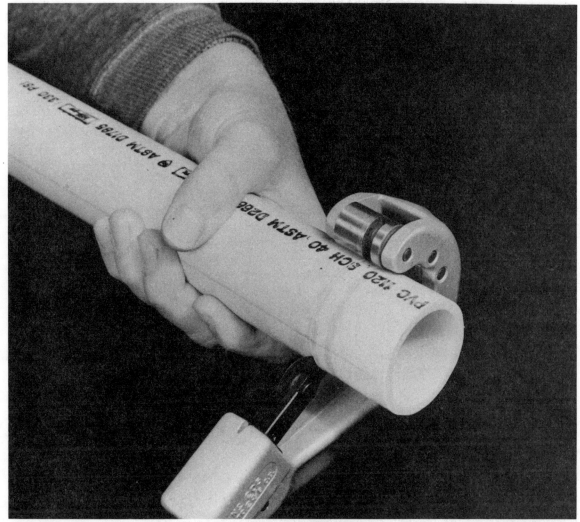

Fig. 5-3. PVC pipe being cut with a cutting wheel (Courtesy of Genova, Inc.).

3/8-inch OD (Fig. 5-5).

In replacing steel pipe, the much smoother inside of the plastic pipe means that smaller sizes can be used to get the same flow rates, and there's the added benefit of hot water staying hotter and cold water colder for longer in the plastic pipe without additional insulation.

CPVC is a part of the family of rigid PVC vinyls made for greater toughness and heat resistance by the addition of an extra chloride molecule. The heat resistance and greater strength make CPVC valuable for all forms of hot and cold water pipe where

pressure is required. The material meets all the requirements of the National Sanitation Foundation for potable (drinkable) water carrying.

Because most fixtures and plumbing appliances come with threaded fittings, they're seldom ready to solvent weld to CPVC pipe. Because of this, adapters are required at the well, water main, appliances, fixtures, and other plumbing devices to adapt the CPVC for solvent welding. There is a complete line available so that you can attach just about any plumbing fixture ever made to a CPVC system (Figs. 5-6 through 5-10).

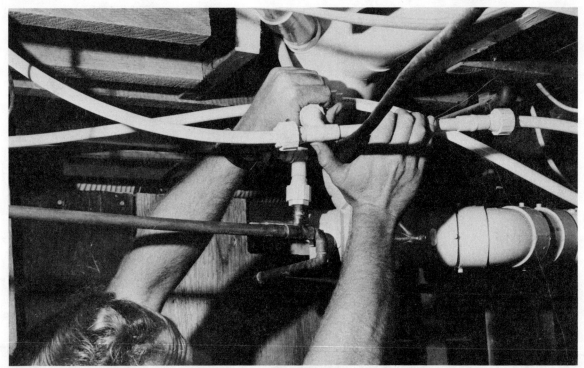

Fig. 5-4. PB tubing can make many bends (Courtesy of Genova, Inc.).

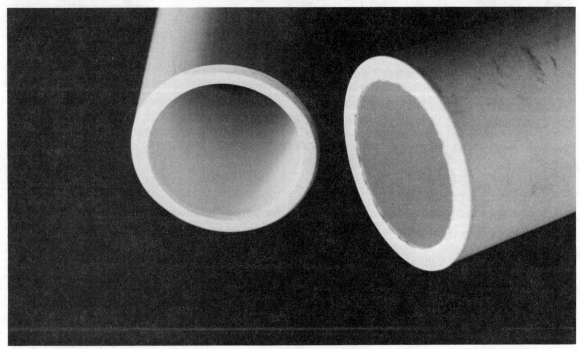

Fig. 5-5. Trimming the end of plastic pipe (Courtesy of Genova, Inc.).

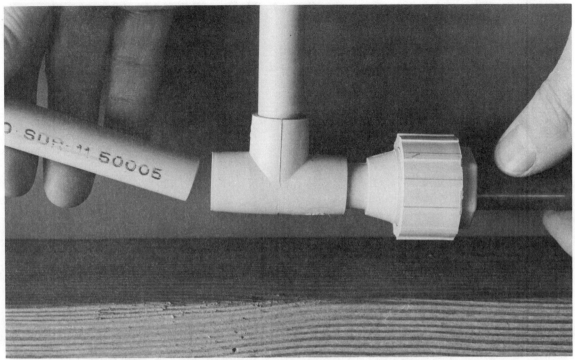

Fig. 5-6. T to transition on the right, and to CPVC pipe on the left (Courtesy of Genova, Inc.).

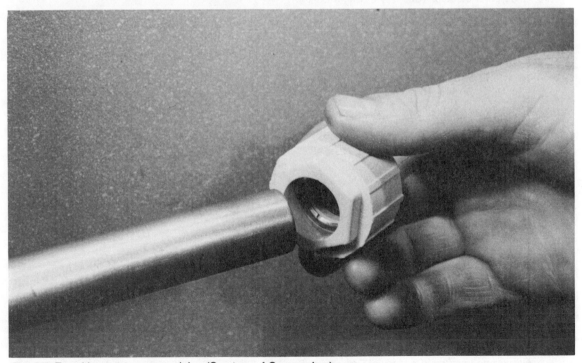

Fig. 5-7. Transition nut to copper piping (Courtesy of Genova, Inc.).

121

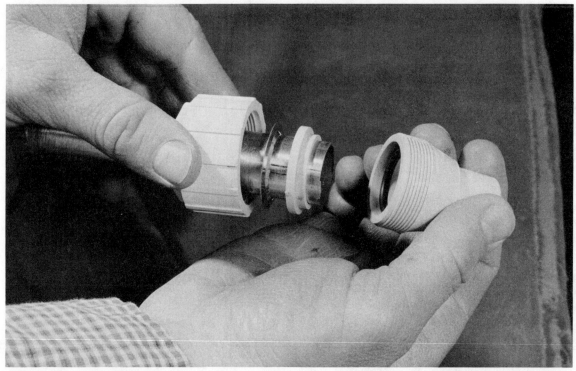

Fig. 5-8. One type of transition (Courtesy of Genova, Inc.).

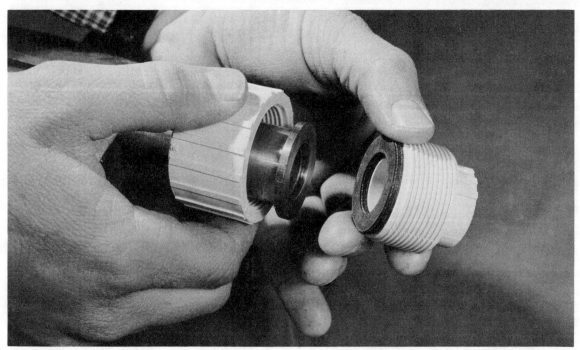

Fig. 5-9. Flange-type transition (Courtesy of Genova, Inc.).

122

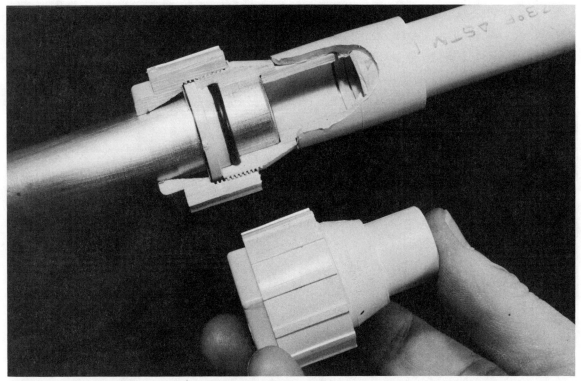

Fig. 5-10. Note O ring in transition fitting (Courtesy of Genova, Inc.).

When working with plastic, a two-step solvent welding process gives the best joints. This starts with a primer/cleaner and is followed with the solvent cement. Essentially, the two-step process assures you that no grease or other weld-ruining debris remains on the joint parts, so that with proper fitting a leak-free joint is certain. With solvent welding there's no chance to back up and begin again. You can't de-solvent weld the joint because it is now one piece. Correct measurements, correct fit of pipe and fittings, and correct two-step application of the solvent weld cement are vital.

As you get ready to solvent weld a fitting, check the pipe end for gouges. Then clean it with primer/cleaner that rapidly removes dirt, grease, oil, and other residues that might interfere with the joint's proper mating. Use a clean cloth to wipe the primer/cleaner around the end of the pipe, and do the same with the inside of the fitting socket. Let it dry before applying solvent cement (Figs. 5-11 through 5-16). Properly done and allowed to cure

for 24 hours, a solvent-welded joint will not fail before the pipe bursts from pressure.

Polybutylene pipe cannot be solvent welded no matter what cement you use. PB must be joined with special adapters (Fig. 5-17).

The major problem with solvent-welded joints is the use of too little cement when making the weld. You don't want the cement to make a mess, but do be generous with the amount you daub on the pipe end (Figs. 5-18 through 5-20).

Transition fittings are used whenever plastic pipe is connected to threaded or sweat-soldered metal pipes and fittings. Only transition fittings should be used on cold and hot water lines for best results, although you can often slip by with threaded CPVC adapters on threaded fittings on cold water hook-ups. On hot water hook-ups, a leak will appear rapidly. The reason is that the metal and the vinyl expand and contract at different rates and this difference is emphasized with wider temperature changes, so specially designed transition

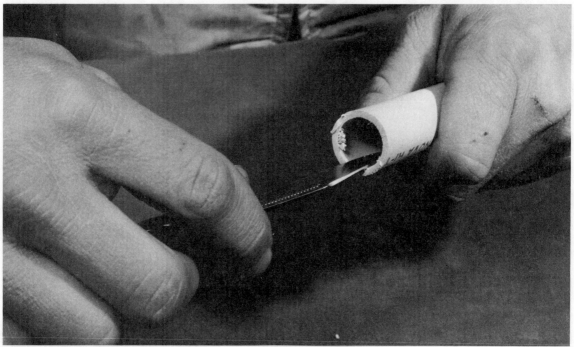

Fig. 5-11. Clean cut (Courtesy of Genova, Inc.).

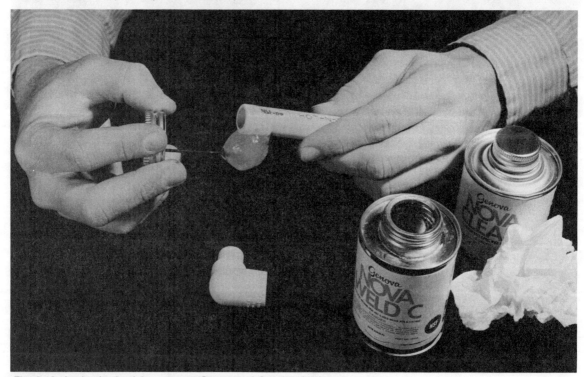

Fig. 5-12. Apply plastic piping cement (Courtesy of Genova, Inc.).

124

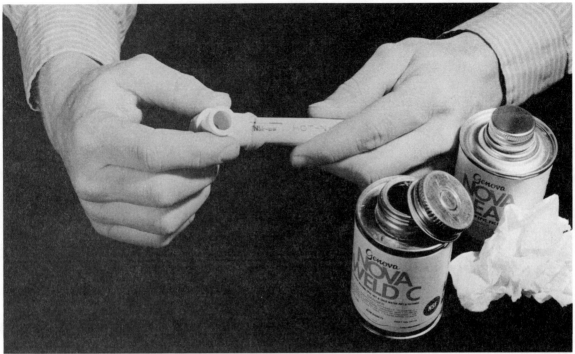

Fig. 5-13. Assemble the joint (Courtesy of Genova, Inc.).

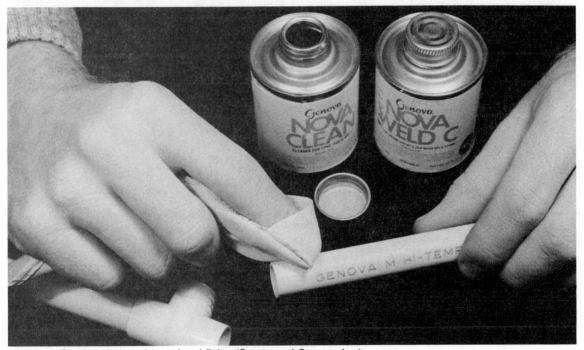

Fig. 5-14. Clean the other pipe end and fitting (Courtesy of Genova, Inc.).

Fig. 5-15. Apply cement to fitting and pipe (Courtesy of Genova, Inc.).

Fig. 5-16. Assemble joint and let dry (Courtesy of Genova, Inc.).

126

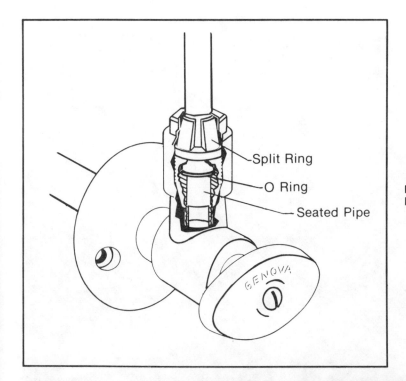

Split Ring

O Ring

Seated Pipe

Fig. 5-17. Adapters for assembling PB pipe (Courtesy of Genova, Inc.).

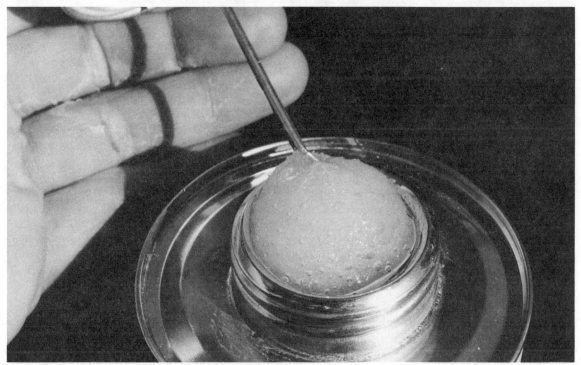

Fig. 5-18. Piping cement applicator (Courtesy of Genova, Inc.).

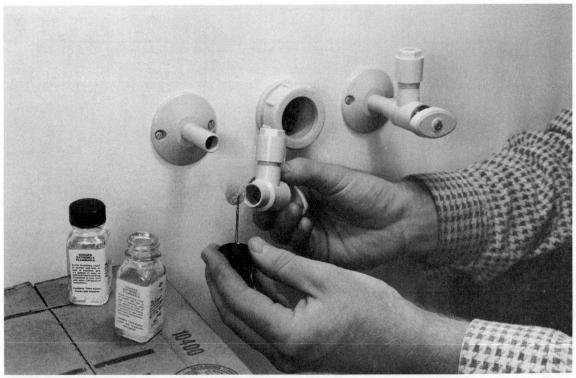

Fig. 5-19. Cement application should be generous, but not excessive (Courtesy of Genova, Inc.).

fittings are required. These fittings present two faces meeting across a rubber gasket so that each face can expand or contract at its own rate without having any effect on the other face. These transition fittings perform the functions of unions so that connections may be disassembled at any time without cutting or heating (Figs. 5-21 through 5-26).

Running plastic pipes is about the simplest of the jobs involved with plumbing, but there are a few rules to follow once you've decided what hooks up where and how the pipe run must go to get to a certain place. You must allow for the distances taken up by the fittings—called make-up. Forgetting make-up means the pipe will be cut too short or too long. Remember to allow for the pipe ends slipping into the fitting sockets. Make your own measurements on all fittings, always subtracting for center-to-end make-up, and remember that all pipe runs will need make-up allowances on both ends.

As an example of make-up, consider a branch to be run down to meet a water heater, tapping from a main supply 3/4-inch line using CPVC 3/4-inch pipe. Stop the main just 9/16 of an inch short of the centerline of the branch pipe's centerline. When you later solvent-weld a 3/4-inch T and the down-pipe, it should align nearly perfectly with the water heater's top tapping. Again, remember that make-ups are needed at both ends of most runs, unless you're using flexible pipe.

You can lay out a plumbing run by positioning the fittings on the floor, spaced as they would be when in their regular installation. Measure, then, face-to-face of each pair of fittings for pipes that will joint them. Add to that overall pipe length the depth of the fitting sockets on both ends, and allow for socket depth 1/2 inch for 1/2-inch pipe, and 11/16 inch for 3/4-inch pipe.

Center-to-end make-up is always subtracted from the required pipe length, but socket depth must be added to the pipe length.

Before doing the final assembly with solvent cement, do a dry assembly of all pipe and fittings,

128

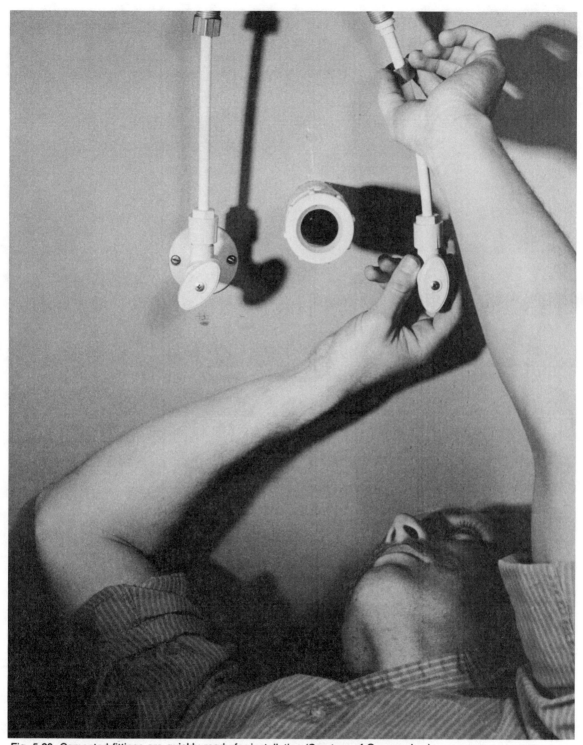

Fig. 5-20. Cemented fittings are quickly ready for installation (Courtesy of Genova, Inc.).

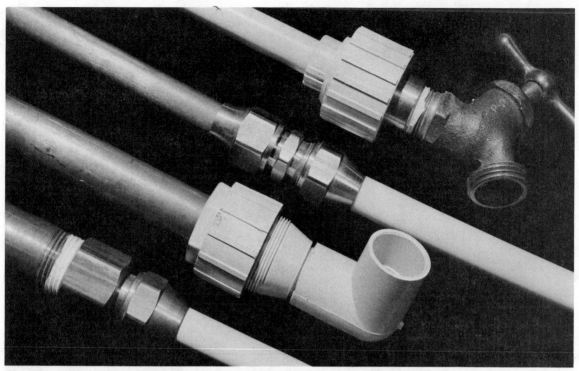

Fig. 5-21. All kinds of transitions and other fittings are available (Courtesy of Genova, Inc.).

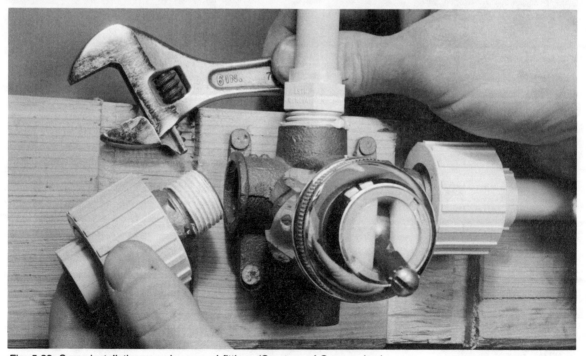

Fig. 5-22. Some installations require several fittings (Courtesy of Genova, Inc.).

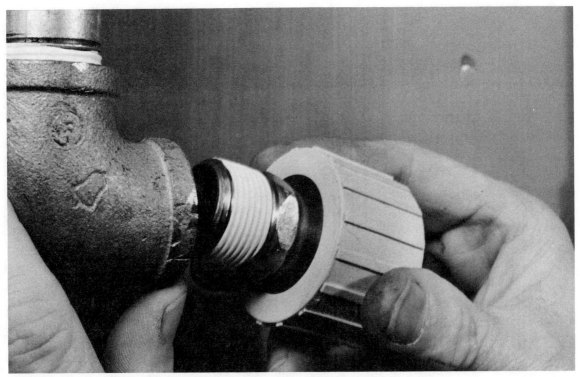

Fig. 5-23. Using plumber's tape to install a fitting (Courtesy of Genova, Inc.).

making sure all lengths are correct and that all fittings are firm fits on their pipes. As soon as the dry-fit check is complete, disassemble the whole works, piece by piece. You will otherwise be taking a chance on solvent welding and missing a section that wasn't disassembled. That non-solvent welded section will leak and will require disassembly and solvent welding after it is discovered when the water is turned on. System design must take into consideration the limitations of the materials being used in construction. Plastic pipe is an easy and rapidly assembled material, but is no exception to the rule. CPVC is rated to withstand 100 pounds per square inch of water pressure, at 180 degrees Fahrenheit, but will take considerably more. Still, the system needs to be held within those design limits.

Because of the limits, air chambers must be used at all fixtures and water-using appliances. If you don't care about the noise the plumbing makes without the air chambers, consider their use as sys-

tem protection from excessive stress created by water hammer (Fig. 5-27).

CPVC and PB pipes should not be restrained; they must be able to expand and contract as required. You must allow for some movement in one or more of the following four manners.

- Always use pipe hangers to support your pipes, and make sure the hangers are made by the same company that made the pipe. These hangers will hold the pipe snugly against the house framing, yet will also permit some end-wise movement without cutting into the pipe. Use at least one pipe hanger for every 32 inches on center (Fig. 5-28).
- Never install long runs of CPVC pipe with it actually touching walls or framing. Leave at least a little space at the ends to allow for expansion. About 1/4 inch for every 10 feet of pipe run is good (Fig. 5-29).

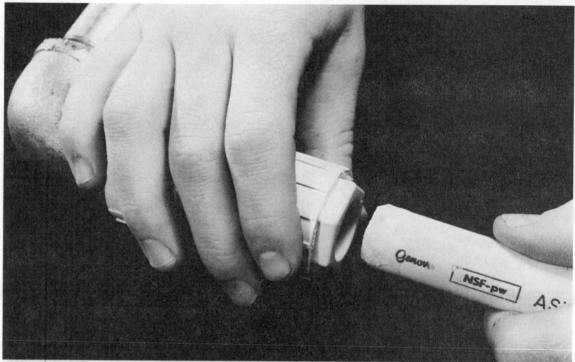

Fig. 5-24. Check the fit after beveling CPVC pipe (Courtesy of Genova, Inc.).

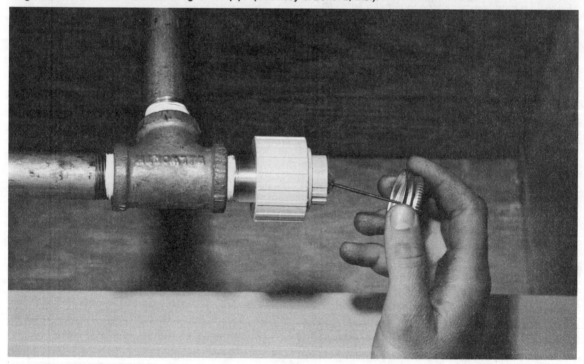

Fig. 5-25. Applying cement (Courtesy of Genova, Inc.).

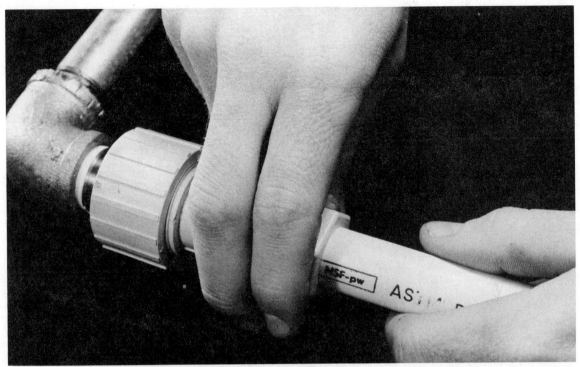

Fig. 5-26. Assembling the fitting and pipe (Courtesy of Genova, Inc.).

Fig. 5-27. Air chamber assembly (Courtesy of Genova, Inc.).

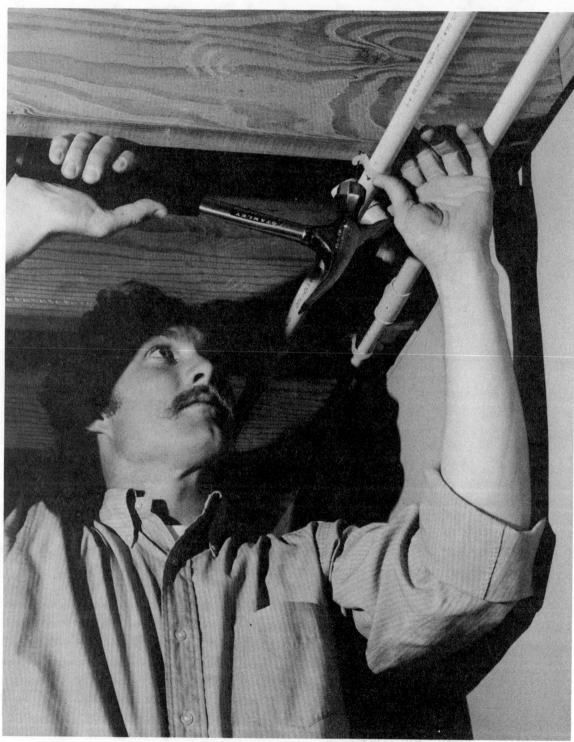

Fig. 5-28. Pipe hangers support while allowing movement (Courtesy of Genova, Inc.).

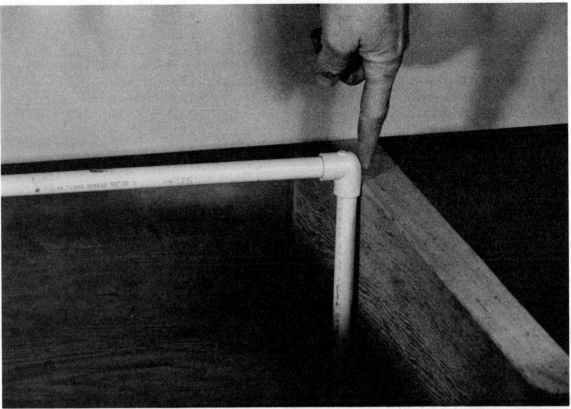

Fig. 5-29. Expansion room is needed on long runs (Courtesy of Genova, Inc.).

■ Make 1-foot offsets (dogleg style) in very long runs of plastic pipe (CPVC). If the pipe run is over 35 feet long, the doglegs ease expansion problems because they bend enough to allow for a substantial amount of size changes.

■ When CPVC risers branch off of CPVC mains they must be unbound and long enough from the main to where they extend through the floor or ceiling to allow for slight movement along the main. Risers should be no less than 8 inches long. PB risers need not meet this standard since the material is flexible, so for very short risers use PB (Fig. 5-30).

Plastic pipe will have to be protected from water burner heat. Use two galvanized steel nipples from 8 to 11 inches long, coming off the top of a gas or oil-fired hot water heater, in order to keep conducted heat built up by long burner runs from reaching the CPVC transition fittings. With electric hot water heaters, you can make direct connections with the CPVC adapters and the tank taps. At the point where the transition fitting is to be installed, wrap a single turn of plumber's tape around the threads to make sure the joint is tightly sealed. Install a line stop in the cold water line, with the arrow pointing down to the tank, so that the cold water can be shut off when the tank must be changed, repaired, or cleaned (never shut this stop off without first shutting off the tank burners, no matter what kind of burners the heater uses). The line stop is installed after the steel nipples, in the CPVC line (Figs. 5-31 through 5-35).

When the installation is made and the water heater is ready to go, start with the lowest setting on your thermostat. If you can make do with that,

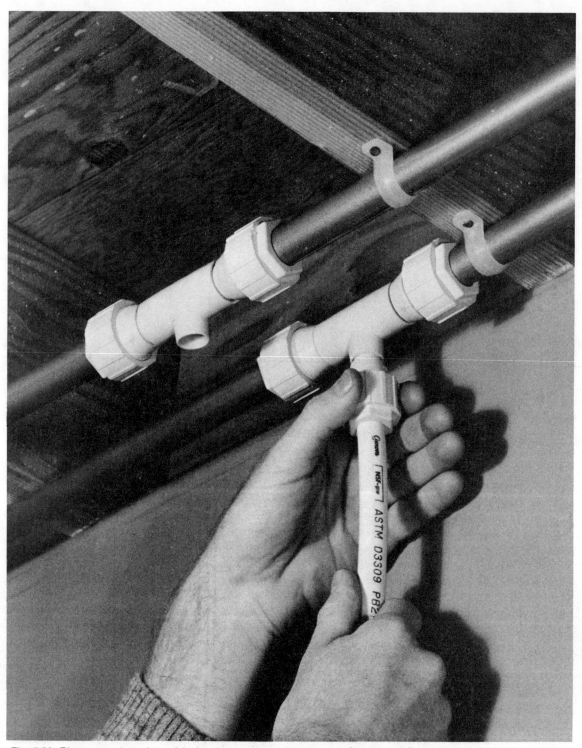

Fig. 5-30. Risers must be at least 8 inches long and remain unbound (Courtesy of Genova, Inc.).

Fig. 5-31. Steel nipples protect plastic from burner heat in hot water heater installations (Courtesy of Genova, Inc.).

Fig. 5-32. A tubing cutter is useful for cutting into old copper pipe runs (Courtesy of Genova, Inc.).

Fig. 5-33. A hacksaw also works well if there is enough room (Courtesy of Genova, Inc.).

Fig. 5-34. A line stop is installed for the water heater (Courtesy of Genova, Inc.).

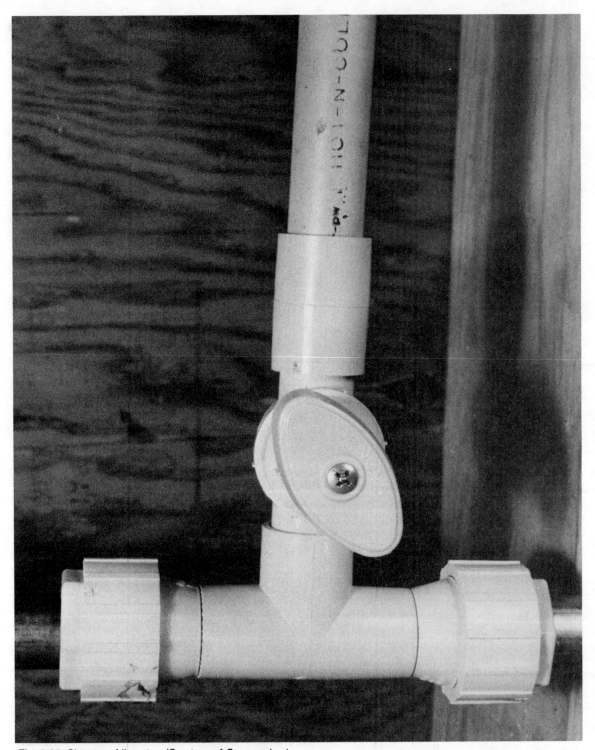

Fig. 5-35. Closeup of line stop (Courtesy of Genova, Inc.).

the amount of energy you consume to heat water will be drastically reduced. If you run out of hot water too quickly, or the water isn't hot enough, then you can turn up the thermostat. Most thermostats will work from 130 to 180 degrees Fahrenheit. Water hotter than 140 or 150 degrees is seldom needed. The highest setting might be needed for fast hot water recovery with a large family.

PB pipe and fittings differ quite a lot from CPVC. While CPVC is a fairly straightforward plastic, polybutylene is a more exotic thermoplastic, suitable for high temperatures and making possible flexible hot and cold water tubing. Flexibility is so great that you can use coils to make 25- and 100-foot-long runs free of joints, with the expansion absorbed by the flexing of the tubing. The movement as the tubing flexes doesn't produce any noise.

The biggest advantage of PB tubing is its flexibility. The ease of installation makes PB nearly ideal for installation in remodeling work, where access to the interiors of walls, floors, and ceilings is liable to be limited.

Polybutylene tubing is best served with special fittings because the material does not lend itself to solvent welding or even simple glueing. Grip fittings are especially made to work with PB pipe runs, and perform two functions at the same time. They not only seal against water leaks, but mechanically hold the pipe so it can't pull or blow out of the fitting. The water sealing is done with an elastomeric O ring and a specially developed split grab ring holds the pipe in place mechanically. A shoulder inside the fitting prevents over-insertion of the pipe, which is inserted until it bottoms, through the O ring and onto the shoulder. Then, the nut on the fitting is tightened and you've got a strong, leak-free joint at the fitting (Fig. 5-36).

It's not as simple as it sounds. The nut has a cone-shaped inner surface to squeeze a cone-shaped outer surface on the grab ring, and the grab ring also has a ridge that digs into the PB tubing to create a slight groove. The ridge remains in the groove and the resulting joint cannot be pulled apart by hand, is water tight, and has tested to hold up to over 11 years of 200 pounds per square inch water

pressure at 180 degrees Fahrenheit (Fig. 5-37). Best of all, the fitting can be taken apart and reassembled as often as is necessary, while the handnut cannot be tightened too much. It bottoms out first.

To make a grip connection to PB, all you must do is cut the PB end off squarely with a knife. The pipe should be cut to the correct length to reach into the fitting, for otherwise nothing will work. Make it the proper length and then allow about 1 1/2 inches for the fitting. Stab it fully into the connector, hand-tighten the nut as much as you can, and that's the job.

Grip adapters come in 3/8-inch, 1/2-inch and 3/4-inch sizes so that PB pipe can be used anywhere in the house. The fittings are made as straight adapters in two styles, angle adapters, angle stops, and Ts. There's just about nothing that can't be done, new or remodeling, with PB pipe for your water supply system. The pipe can be buried in the ground or run through walls with no extra protection.

You'll also find PB pipe in the form of ready-to-use riser tubes, in 3/8-inch size. For fast hookup of fixtures to water supply systems, there's nothing to beat them. You can buy them bullet-nosed for connecting sinks and flange-ended for connecting toilets. The PB is very flexible and nearly impossible to kink. It makes superb replacements for older flexible (and kinkable) copper risers. Both styles come in 12- or 20-inch lengths, with the bullet-nosed style also sold in 3-foot lengths.

There's just one caution: when you use a grip connection with a chromed brass riser, you'll have to substitute a serrated metal grab ring, but the metal ring is included in the package. If the riser being connected is PB, throw the metal ring away to make sure it's not used, because the metal could cut the PB tube and cause a leak (Figs. 5-38 and 5-39).

Choosing materials is not complicated. Both CPVC and PB are suitable for use with any portion of any water supply system on the inside of the house. PB also can be used in a below-ground trench leading to the house, from a well or from a city water main. So either is suitable for all uses, but there are features other than simple pipe

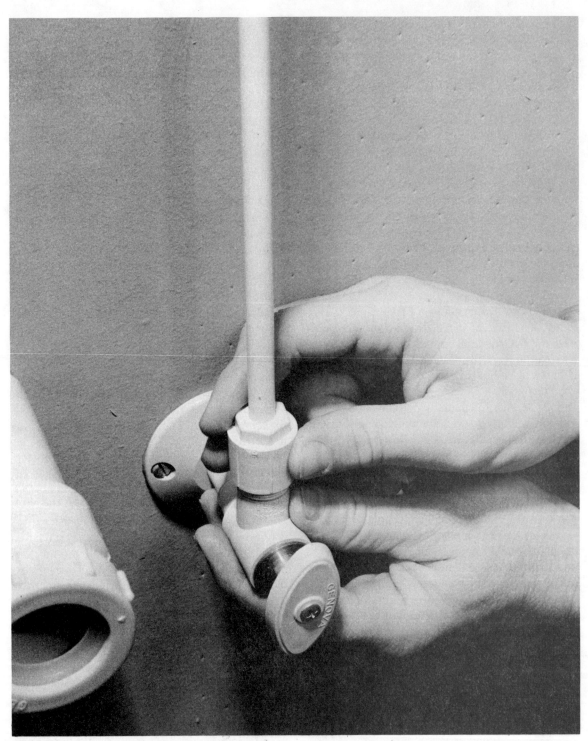

Fig. 5-36. Line stop and riser (Courtesy of Genova, Inc.).

Fig. 5-37. Parts of line stop (Courtesy of Genova, Inc.).

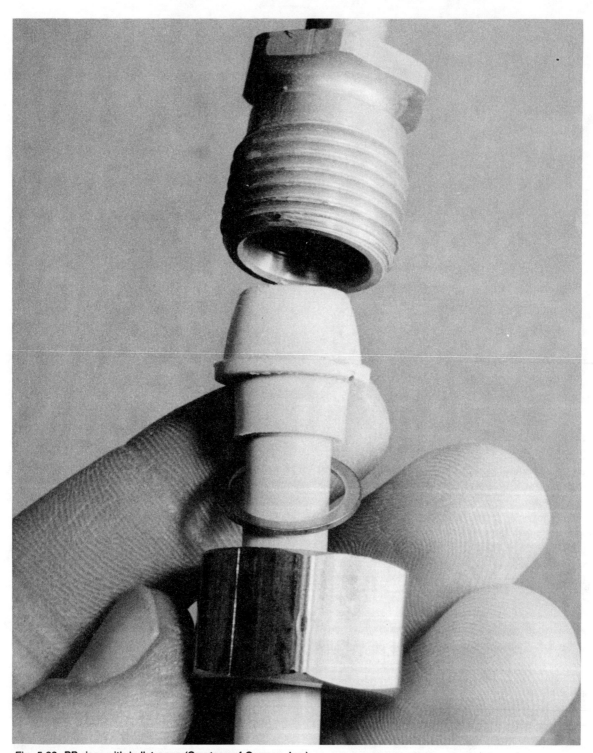

Fig. 5-38. PB riser with bullet nose (Courtesy of Genova, Inc.).

144

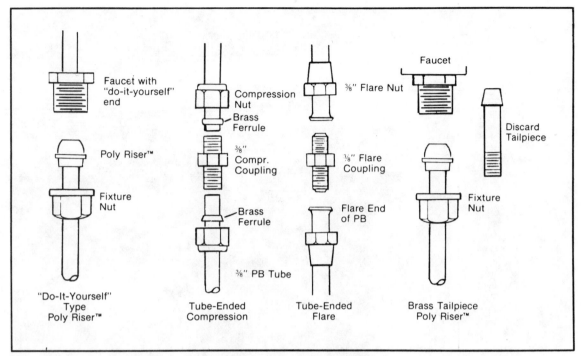

Fig. 5-39. Faucet connections using polybutylene (Courtesy of Genova, Inc.).

strength (bursting strength) and heat resistance to consider. First, rigidity can be a help in some situations and a hindrance in others. In addition, there's a cost factor; PB is a bit more expensive.

Generally, for a new system you would consider running 3/4- or 1-inch PB into the house, carrying it to a water softener, a water heater, the outdoor water hose bibbs, and any other such outlets, using 3/4-inch CPVC branches and fittings (Fig. 5-40). The rigidity of CPVC makes the final installations look neater. From the house mains for hot and cold water, you could branch to the kitchen sink, bathroom, laundry, and hose bibbs, using either 1/2-inch CPVC or PB. PB branches to the lavatory, toilet, and dishwasher may be done with 3/8-inch pipe (Fig. 5-41). Use the CPVC for a neat looking job where the runs will show, and the PB for spots where rigid pipe would be difficult to run. No matter what the rest of the runs are like, swap to PB beneath all sinks and for supply risers to toilets and other fixtures, using 3/8-inch risers. The riser will connect directly to most faucets, using a 3/8-inch fixture flange nut, and those it doesn't fit immedi-

ately, it will readily adapt to (Figs. 5-42 and 5-43).

When you're remodeling, PB is the best way to go unless you wish to gut large areas of the house. It's the only commercially available pipe, for both hot and cold water supply lines, that can be fished through holes in the framing. There are other materials on the market providing a flexible cold water line, but PB is the only one that is usable with both hot and cold water. PB costs more than other types of pipe, but can more than make up the extra cost with labor savings and the savings in fittings such as elbows. In fact, PB can save a lot of time in measurement, because it can be readily flexed around corners that would otherwise require possibly eight, ten or even more separate measurements, cuts and fits.

Throughout this book you'll run into the word "street" applied to various items. In plumbing work, street means pipe sized, rather than fitting sized. In other words, a street fitting has one that slips into another fitting socket, as would a pipe. A 90-degree street elbow is used to change directions from a fitting socket. Should you use a regu-

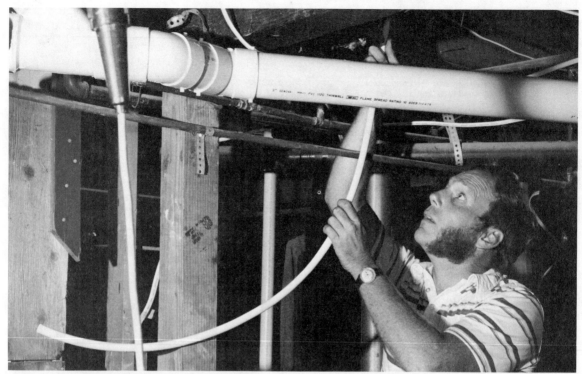

Fig. 5-40. Running in PB (Courtesy of Genova, Inc.).

Fig. 5-41. Preparing for branches (Courtesy of Genova, Inc.).

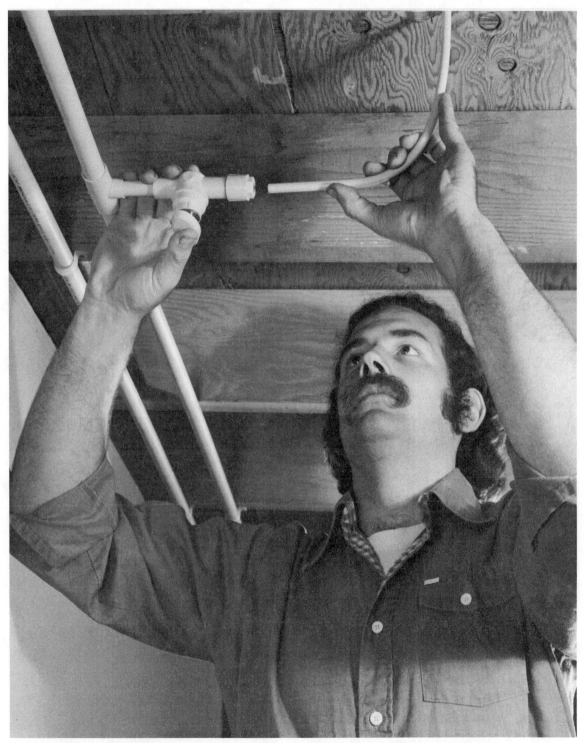

Fig. 5-42. PB to CPVC mains (Courtesy of Genova, Inc.).

Fig. 5-43. PB risers (Courtesy of Genova, Inc.).

lar fitting for this change, you'd have to prepare a short stub of pipe to go between the two fittings.

A universal adapter is a useful fitting for some odd spots and needs. Using this adapter, you can join CPVC fittings to copper tubing with no sweat soldering needed. In fact, you don't even need any tools because it's a push and tighten by hand operation that can be done in seconds. The universal adapter will connect to CPVC pipe without solvent welding (Fig. 5-44).

Line stops of plastic, both in 1/2-inch and 3/4-inch sizes, offer very high flow rates (the above are street sizes). Used directly, the line stop fits 1/2-inch line, while the addition of two 3/4-inch couplings will turn it into a 3/4-inch valve for use as a house main shut-off valve.

USING PLASTIC IN THE DWV SYSTEM

Vinyl excels as DWV pipe. The corrosion resistance of the pipe is phenomenal. Vinyl pipe, in several forms, is used in chemical plants to handle strong acid and alkaline solutions. Metal pipe of almost any kind would disintegrate when used to transport these chemicals.

DWV pipe is made of PVC because it doesn't need the high temperature handling capabilities of supply pipe provided by the extra chloride molecule in CPVC. Joints are still made by simple solvent welds, and the pipe is very light weight, with the common 10-foot-long sections easily handled. A 2-inch diameter, 10-foot section of PVC DWV weighs only 6 pounds, which makes working hard-

Fig. 5-44. Adapters (Courtesy of Genova, Inc.).

Fig. 5-45. PVC pipe is easy to work (Courtesy of Genova, Inc.).

to-get-at places a great deal easier on the muscles (Fig. 5-45).

Another advantage is resilience. Hammer blows that would dent copper DWV beyond use simply bounce off PVC so that damage from rough handling, back filling, temperature changes, and vibration—all common hazards for DWV pipe—are no problem with PVC. Like other forms of plastic pipe, there is no need to worry about electrolytic action destroying either the pipe or some other part of the plumbing system. No dissimilar metals are involved and the PVC is resistant to fungi, bacteria, and generally bad soil conditions, as well as being resistant to ultraviolet light. PVC can be left exposed to direct sunlight with no harmful effects.

With high resistance to chemical action, PVC DWV systems can also be treated to regular doses of chemical drain cleaners with no signs of trouble. With the nearly mirror smooth interior passages of the DWV offering minimum flow resistance, there should be less need for such cleaners over the years,

as the smooth finishes tend to stay smooth for a long time, thus resisting clogging actions. Hot drain water also does not affect PVC, and the pipe will not support combustion, which keeps fire from traveling along the pipes. Some plastics do support combustion and are not generally approved for building because of that feature.

In general, PVC pipe is available in five diameters, with fittings to match each diameter: 6-inch, 4-inch, 3-inch, 2-inch and 1 1/2-inch. In almost every case, the largest required size for residential use would be 4 inches.

Two different lines of DWV are made by many companies: Schedule 30 DWV and Schedule 40 DWV. Schedule 30 was developed exclusively for use in home plumbing and has slightly thinner walls than does Schedule 40, so it can fit inside stud walls of standard size (today's interiors on those stud walls are 3 1/2 inches deep). A 3-inch diameter Schedule 30 DWV pipe will fit. In fact, the material is designed so that the entire plumbing stack, including fittings, will fit inside a standard stud-framed wall. Standard Schedule 40 3-inch pipe will *not* fit Schedule 30 fittings. The two cannot be mixed.

It is wise to use the In-wall Schedule 30 pipe wherever 3-inch diameter pipe is required in your bathroom installation, as well as any other areas you might be updating during this remodeling. Smaller sizes will fit Schedule 30 fittings. You won't have to fur the wall with lath or furring strips to allow room as you would with Schedule 40 pipe and fittings. In other words, a Schedule 30 3-×-1 1/2-inch T will fit Schedule 30 3-inch diameters, and the standard 1 1/2-inch DWV at the smaller branch socket.

When it's imperative to use Schedule 40 DWV pipes in a standard stud wall, count on having to fur the walls about 1 inch extra to accommodate the extra diameter of the pipe. To order DWV pipe, get all 3-inch diameter needs in Schedule 30 and all else in Schedule 40. The only time you'll need an adapter between the two is to use 4-inch Schedule pipe.

Fittings for DWV pipe follow the same procedures as fittings for supply lines of PB and CPVC. Get the whole package of materials made by the same manufacturer to assure yourself of the best possible fit at joints and fittings. Using fittings and pipe from one manufacturer will cut down on mismatching problems from slight variations in the same product (Figs. 5-46 through 5-51). See Table 5-1 for DWM standards.

Working with PVC DWV is similar to working with CPVC because both are joined with solvent-welding techniques and materials, but PVC DWV is on a slightly larger scale. Solvents for welding are made specifically to work effectively in either warm weather or at cool temperatures. Each solvent is designed to develop 375 pounds of resistance to pull-out on a 1 1/2-inch PVC pipe after a five minute setting time. The cans come with daubers that work well up to 2-inch pipe sizes, after which you'll want a small paint brush of about half the diameter of the pipe (Fig. 5-52). As with CPVC, start by using a combination cleaner made of tetrahydrofuran and methyl ethyl ketone on a

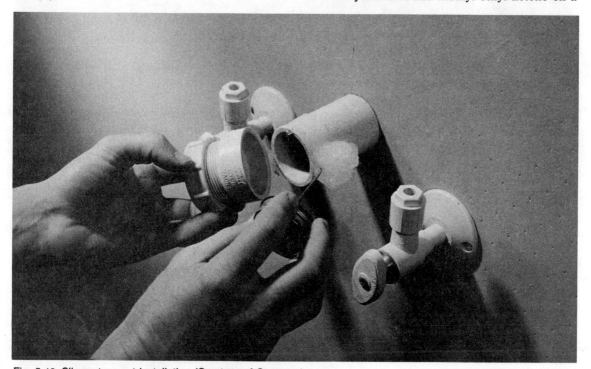

Fig. 5-46. Slip-on trap nut installation (Courtesy of Genova, Inc.).

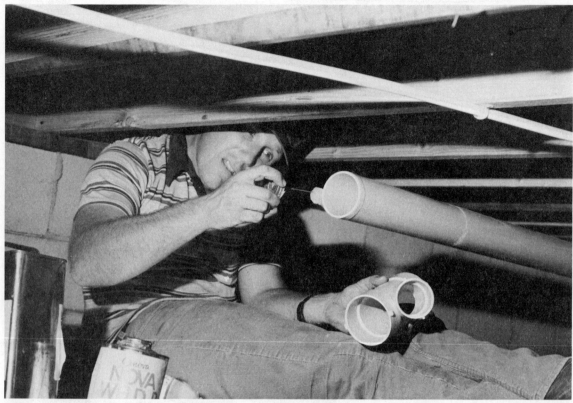

Fig. 5-47. DWV Ys for Schedule 30 go on easily (Courtesy of Genova, Inc.).

Table 5-1. ASTM Standards.

ASTM DWV STANDARDS
D2661 (ABS)
D2665 (PVC)

PIPE DIMENSIONS AND TOLERANCES

Nominal Size	Outside Diameter Average	Tolerance	Out-of-Round	Wall Thickness Minimum	Tolerance
3″	3.500″	±0.008″	±0.015″	0.216″	−0.000″ +0.026″

FITTING DIMENSIONS AND TOLERANCES

Nominal Size	Socket Entrance Dia. Average	Tolerance	Socket Bottom Dia. Average	Tolerance	Socket Depth	Wall Thickness (min.)
3″	3.520″	±0.015″	3.495″	±0.015″	1 1/2″	0.219″

(Courtesy of Genova, Inc.)

Fig. 5-48. Installing a large fitting (Courtesy of Genova, Inc.).

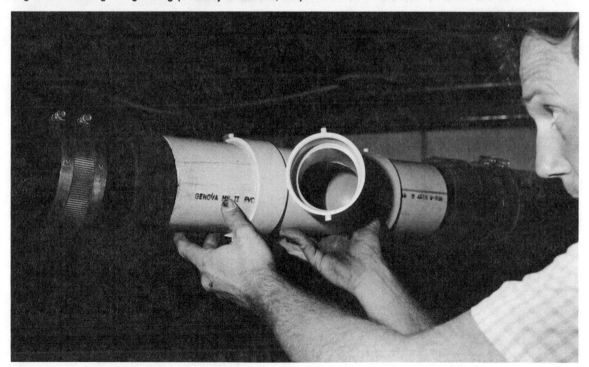

Fig. 5-49. Installing PVC piping on old lines (Courtesy of Genova, Inc.).

153

Fig. 5-50. A miter box makes the best cutting device (Courtesy of Genova, Inc.).

Fig. 5-51. PVC fitting adapts to cast iron pipe (Courtesy of Genova, Inc.).

154

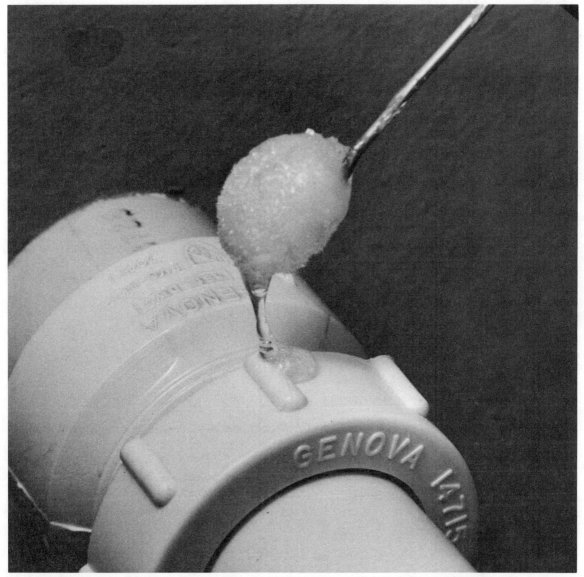

Fig. 5-52. The dauber, with fresh cement, is fine with DWV up to about 2 inches in diameter (Courtesy of Genova, Inc.).

clean rag to remove residue. Pour some solvent into a clean coffee can or other can and dip the brush into it, applying a liberal coating to the pipe end. Dip the brush once more and coat the fitting socket interior. Be liberal but neat with the cement as it requires plenty to form a leak-free joint.

Use a miter box for square pipe ends when making cuts, or you can use a pipe cutter with a special plastic cutting wheel. Once pipe ends and fitting sockets have been cleaned, lay them on a clean piece of lumber to keep them from getting dirty again.

Carefully check each pipe end for deep scratches, abrasions, and hairline cracks and cut off and discard any damaged ends. Use a coarse file or sandpaper to chamfer the pipe end all around,

Fig. 5-53. When working out of place, keep materials out of dirt by cutting on a board (Courtesy of Genova, Inc.).

aiming at a 45-degree angle so that the pipe will enter the fitting easily and cleanly.

When DWV pipe is being solvent welded out of place, do it across a pair of 2- × -4s as a way of keeping the aligned and ready-to-glue material off the floor and out of the dirt (Figs. 5-53 through 5-58).

Pipe alignment is of particular importance with plastic. Degree-marked pipe helps in getting each fitting properly aligned during the fitting process and can be used during the solvent-welding process

1. Cut to length squarely and allow for makeup dimension (depth of fitting socket). Use a fine-tooth saw or a pipe cutter with a special vinyl cutting wheel.

Fig. 5-54. Step 1 in solvent welding (Courtesy of Genova, Inc.).

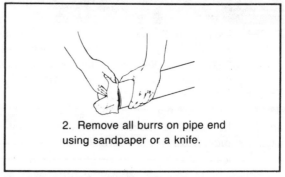

2. Remove all burrs on pipe end using sandpaper or a knife.

Fig. 5-55. Step 2 in solvent welding (Courtesy of Genova, Inc.).

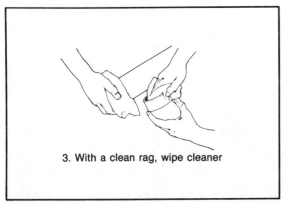

3. With a clean rag, wipe cleaner

Fig. 5-56. Step 3 in solvent welding (Courtesy of Genova, Inc.).

as well if you can remember which mark is which during the process of assembly (assuming you're cutting, checking fit, and going on with the entire system before solvent welding.)

Expansion allowances must be made with all types of pipe over long runs and PVC pipe is no different in the fact that it expands and contracts with changes in temperature. Normally, directional changes in DWV runs will make up for such movement, but with unusually long runs that have only short offsets of 45 or 90 degrees following them, you'll need to provide supports, tightly clamped to the pipe, to prevent extra heavy flex-loading of the fitting. If the directional change is followed by another long run of 20 pipe diameters or more (for example, 5 feet, or 60 inches, for 3-inch pipe), strap loosely to allow free movement (Fig. 5-59).

All horizontal runs of PVC DWV must be supported at intervals no greater than 4 feet, which is every third joist if your house is on 16-inch centers for framing, every other joist if it's on 2-foot centers. Rest vertical runs on wood blocking at the bottom ends, with extra support provided by branching runs.

Drainage runs should slope 1/4 inch per foot towards the drain and you should use care in selecting fittings to make sure they're all meant for drainage. They have no sharp turns. Runs in DWV pipe with sharp turns are meant only for use as venting. If you must use Ts or Ys from drainage fitting lists for vents, install them upside down (Fig. 5-60).

Threaded fittings in PVC pipe call for the use of a strap wrench. Do *not* use a pipe wrench of any other type. (Although in an emergency, with a rag or duct tape on the pipe around the jaws, the teeth won't do too bad a job of chewing up the vinyl pipe.) When installing screw fittings, dry-fit things first and count the number of turns needed to make the fitting hand-tight. Disassemble. When getting ready to reassemble, apply a single turn of Teflon plumber's tape to the first 3/4 inch or inch of the screws. You can also use a non-hardening pipe dope, but the tape is less messy going on and less mess to remove and replace later if you have to dis-

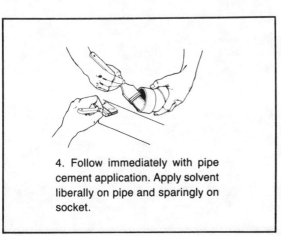

4. Follow immediately with pipe cement application. Apply solvent liberally on pipe and sparingly on socket.

Fig. 5-57. Step 4 in solvent welding (Courtesy of Genova, Inc.).

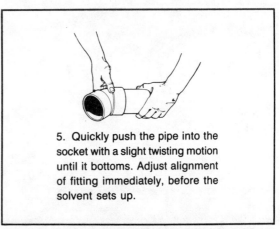

5. Quickly push the pipe into the socket with a slight twisting motion until it bottoms. Adjust alignment of fitting immediately, before the solvent sets up.

Fig. 5-58. Step 5 in solvent welding (Courtesy of Genova, Inc.).

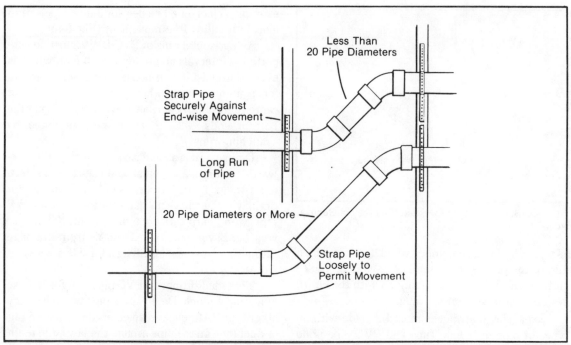

Fig. 5-59. Pipe expansion allowances (Courtesy of Genova, Inc.).

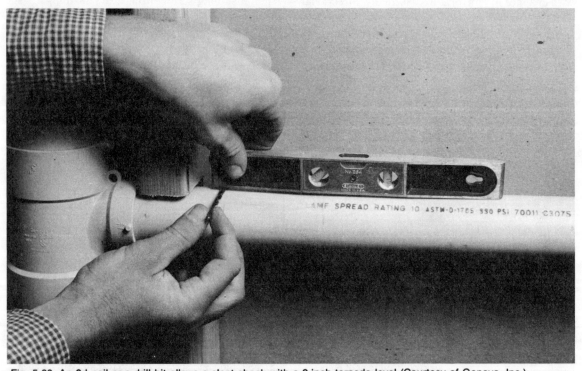

Fig. 5-60. An 8d nail or a drill bit allows a slant check with a 9-inch torpedo level (Courtesy of Genova, Inc.).

158

Fig. 5-61. Modern vent flashing (Courtesy of Genova, Inc.).

assemble the fitting. Now, screw in the fitting the correct number of turns to get it hand-tight without the tape or pipe-dope and give it one or 1 1/2 turns extra with the strap wrench.

If part of your existing system is made of ABS plastic, solvent welding will work between ABS and PVC if great care is used during the job. The extra care is needed because ABS is not as chemically resistant as PVC, so the solvent's action may soften the ABS to the point where it collapses. Use just enough solvent to make the joint, without being as generous with the cement as you would in a pure PVC solvent weld. With PVC you cannot use too much cement, but with ABS you can.

Fittings of various kinds are available for DWV systems of PVC. There is a pop-top toilet flange that is used to join the toilet to the DWV system. It has a flashed-over opening that removes easily and also has teeth along the edge of the flange bolt slots. The teeth serve to hold the toilet bolts in place

as you set the toilet bowl.

Metal flashing over vent stacks, on the roof, cause problems of sealing with plastic DWV pipe because their expansion rates are markedly different, making a good, long-lived seal nearly impossible around plastic pipe. Snap-fit thermoplastic roof flashings are available with soft collars for the pipes that require no caulking and go on very quickly, solving problems and sealing well. They come in models to fit most sizes of vent pipe (Fig. 5-61).

A special waste and vent fitting to take the place of the sanitary T under the floor, behind the toilet, is made in both Schedule 30 3-inch and in 3- and 4-inch Schedule 40. The fitting accepts the toilet's vent stack and drain line at full size, while a pair of reduced side fittings will take 1 1/2- or 2-inch basin or tub/shower waste lines. If the side tappings aren't needed, solvent weld plugs close them.

At its lower end, the special waste and vent fit-

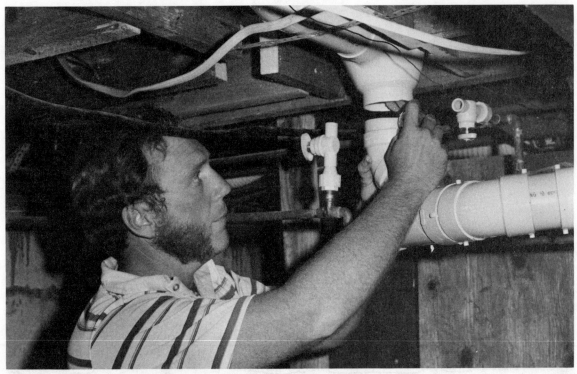

Fig. 5-62. Installation of special waste-vent fitting (Courtesy of Genova, Inc.).

ting takes either of two types of bottom caps that are solvent welded into place. Both accept the full size of the main stack and one has a 1 1/2-inch tapping for an additional drain or vent run (Fig. 5-62).

This special waste or vent fitting is available in either single or double configuration so it may be used with one or two toilets, with two-toilet drainage lines entering the double configuration fitting back-to-back.

Some companies have put together kits that contain all the fittings you would normally need to perform an ordinary bathroom DWV installation, right on up through the roof flashing. It simplifies selection considerably.

PLUMBING WITH COPPER

When updating a system or remodeling, you might need to work with copper plumbing pipes and fittings. While not as easy to use as plastic, copper is still lightweight and reasonably easy to handle and install.

The first step will be to remove whatever old sections of pipe need to come out. Brace the pipe well to prevent too much movement and to keep cut ends in place. A good way to brace the pipe is by wrapping it every few feet with plumbers tape and nailing the end of the tape to handy joists or studs.

A fine-toothed hacksaw will easily cut through copper pipe. Or the pipe can be disconnected by melting the soldered joints with a propane or butane torch. Many fittings and unions will simply unscrew.

New copper pipe can be cut to the necessary lengths for installation with a pipe cutter fitted with a copper pipe blade. A hacksaw can be used also, but it will not make as straight a cut as the pipe cutter. Once the pipe is cut, you will need to file or sand off burrs from both the inside and outside of the pipe.

Measuring is simple for copper pipe installation. Just measure the distance needed between fittings and add the distance the pipe will extend into fittings.

Copper pipe and fittings can be joined in several ways. Soldering is probably the best, but cannot be used in every situation, sometimes because of joint location. Soldered joints are used for most copper fittings that have smooth interiors.

The pipes must be dry to make a successful soldered joint. With steel wool, sandpaper, or an emery cloth, polish about 1/2-inch of each inside end of the fitting and the last inch on the outside of the pipe. Apply soldering flux to the polished inside of the fitting and the outside of the pipe end. Once the fitting is on the end of the pipe, turn both a couple of times to spread the flux. Place the fitting into the proper position and heat it evenly with a butane or propane torch. Remove the torch and touch the solder to the edge of the fitting. Continue until a fine line of solder is showing around the entire fitting. Wipe away excess solder with a damp rag before it dries. Only a little solder should show between the fitting and pipe.

To swage copper pipe for soldering, insert the swaging tool into the end of the pipe and hammer it into the pipe to where the head of the tool is the largest in diameter. It will then be soldered in the same manner as a fitted joint.

A flared joint can be used in places where a soldered joint is not possible. The flare nut will go over the end of the pipe with the tapered end facing away from the end of the pipe. With the end of the pipe clamped into a flaring tool, screw the ram into the end of the pipe. Remove the flaring tool and press the tapered end of the fitting into the newly flared pipe. Screw the nut onto the body of the fitting, using two wrenches to tighten the fitting.

A compression fitting can be completed by sliding the compression nut over the end of the pipe with the large shoulder turned away from the end. Put on the compression ring and screw the nut onto the body of the fitting with the threaded body of the fitting against the end of the pipe. Once the compression ring is tightened, a watertight seal is achieved.

Copper pipe must be supported every 6 to 8 feet once it is joined and run. Special hangers are available. Wrap the pipe with electrician's tape at every spot where a hanger will be used.

PLUMBING WITH GALVANIZED PIPE

If you are working with a plumbing system in a home of more than 20 years, you might need to know how to handle galvanized pipe. If a section of pipe needs to be replaced, it is best to replace it with new galvanized pipe. If you are extending the system, however, you could choose to use either copper or plastic pipe.

Galvanized pipe fits together with threads. You can often buy the length pipe you need with both ends already threaded. If you need a special size, see if the store will thread the end for you. If not, threading can be done with a pipe threader usually available at rental outlets. A pipe vise or bench vise with jaws for pipe will also be needed to hold the pipe steady for threading. Fit the head of the threader into the threading handle and slip it over the end of the pipe to be threaded. While rotating the handle clockwise, apply force toward the body of the pipe. As the threader cuts into the metal, quit pushing, but continue the turning of the handle. As you turn the threader, apply cutting oil. Stop threading when the pipe is one thread past the end of the threader's head.

Before joining the pipe, apply pipe joint compound or fluorocarbon tape to the threads. Screw the pipe and fitting together. Use two pipe wrenches to tighten the connection.

Galvanized supply pipe can be cut in two with a coarse-toothed hacksaw. Use two wrenches to uncouple the pipe from the fitting.

New galvanized pipe can be cut in the same manner as copper pipe with a pipe cutter and a blade specially for galvanized pipe. A large variety of fittings are available for use with galvanized pipe. Pipe must be supported every few feet in long runs.

PLUMBING WITH CAST IRON

The DWV pipe in many homes is made of cast iron. When it comes time to repair or replace cast iron pipe, seriously consider switching to the lighter and easier to use plastic.

By far the easiest way to remove cast iron pipe is to rent a DWV cutter from a rental store.

If you must replace some of your plumbing with new cast iron, choose hubless because it is much easier to install than hub cast iron pipe. To find out how much new cast iron pipe you need, simply measure between the cut ends of the removed section. Your new pipe can be cut with the same DWV cutter you used to remove the old pipe.

The new pipe will be connected to the pipe in the system with a neoprene gasket placed over the end of the existing pipe and a stainless steel band over the end of the new pipe. With the ends of the two pieces together, slide the gasket over the joint and the band over the gasket. The band can be tightened with a screwdriver as needed. Because of its excessive weight, cast iron should be supported at least every 5 feet with plumber's tape.

RUNNING PLUMBING PIPE

If your bathroom project calls for any kind of major change in the plumbing pipes, a detailed map of the entire plumbing system for your home will be useful. You can make your own map by simply tracing out all of the plumbing throughout the house. Measure everything and make a scale drawing of the whole system. Start in the basement and follow through all the way to the attic.

Open up the walls that you need to work inside and fit everything together for a dry run as described earlier in the section about plumbing with plastic. With plastic pipe you will have the option of replacing pipe without opening walls to any great extent. With the more rigid pipes you will have no choice but to open walls for removal and replacement. Once you have all of the new piping laid out and are sure that all supplies are on hand you can begin the work. Turn off the water to the house and start replacing or adding to pipes. When all of the major pipes are in place and connections firmly placed, you will be ready to move on to fixture connections.

Chapter 6

Light, Heat, and Ventilation for the Bathroom

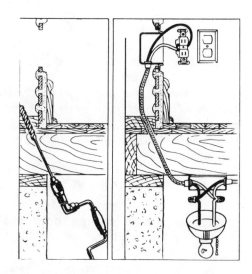

Y OU NEED NOT BE AN ELECTRICIAN TO MAKE repairs or changes in your bathroom's electrical system, or even to wire a new bathroom.

Of course, be sure to first check your local codes for specifications and to learn how much of the work you will be allowed to do yourself. It will help to be familiar with the following terms in order to work with electricity.

Electric current can be compared to a current of water. The more current there is in a wire, the more light, heat, and power it will produce.

The ampere is the measurement of the amount of electric current flowing through a wire at any given time. Fuses, switches, and outlets are rated in amperes. That rating determines the size of the wire or cable needed for safe operation.

The volt is the unit of electric pressure that forces amperes to flow through the wires. For example, an appliance using 5 amperes at 110 volts will consume 550 watts.

The kilowatt hours are units of electrical work. This unit is used because the watt is too small a measurement for most purposes. A kilowatt hour is 1000 watts consumed over a period of one hour. Meters register power consumption in kilowatt hours.

Voltage drop is the decrease in electric pressure. It is caused by wires of inadequate size in the house wiring system or by circuits having more outlets than the power source can serve.

Conductors and insulators control the flow of electricity. Conductors, usually copper wire, transmit electric current. Insulators, usually made of porcelain, glass, rubber, silk, or certain plastics, serve as protective shields to keep current under control. Inadequate insulation permits current to escape from the wire, causing a serious fire hazard.

Electric circuits are closed systems through which current runs from a power source to outlets where it is used and back to the power source. There are two types of circuits: series and parallel.

In a series circuit, current passes through several outlets one after the other, each taking from the current the amount of power it needs. Every outlet in the circuit must continue to work if the others are to function. If a light burns out or is removed the circuit is broken. Series wiring is rarely used in the home.

Parallel circuits are standard for most house wiring. In these circuits, any outlet may be cut in and out without affecting the others. Too many outlets in use on any one circuit at a time will drain more current than the circuit is designed to carry, producing a serious voltage drop.

Current consumption in the home is measured by a meter. The standard measurement is the kilowatt. Electric meters are of two types. The newer meters have direct-reading, four-place counters. Old meters have four dials, each numbered from one to ten. The pointers on the first and third dials turn counterclockwise while the second and fourth turn clockwise. Read from left to right to determine consumption.

BATHROOM WIRING

Your home is probably wired with either a two-wire or three-wire system leading into the house, depending largely on local electrical codes at the time the home was built.

Many pre-1940 homes contain a two-wire system. The two wires leading to the house carry 115 volts from a pole or underground cable to the electrical meter and on into the main power panel. From there electricity is distributed throughout the house.

In a two-wire system the white wire is neutral and is probably grounded at the power panel by an attachment to the water pipe. The black wire is the "hot" wire. Both carry current and care must be taken when working near them. A two-wire system might not be adequate for all of the electrical appliances used in modern homes.

Houses now are normally wired with the three-wire system, which provides both 115 and 230 volts, adequate for most home usage. In the three-wire system, two of the wires are hot and the third is neutral. The hot wires are usually black and red, while the neutral is white. All three feed into the main power panel and are branched out from there.

Wiring in your bathroom provides power for lighting, heating, and ventilation. If the wiring is inadequate or not in the proper position for your new plans, you will have to add to or modify the system. In a new room, of course, you will need to put in all new wiring.

Local building codes will again tell you what you can do and what materials you can choose from for your project.

If your plans call for adding switches, outlets, or a new lighting fixture, you might be able to run the wire from the power source in an existing outlet to a new position. The wire can be routed through a wall, attic or basement, or even behind a baseboard.

To extend wiring through a wall, first be sure to turn off the power to the circuit on which you are working. Remove the cover plate from the existing power source and remove the "knockout" hole for cables in the direction you need to run your wire. Pinpoint your new fixture location and with a keyhole saw cut out a spot in the wall for the fixture. After stripping 6 inches of outside insulation from one end of the cable, feed the cable through the knockout of the original power source and out the new wall opening. Tighten the cable clamp at the first outlet. Strip about 1/2 inch of insulation from the wires at the new opening and put them through the knockout of the new box. After the cable clamp is tightened, match the new wires at the first source and replace the outlet. At the new fixture, connect the black wire to the brass terminal, the white wire to the white terminal, and the ground to the green hex head screw. You are now ready to connect your new outlet or fixture.

If you have opened the walls for new plumbing or other changes, it will be a simple matter to run electrical wiring to anywhere you need it before the walls are closed up again. Be sure to check all local codes governing home wiring and only perform those tasks you understand and you are allowed by law to attempt.

Often the only rewiring in a bathroom will be in the area of the lights, which are usually around the medicine cabinet (Fig. 6-1), and for a ventilator/heater/fan. Most codes for bathrooms require that there either be a window in the room or a ventilator and fan.

Equipment and materials for electrical wiring will vary from job to job, for one person might

Fig. 6-1. Sidelights for an old-fashion bathroom cabinet (Courtesy of NuTone).

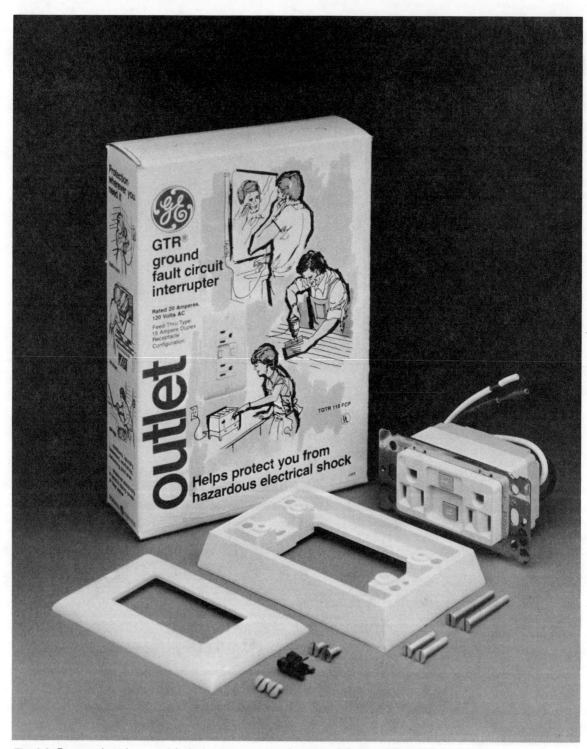

Fig. 6-2. Receptacle-style ground fault circuit interrupter (Courtesy of General Electric).

quire several lights in the room, while another family is happy with an overhead light and the lights on or near the medicine cabinet mirror (if any). Heaters and ventilators and their controls come in a wide variety and the wiring for those can get involved. The following are general guidelines. Follow the directions from the manufacturer for the installation of any lights, heaters, or ventilator/fans.

The National Electric Code gives a list of electrical needs for bathrooms. The first is a receptacle near the basin. This gives you a spot to plug in a hair dryer, electric razor, or other such items. The NEC states that all 120 volt, 15 and 20 ampere receptacle circuits in bathrooms must have ground fault circuit interrupters (GRIs and GFCIs) as protection (Figs. 6-2 and 6-3).

Ground fault circuit interrupters are electronic feedback-reading devices designed to prevent, or cut back on, the incidence of electrocutions from ground faults. Ground faults are problems when someone touches a hot wire on an appliance having a defect that keeps it from being properly grounded, so that the appliance is "hot" all the time. The GFCI provides an electronic watchdog circuit on the two conductors in a circuit (the hot and neutral wires). The current in these two wires should always be equal so the GFCI is set to sense a difference of more than 5 milliamperes, at which it automatically trips the circuit breaker, cutting power to that circuit. The power interruption is supposed to take place in less than a fortieth of a second, which is usually fast enough to prevent major harm to anyone in normal health. It doesn't feel good, but it should not be harmful.

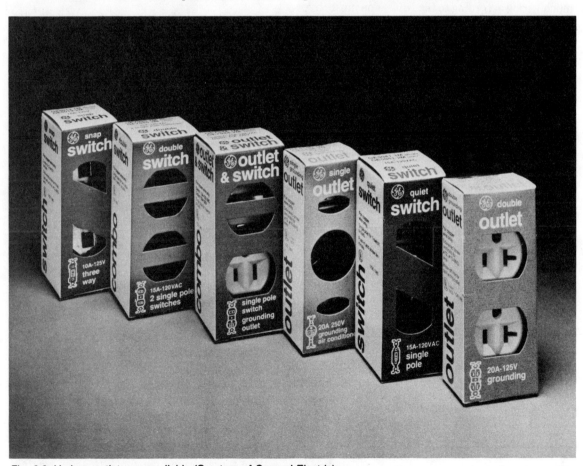

Fig. 6-3. Various outlets are available (Courtesy of General Electric).

GFCIs come in three basic forms. One fits into the service entrance pane, in place of the standard circuit breaker, while another style fits into the receptacle box in place of a standard receptacle (there's still a receptacle there, but it's protected). A third type simply plugs into the receptacle. On new installation work, you can't use the last because they're too easily removed. Some receptacle replacement types protect that receptacle and everything beyond on the same circuit. It makes sense to replace the circuit breaker and cover all the circuits that way.

Bathroom lighting circuits do not require the same protection and probably don't need it. They'll be protected if they're on the same circuit as receptacles protected ahead of them.

The average bathroom doesn't require too much wiring according to the NEC. You must have just that single receptacle (a standard double outlet receptacle is used), and at least one lighting circuit. In small baths the lights mounted near the medicine cabinet will be enough for most people. A second lighting circuit prevents blackout problems should the first circuit be overloaded while you're in the shower or shaving. If, for instance, the first lighting circuit comes off a dining room circuit and someone turns on an appliance that draws enough to pop the breaker, a second lighting circuit coming off one of the bedrooms or the hall lighting circuit keeps you from being in the dark for too long.

You'll have to have a circuit capable of handling a ventilating unit if there is no window in the room.

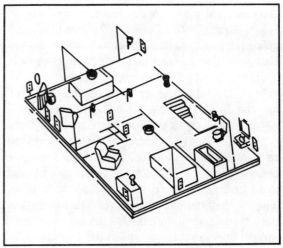

Fig. 6-5. Wiring circuit for two bedrooms and bath (Courtesy of Sears, Roebuck & Co.).

This circuitry will depend on the type of ventilator you add. Some require very little amperage and can go on any lighting circuit that is not already overloaded, while others require a separate circuit, and sometimes even a "small appliance" circuit. Such a circuit will use a minimum cable size of 12, with a 20-ampere circuit breaker capable of carrying a 33 1/3 percent greater current load than the standard 15-ampere circuit. Total lighting circuit loads are often figured at around 1500 watts, though that's a shade on the low side. Using standard formulae, a 120-volt system should take 1800 amperes and a voltage drop to 110 would still give a power capacity of 1650 watts (about the maximum of most electric heaters). Still, upping the circuit to 20 amperes provides a capacity of either 2400 watts on the high side or 2200 watts on the low side, both considerably better than with a 15-ampere circuit.

Any 20-ampere circuit should be able to carry the load from any available heater/ventilator/light appliance now on the market, so you still have a wide array from which to make your choice.

Residential electrical wiring is not really a complex job. There are some basic requirements to keep in mind to ensure a safe and efficient job. As mentioned earlier, never work on a circuit that has power to it. It's a simple matter to flip the circuit breaker or pull the fuse on any circuit being worked on, and there is a simple check to show whether

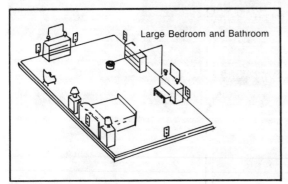

Fig. 6-4. Properly placed wiring circuit (Courtesy of Sears, Roebuck & Co.).

a circuit is powered or unpowered. Always remember that neatness does count when wiring. The proper slant on insulation when trimming it, getting a loop just so when attaching wire to a terminal and not nicking a wire when trimming insulation add up to a safe installation because the neatness prevents problems from shorts and high resistances, or from having a wire break along a nick (Figs. 6-4 and 6-5).

Making certain all terminal connections are secure and that each cable passing into a metal box has a collar is also necessary. The working of a cable back and forth over time will eventually wear the insulation away, allowing the cable to contact the box. If you use plastic boxes, the cable wear is less abrupt, in fact not really likely, and a short is also unlikely. Most installations are made with galvanized steel boxes and a short from the cable to one of these is a serious matter. Secure terminals prevent arcing, which could rapidly build up high resistance and burn through a connection. A loose terminal is a sore spot anyway because it can be a point of varying high resistance, causing lights

to flicker and dim, or heaters to cycle oddly, or several other problems. You can see the many reasons that neatness really does count in electrical installations.

Cable installed in stud walls generally is run unprotected except for the studs, unless it's run in notches. When run in notches, a protective plate is required. These protective plates are useful even when the cable is run through a bored hole if the wall is open so that you can tap the plates, which have little V points to hold them in place, into the stud. No code requires these and it would not be worthwhile to open a wall up when fishing cable to install them, but whenever possible use the plates because it means that someone later driving a long nail into a stud won't be poking it through the cable.

TOOLS FOR WORKING WITH ELECTRICITY

Tools required for wiring are similar to tools for general carpentry, with a few additions (Fig. 6-6). A 1/2-inch drill with a right angle off-set attachment and a bit 18 inches long and 1 inch wide is useful for this sort of work. The long bit isn't always es-

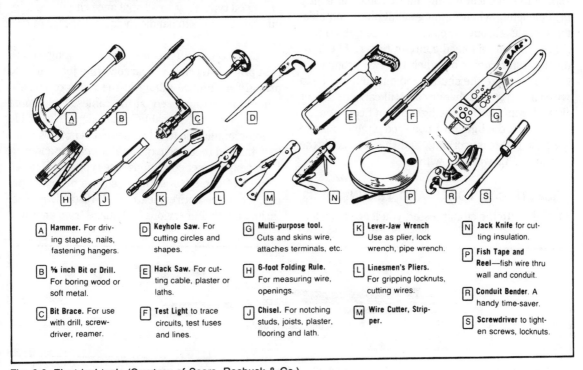

A **Hammer.** For driving staples, nails, fastening hangers.

B **⅝ inch Bit or Drill.** For boring wood or soft metal.

C **Bit Brace.** For use with drill, screwdriver, reamer.

D **Keyhole Saw.** For cutting circles and shapes.

E **Hack Saw.** For cutting cable, plaster or laths.

F **Test Light** to trace circuits, test fuses and lines.

G **Multi-purpose tool.** Cuts and skins wire, attaches terminals, etc.

H **6-foot Folding Rule.** For measuring wire, openings.

J **Chisel.** For notching studs, joists, plaster, flooring and lath.

K **Lever-Jaw Wrench.** Use as plier, lock wrench, pipe wrench.

L **Linesmen's Pliers.** For gripping locknuts, cutting wires.

M **Wire Cutter, Stripper.**

N **Jack Knife** for cutting insulation.

P **Fish Tape and Reel**—fish wire thru wall and conduit.

R **Conduit Bender.** A handy time-saver.

S **Screwdriver** to tighten screws, locknuts.

Fig. 6-6. Electrical tools (Courtesy of Sears, Roebuck & Co.).

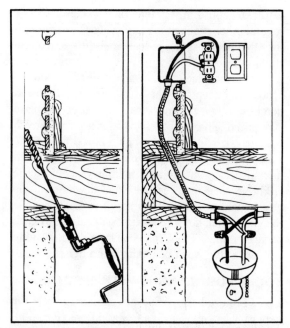

Fig. 6-7. Using the long bit for cable work (Courtesy of Sears, Roebuck & Co.).

trician's screwdriver, which is a long-shanked (at least 10 inches) 1/8- or 3/16-inch blade screwdriver. A pair of wire cutting pliers is handy; the heavier lineman's styles are excellent. A pair of long-nose pliers is a big help in forming the loops for terminals and often in applying those loops to terminal screws your fingers won't reach. An electrician's pocket knife is exceptionally useful. You will need wire nuts in at least two of the three most readily available sizes. Each size usually fits two sizes of wire, such as 12 and 14 or 16 and 18 (Table 6-1 and Fig. 6-10).

You will need electrical cable that is more than one wire made up into a single unit, so that standard 12-2 with ground (three wire) cable is normal, as is 14-2WG. Lighting circuits require cable no lighter than number 14 on their 15-ampere circuitry and all new circuits must be of the type using grounds. (Non-grounded circuits—wires, cables, and receptacles—may only be used as replacements on old circuitry.) In almost every case, if replacement extends beyond a switch or a receptacle, it's best to change that individual circuit to the grounded type. Any small appliance circuits require number 12 cable to handle their 20 amperes of current (Table 6-2).

Cable types differ considerably, making significant price difference in a large wiring job, with the primary difference falling in the types of sheathing and insulation used on the cables. For almost all indoor uses, NM cable is sufficient. NM cable is non-metallic sheathed cable that is not designed to withstand repeated exposure to weather and wet. If you expect wet conditions, use type NMC cable. Type NM cable has an inner sheath of heavy paper, while the entire sheath of NMC cable is plastic and nearly impervious to damage from anything

sential to electrical wiring, but it comes in handy in remodeling when running small pipes and electrical cables through areas already assembled (Fig (Fig 6-7). You will need a circuit tester. The light on the tester comes on when the two prongs are touched—one to the neutral and one to the hot—to wires in a circuit if that circuit still carries current (Figs. 6-8 and 6-9). If the light doesn't come on, always check the light on a powered circuit to make sure the tester is working, and then re-check the circuit you're working with.

ELECTRICAL TOOLS AND TECHNIQUES

In addition to the circuit tester, you'll need an elec-

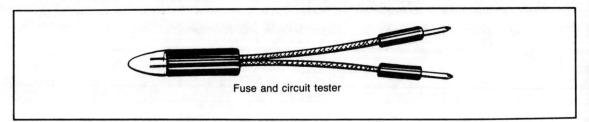

Fuse and circuit tester

Fig. 6-8. A universal tester (Courtesy of Sears, Roebuck & Co.).

Table 6-1. Wire Connectors or Nuts.

Color		Voltage Rating	Use For	Temp. Rating	Wire Combination Range
Shown Actual Size	Orange, Small	600 Volt Maximum for Building Wiring 1,000 V Max. in Fixtures and Signs	Copper/copper Aluminum/aluminum Copper/Aluminum	105°C (221°F)	Joins No. 22 thru 14 AWG Min. 3 No. 22 Max. 3 No. 16 & 1 No. 18
	Yellow, Medium	Same as above	Same as Above	105°C (221°F)	Joins No. 18 thru 12 AWG Min. 1 No. 14 & 1 No. 18 Max. 2 No. 14 & 3 No. 16
	Red, Large	Same as Above	Same as Above	105°C (221°F)	Joins No. 18 thru 10 AWG Min. 1 No. 12 & 2 No. 18 Max. 2 No. 10 & 1 No. 12

(Courtesy of Vaco)

other than mechanical objects. You'll need to make entire runs with NMC if you decide to use it at all, because the NEC forbids cable or wire splices outside junction boxes.

Exposed wire runs need protection from mechanical damage, which means a fastener of some type at 4 1/2-foot intervals and within 1 foot of any box. Staples are still code-allowed, but straps are preferred by most top-notch electrical workers because there's less chance of damaging the insulation of the cable by driving a staple in too far. Staples serve as well as clamps and are far cheaper, so careful driving can prevent damage. Drive staples so the bar just touches the cable, as you would a finish nail to wood molding. A 13-ounce claw hammer works well for driving staples. Any exposed wire runs in unfinished areas, attic or basement, must also be protected from mechanical damage. Do this by running the cable through holes in the framing members, or along the sides of the beams, joists, and studs if the wire run is parallel to them (Figs. 6-11 through 6-14). In those cases where holes cannot be drilled in the materials, the cable can be placed on a running board nailed to the beams or joists (usually a piece of 1- x -2 is nailed to the beams or rafters before the cable is installed). If you install cable above your bathroom, through an unfinished attic space for instance, you'll need protective runners along each side of the cable to help prevent mechanical damage whenever the cable can't be run through holes or notches in the beams and ceiling joists (Figs. 6-15 through 6-19).

Mechanical protection can also be provided by thin wall conduit, but this is seldom seen anymore indoors, as the new plastic sheathed cables take a battering a lot better than did some of the older styles of cable.

When working with any household wiring

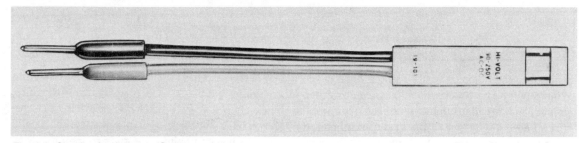

Fig. 6-9. Simple circuit tester (Courtesy of Vaco).

Table 6-2. Wire Size and Ampacity.

Adequate Wire Sizes . .
Weatherproof Copper Wire

Load in Building Amperes	Distance in Feet from Pole to Building	*Recommended Size of Feeder Wire for job
Up to 25 amperes, 120 volts	Up to 50 feet	No. 10
	50 to 80 feet	No. 8
	80 to 125 feet	No. 6
20 to 30 amperes, 240 volts	Up to 80 feet	No. 10
	80 to 125 feet	No. 8
	125 to 200 feet	No. 6
	200 to 350 feet	No. 4
30 to 50 amperes, 240 volts	Up to 80 feet	No. 8
	80 to 125 feet	No. 6
	125 to 200 feet	No. 4
	200 to 300 feet	No. 2
	300 to 400 feet	No. 1

*These sizes are recommended to reduce "voltage drop" to a minimum

Ampacities of Copper Wires

Wire size	In Conduit or Cable		In Free Air		Weather-proof Wire
	Type RHW* THW*	Type TW, R*	Type RHW* THW*	Type TW, R*	
14	15	15	20	20	30
12	20	20	25	25	40
10	30	30	40	40	55
8	45	40	65	55	70
6	65	55	95	80	100
4	85	70	125	105	130
3	100	80	145	120	150
2	115	95	170	140	175
1	130	110	195	165	205
0	150	125	230	195	235
00	175	145	265	225	275
000	200	165	310	260	320

*Types "RHW," "THW," "TW," or "R" are identified by markings on outer cover

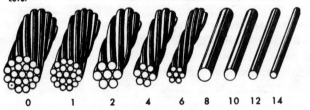

0   1   2   4   6   8   10   12   14

Actual size of copper conductors. Note the larger the gauge number the smaller the diameter of the wire.

(Courtesy of Sears, Roebuck & Co.)

remember the color code. The green wire is the ground wire. The covering will be green or green striped, and any uninsulated wire is also a ground wire. These always go to the green terminals of receptacles and are not fused under any circumstances. The other two colors in residential wiring are white and black. White always goes to white, black always goes to black. Some wiring set-ups, shown later, for three- and four-way switches, will require that you paint wire ends to match colors.

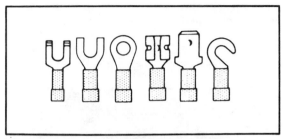

Fig. 6-10. Wiring terminals (Courtesy of Vaco).

Controversy still seems to exist over the use of aluminum wiring in homes. Aluminum is a self-limiting oxidizer. When the surface of non-treated aluminum oxidizes to a certain point, no further oxidation can take place because the oxides seal the metal off from oxygen penetration. Special terminals are available and must be used if aluminum wire is used in a system. Aluminum also is susceptible to stress at any junction, which adds to the chances of higher resistance. For bathroom wiring it is generally wise to avoid using aluminum wiring if possible.

Wiring mechanics are relatively simple. Junctions can be made only in boxes, up to the limits of any particular box size. Check local codes for variations on these limits. Use only wire nut, screw-on connectors, unless a soldered connection is imperative. When you get to wire stripping, start by slitting the cable. Then separate the wires and strip each wire back 1 1/2 inches, making sure the insulation edge left tapers to the wire and the wire is not nicked. When screw terminals are used, the wire loop made should have its open end facing the direction in which the screw turns down and should leave a gap of about 1/4 the circumference of the loop (this will close up part way as you turn the screw down). Any pigtail of wire extending beyond this will interfere, and needs to be cut off (Fig. 6-20).

You will save time by selecting stab-in terminal type receptacles and switches. A simple push gets the wire in place. You will find a few differences in brands, so check the instructions on the packaging or the included instruction sheet if you buy in bulk, to see just what else will be needed and what length of bare wire you need to have.

Box type is pretty much determined by the job it must do, with rectangular boxes for switches and

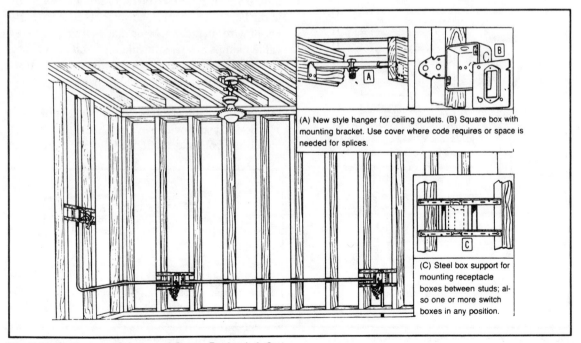

(A) New style hanger for ceiling outlets. (B) Square box with mounting bracket. Use cover where code requires or space is needed for splices.

(C) Steel box support for mounting receptacle boxes between studs; also one or more switch boxes in any position.

Fig. 6-11. Cable runs (Courtesy of Sears, Roebuck & Co.).

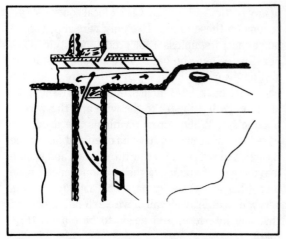

Fig. 6-12. Fishing cable (Courtesy of Sears, Roebuck & Co.).

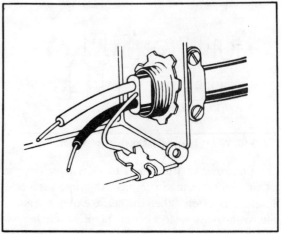

Fig. 6-14. Installing cable clamps (Courtesy of Sears, Roebuck & Co.).

receptacles, and octagonal boxes, or round boxes, for light fixtures and junctions. Rectangular boxes can usually be "ganged." That is, one or more sides can be removed and two or more boxes hooked together to make a larger box. You'll note double entry switches, switch and receptacle boxes and so

forth are all made with ganged boxes. Junction boxes must have covers no matter where they're located. Switch boxes, receptacle boxes, and fixture boxes must also be covered, though fixtures often serve as covers on their boxes.

Unspliced wires passing through boxes are not counted as a part of the contents, nor are wires running from an appliance or fixture to wires already in the box. Cable clamps, however, reduce the number of wires in the box by one, no matter how many cable clamps are used, while a switch or receptacle in the box also reduces the allowable number of wires by one. Bare grounding wires entering a box from nonmetallic sheathed cable also reduce the number of allowable wires by one. (Table 6-3.)

Boxes come with several different types of mounting brackets to fit wall types. Boxes also

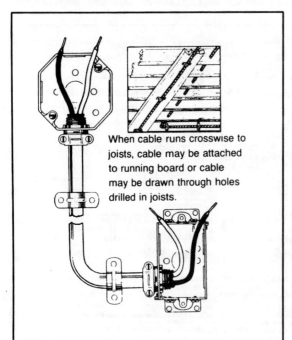

When cable runs crosswise to joists, cable may be attached to running board or cable may be drawn through holes drilled in joists.

Fig. 6-13. Installing non-metallic cable (Courtesy of Sears, Roebuck & Co.).

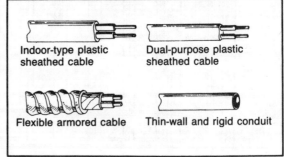

Indoor-type plastic sheathed cable

Dual-purpose plastic sheathed cable

Flexible armored cable

Thin-wall and rigid conduit

Fig. 6-15. Cable types (Courtesy of Sears, Roebuck & Co.).

174

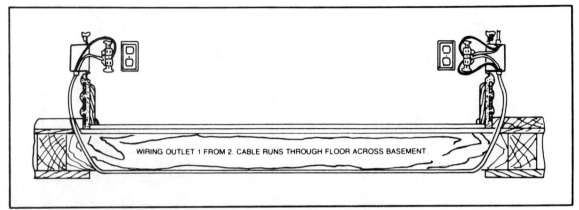

Fig. 6-16. Running cable under a floor (Courtesy of Sears, Roebuck & Co.).

come without brackets but those with brackets are easier to install. Ceiling boxes for lights are available with adjustable hangers that nail between the rafters.

Boxes are wired up with at least 8 inches of wire protruding from each box. This assures you of sufficient wire to either join wires or reach terminals on a switch.

Select any switches you need for the voltage and amperage of the circuit you're installing. In most cases switches for 110 and 120 volts will handle up to 25 amperes of AC. Read the labels to be sure.

Wiring a room or house requires planning and care so that everything comes out even. The craftsmanship needed to install modern electrical cable and accessories is easily gained. Check local building codes before beginning any wiring changes. In some areas it is illegal to do any electrical work without a license, while in others the work must be inspected by a licensed electrician before it passes. Figures 6-21 through 6-31 will guide you step by step through many wiring situations not previously covered.

LIGHTING

While daylight from a strategically placed window is the best for shaving, applying make-up, and other bathroom activities, it is not always available. Your bathroom will have to include some artificial light.

The well-lighted bathroom has good, glare-free general illumination as well as properly placed area lights at the basin or dressing counters. The lights at the basin or dressing counter should be located so that the light shines on the face, not the mirror.

To light the head and face without deceptive shadows requires light from three directions—above and both sides—plus reflected light from white or neutral surfaces below. Lighting at the mirror will illuminate a small or average bathroom adequately. A large or compartmented bathroom will require additional ceiling or localized lighting.

The lights at the basin should be about 30 inches apart with the center of the light bulb 60 inches above the floor. Center the ceiling light above the front edge of the lavatory. Fluorescent units are recommended for uniform shadow-free lighting. Such units should be long enough to throw light on the vertical planes of the face. Because they

Table 6-3. Box Capacities.

Type of Box	Size (inches)	Max. No. of Wires		
		#14	#12	#10
Outlet (round	4 × 1 1/4	6	5	5
or octagonal)	4 × 1 1/2	7	6	6
	4 × 2 1/8	10	9	8
Switch	3 × 2 × 1 1/2	3	3	3
	3 × 2 × 2	5	4	4
	3 × 2 × 2 1/4	5	4	4
	3 × 2 × 2 3/4	7	6	5
	3 × 2 × 3 1/2	9	8	7

(Courtesy of Sears, Roebuck & Co.)

175

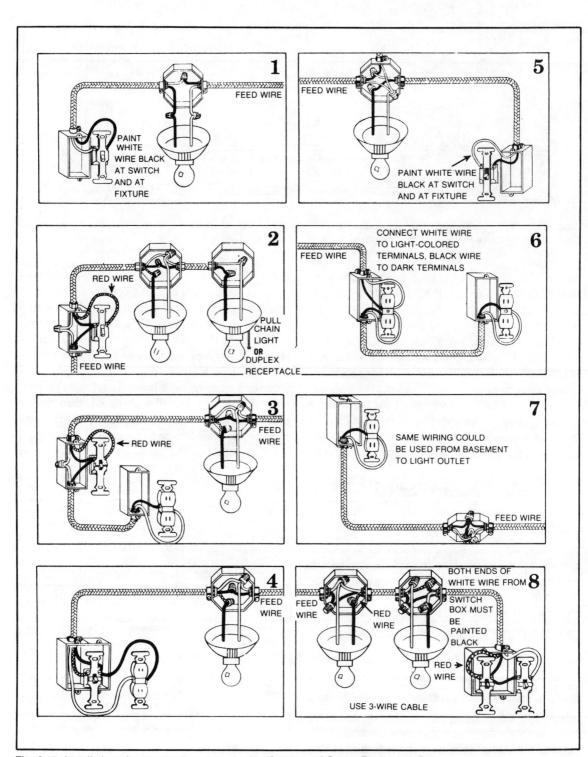

Fig. 6-17. Installation of some simple switch circuits (Courtesy of Sears, Roebuck & Co).

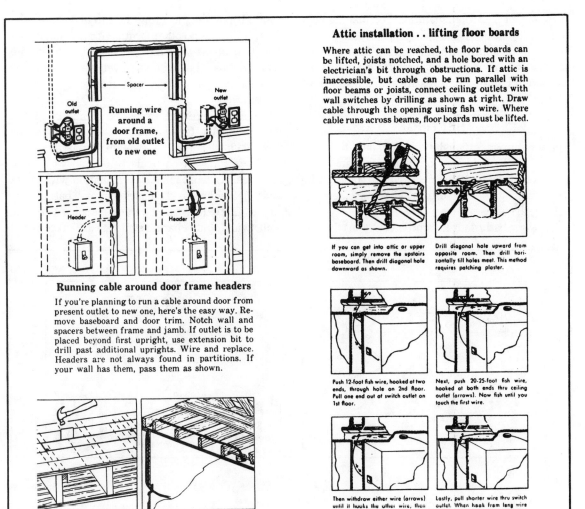

Where attic can be reached, the floor boards can be lifted, joists notched, and a hole bored with an electrician's bit through obstructions. If attic is inaccessible, but cable can be run parallel with floor beams or joists, connect ceiling outlets with wall switches by drilling as shown at right. Draw cable through the opening using fish wire. Where cable runs across beams, floor boards must be lifted.

Running wire around a door frame, from old outlet to new one

Spacer

Old outlet

New outlet

Header Header

If you can get into attic or upper room, simply remove the upstairs baseboard. Then drill diagonal hole downward as shown.

Drill diagonal hole upward from opposite room. Then drill horizontally till holes meet. This method requires patching plaster.

Push 12-foot fish wire, hooked at two ends, through hole on 2nd floor. Pull one end out at switch outlet on 1st floor.

Next, push 20-25-foot fish wire, hooked at both ends thru ceiling outlet (arrows). Now fish until you touch the first wire.

Then withdraw either wire (arrows) until it hooks the other wire, then withdraw second wire until both hooks hook together.

Lastly, pull shorter wire thru switch outlet. When hook from long wire appears, attach cable and pull thru wall and ceiling.

Running cable around door frame headers

If you're planning to run a cable around door from present outlet to new one, here's the easy way. Remove baseboard and door trim. Notch wall and spacers between frame and jamb. If outlet is to be placed beyond first upright, use extension bit to drill past additional uprights. Wire and replace. Headers are not always found in partitions. If your wall has them, pass them as shown.

Fig. 6-18. Attic installation (Courtesy of Sears, Roebuck & Co.).

give a harsher quality of light, incandescent units are not recommended for mirror lighting, unless they are recessed behind diffusing glass and located no more than 18 inches apart, centered over the sink counter.

For enclosed showers or baths, vapor proof (water-tight) recessed incandescent units with diffusing glass may be used. A matching recessed unit can be used in an enclosed toilet compartment. Infrared lamps are sometimes used in recessed fixtures for bathrooms to provide immediate heat when needed.

Because it is easy to touch water and metal while switching on lights in the bathroom, make certain that lights are controlled by wall switches out of reach of anyone in the bathtub or shower, or anyone using a water faucet (Figs. 6-33 through 6-34). Defective wiring and frayed cords on electrical equipment can result in severe electrical shock. Locate a grounded convenience outlet near the basin counter at a comfortable height for electrical appliances used in the bathroom.

Many types of specialty lights are available for bathroom use, including sun lamps. As you are shopping for bathroom materials and making your bathroom plans, consider the special needs of members of your family. Do you have a sun worshipper? Do you need a grow light for plants in the bathroom? Lighting fixtures are available for most all lighting needs.

HEATING

Every bathroom or wash-up area should be ventilated either by a window or an exhaust fan. Natural or forced ventilation is necessary to comply with local building codes and to meet requirements of lending agencies.

If your bathroom is ventilated by a window,

avoid, if possible, locating the tub under the window. If there is no other location for the tub, a window that opens with a crank is easier to operate than a double-hung window. Even where a window is present it is preferable to include an exhaust system.

To help prevent excessive humidity in the house, exhaust fans vented to the outside can be installed in all bathrooms, whether or not they have windows. Fans are particularly necessary in humid climates. Exhaust fans in combination with lights and a heater are good choices for small bathrooms. Lights and exhaust fans can be installed with one wall switch, but separate switches are preferred if

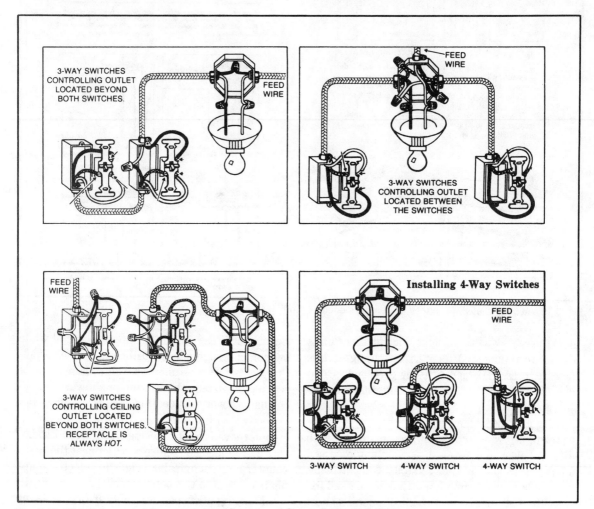

Fig. 6-19. Wiring 3-way and 4-way switches (Courtesy of Sears, Roebuck & Co.).

Joining ends of 2 wires together is a splice. To make splices as strong as a continuous piece of wire, the job must be done well. Otherwise trouble will result.

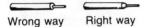

Wrong way   Right way

Cutting wire. Remove insulation by cutting at a slant . . . as in sharpening a pencil. Expose 1/2 inch of copper conductor. Remove all parts of insulation, but not tin coating which helps soldering.

Combination Wire Cutter and Stripper. Makes a handy tool that cuts and strips clean all sizes of solid or stranded copper wire. Use also for looping wires under screws.

Wrong way   Right way

Connections at screw terminals. Bend end of metal wire into a loop to fit around screw. Be sure to attach loop in direction in which screw turns when tightening as illustrated above.

Plastic Tape does a faster, neater, cleaner job than rubber and friction tape. Easier to handle takes less space in boxes. Does the work of both rubber and friction tape. Water-proof, acid-proof.

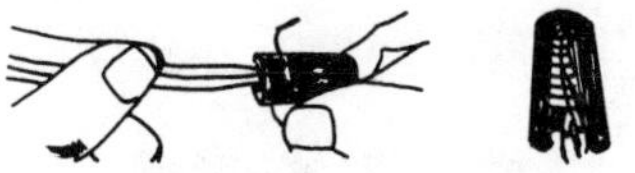

Solderless connectors eliminate the need for soldering joints. Made of insulating material so wires need not be taped . . . short circuits can't occur. Just screw connector over wires as shown.

Fig. 6-20. Wiring techniques (Courtesy of Sears, Roebuck & Co.).

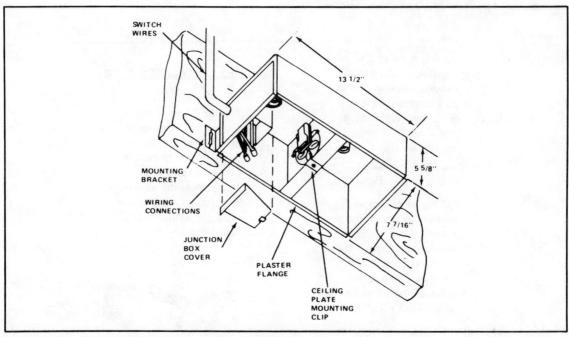

Fig. 6-21. Mounting the lighting box (Courtesy of NuTone).

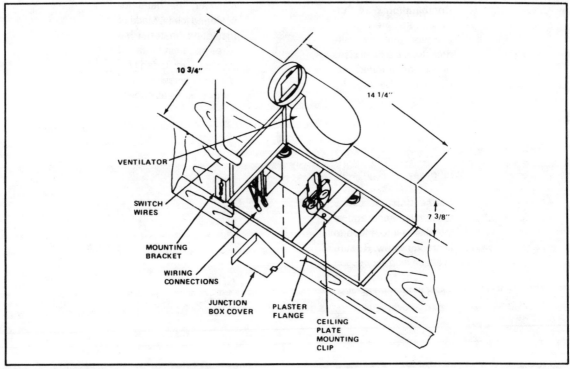

Fig. 6-22. Installing the fan (Courtesy of NuTone).

180

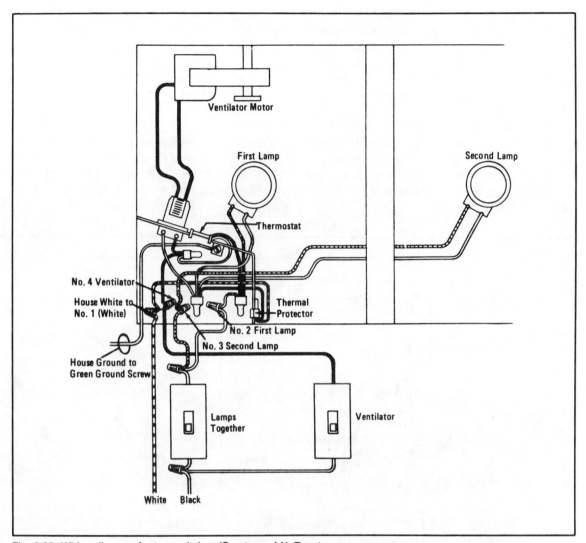

Ventilator Motor

First Lamp

Second Lamp

Thermostat

No. 4 Ventilator

House White to
No. 1 (White)

Thermal
Protector

No. 2 First Lamp

No. 3 Second Lamp

House Ground to
Green Ground Screw

Lamps
Together

Ventilator

White   Black

Fig. 6-23. Wiring diagram for two switches (Courtesy of NuTone).

such an installation is permitted by codes and ordinances. Because ceiling ventilators are most commonly used, we will go through the procedure for installing this type. The ceiling ventilator will probably be composed of a housing, a fan-motor assembly, and a shield.

Select the ceiling location for the fan between joists and cut an opening in the ceiling slightly larger than the ventilator housing. Position the edge of the hole so that the housing can be fastened to a joist for support. Screw the housing to the joist, with the lip flush with the ceiling. Have a helper

mount the fan-motor assembly in the housing while you make the electrical connection. Turn on the power and flip the wall switch to verify operation. The last step is to install the shield over the fan.

Don't forget to plan for auxiliary heat in the bathroom. Even if you have a central heating system, you should consider installing a separate bathroom heater. There will be times when it is too warm to run the central heating, but it would be more comfortable at bath or shower time to have a little heat in the bathroom. There are several types of heaters from which to choose.

A typical ceiling unit installed over the bathtub includes a heater, light, and ventilator fan. These can be used separately or all together. Other popular bathroom heaters include radiant type for either wall or ceiling installation. Infrared heat bulbs are also available that provide light as well as radiant heat.

Plan the location of your heater carefully. Place any wall heater where there is no possibility of a person being burned on it, or of towels or curtains catching fire from it. Portable heaters are not recommended as the general source of heat for the bathroom.

Most bathroom heaters are easy to install. With the variety available, it is best to follow the instructions on the unit that you choose. Always be sure to work on electricity with the power turned off and to follow the coding on the wires.

SAFETY

Bathroom safety requires a great deal of thought and effort. Construction safety is one point to consider, but safety in use is another point. People, usually children, do drown in the bathroom. It requires only a few inches of water to drown even an

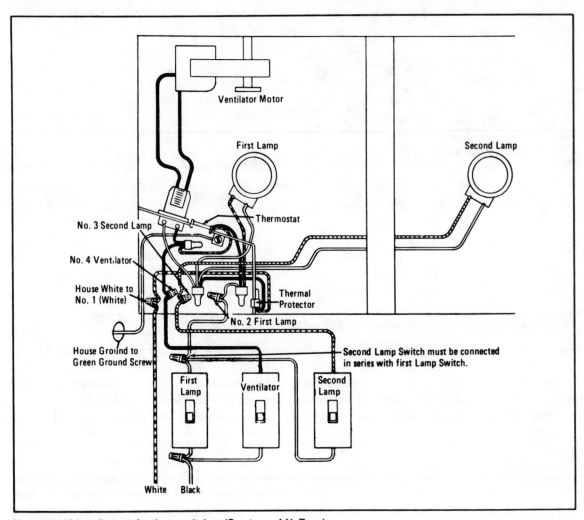

Fig. 6-24. Wiring diagram for three switches (Courtesy of NuTone).

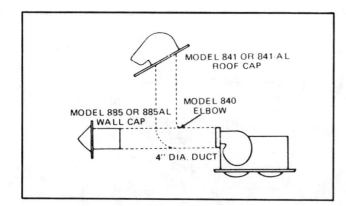

Fig. 6-25. Installing the vent outlet
(Courtesy of NuTone).

MODEL 841 OR 841-AL
ROOF CAP

MODEL 840
ELBOW

MODEL 885 OR 885AL
WALL CAP

4" DIA. DUCT

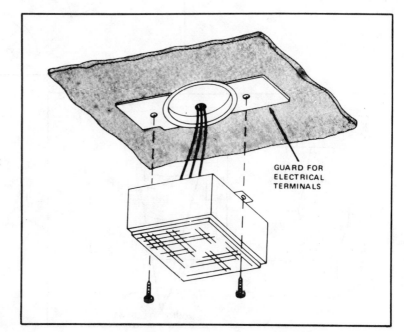

Fig. 6-26. Installing a bathroom light
(Courtesy of NuTone).

GUARD FOR
ELECTRICAL
TERMINALS

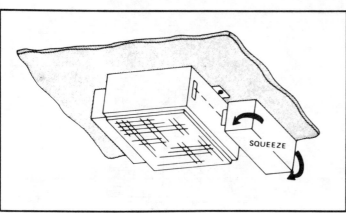

Fig. 6-27. Few tools are needed
(Courtesy of NuTone).

SQUEEZE

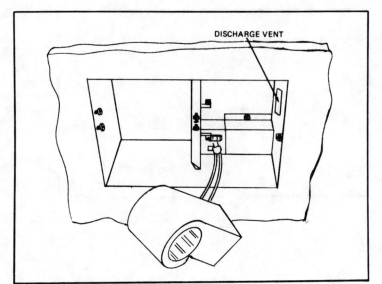

Fig. 6-28. Hooking up the vent fan (Courtesy of NuTone).

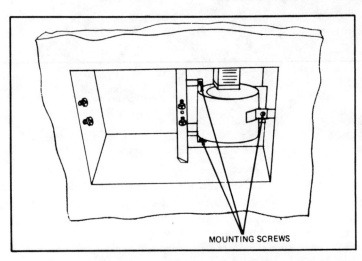

Fig. 6-29. Mounting the vent fan (Courtesy of NuTone).

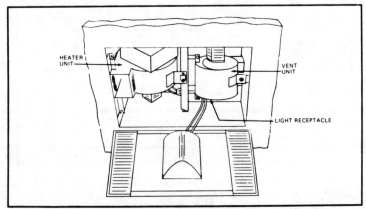

Fig. 6-30. Installing the cover (Courtesy of NuTone).

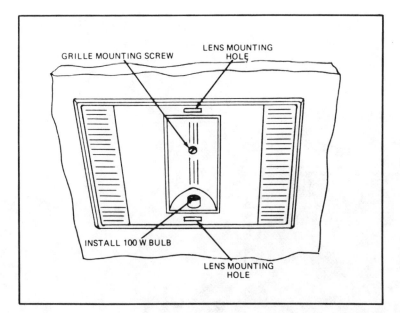

GRILLE MOUNTING SCREW

LENS MOUNTING HOLE

INSTALL 100 W BULB

LENS MOUNTING HOLE

Fig. 6-31. Finishing touches (Courtesy of NuTone).

adult. The curiosity of a child can lead to all kinds of problems.

The design of the bathroom must place safety on the top of the list. Select products for the roles they can play in adding to your family's safety, as well as to convenience and comfort. Luxury and sanitation are all very well, but getting bruised to attain them is not. Install grab rails in the shower bath areas, and if there are elderly or infirm people in your home, install assist bars at the toilet and other fixtures where they might have to rise from a seated position. Make certain all glass used in tub and shower doors when they're enclosed is tempered. Tempered glass is far stronger than regular glass and, if it should break, forms small, more or less smooth-edged shards instead of

Fig. 6-32. Sockets should be away from baths and grounded (Courtesy of NuTone).

Fig. 6-33. Be careful of standing in water when switching on lights (Courtesy of NuTone).

Fig. 6-34. Decorator switch and clothes hook for your bathroom. (Courtesy NuTone).

sharply pointed spears. If you can't afford tempered glass, use plastic, never plain glass. Plastic is much safer than plain window glass. Plastic will scratch and discolor, which tempered glass won't, but it is cheaper.

Select your tub and shower units from those with non-skid bottom surfaces and never use rugs on the floor without applying a non-skid backing to them. Most bathroom accidents are from falls; non-skid surfaces (including tile and other flooring materials), non-skid backing on rugs, and grab rails will all help to reduce accidents. Accidents still happen occasionally, and that's when plastic or tempered glass is invaluable.

In Great Britain it is illegal to run electrical circuits to bathroom outlets in new construction, but it isn't in the United States, so a ground fault circuit interrupter should be installed on any bathroom circuit. These do add appreciably to circuit cost but they feed back a signal that cuts current if there's any kind of problem, and they do it in milliseconds to prevent electrocution, or help prevent it. Even with GFCI circuits, no appliance should ever be touched with wet hands if it is electrically powered.

Always check water temperatures before stepping into a tub or shower. In most cases too-hot water will just cause you to back off, but if you should slip there could be a scalding problem. If you can, install, or have installed, a thermostatic water pressure valve to balance the shower temperature, keeping it on or near a constant temperature. Cutting the temperature back on your hot water heater to about 115 degrees Fahrenheit (from the more common setting of 145 degrees and up) not only cuts down on the chances of scalding someone but also saves energy over the long run.

Never place electrical appliances such as radios where they could fall into a tub, shower, or basin. If you must have music with your bath, see about installing an in-the-wall unit, or place the radio on a low shelf—well away from any other fixture or appliance. Never use an electrical appliance, such as a razor or hair dryer, over a basin full of water or with the water running.

Chapter 7

Installing Bathroom Floors, Walls, and Ceilings

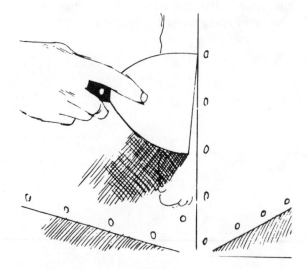

INSTALLING CERAMIC TILE PROBABLY ISN'T AS hard as selecting the tile itself. There are many manufacturers and styles on the market.

INSTALLING CERAMIC FLOOR TILE

The Tile Council of America represents a majority of American tile manufacturers, and as you can see from the illustrations throughout the book, there are many beautiful bathroom tiles available. Imported tiles also offer good quality the look of luxury and, though they're sometimes a bit harder to locate than American brands. Ceramic tile is the most expensive wall and floor covering, but if the proper adhesive and grout are used the tiles will stay put as long as you want them and will need only minor touch-ups to the grout over the years. Silicone rubber grouts clean up easily, usually with alcohol, and don't mildew or turn to powder as easily as older grouts (Fig. 7-1).

Because of its permanence, ceramic tile is harder to select for style. It's something you'll have to live with for many years (Fig. 7-2).

In many instances you can select accessories—towel bars, soap dishes, etc.—in matching or contrasting ceramics, to be put in as the tile is being installed (Fig. 7-3). Wall tile is not necessarily suitable for and will not wear well on floors. Italian tiles are graded from one to four, and marked. One is for walls, while four is for heavy duty use such as the tile in public restrooms.

Because foreign-made tiles are a bit harder to handle, we'll first consider a type from Italy and then move into the installation of American-made tiles. Read the entire section pertaining to your type of tile before starting the project.

Italian tile installation begins with the assembly of the needed tools and materials. First check the floor to make sure it is not flawed. You'll need:

—Galvanized wire lath and rails.

—A masonry fortifier (this is a latex additive that adds bonding power to masonry).

—Thin set mortar.

—Grout.

—A trowel notched at 1/2-inch intervals 1/2 inch deep.

Fig. 7-1. Good grouting shows up in this tile bath (Courtesy of Tile Council of America).

—A hammer.
—A large sponge.
—A pail.
—A squeegee.
—Tile cutters.
—Lemon oil.
—Cloth.
—Plenty of tile and border tile to do the job.

Before starting the work you need a graph drawing of the room to make a tile layout. Once this layout is laid and all else assembled, spread the tar paper (use 15-pound) over the floor to be tiled. This is to protect the wood floor while you're using wet masonry. Then lay galvanized wire lath on top of the tar paper, nailing it at 6-inch intervals (Fig. 7-4).

Mix the masonry fortifier and the thin set mortar according to package directions.

Lay out for room center with a chalk line, and spread the mortar to cover one section of floor, spreading enough so you can work for about 45 minutes laying tile, or in 2-×-3-foot sections. Spread the mortar on evenly to cover the wire lath and then add a bit more and use the trowel to "comb" it, to produce a mortar surface with a ripple effect (Figs. 7-5 and 7-6).

Each tile is set into the mortar with a twisting adhesion is over the entire surface (Fig. 7-7). Leave a 1/16-inch space between the tiles for grouting. With this form of tile, you'll need spacers if you wish to lay tile with larger grout lines. Your tile dealer will have to be able to get the spacers for you.

Tiles set in this manner are carried right on un-til the floor is finished. You must then stay off the set tiles for at least 24 hours for the mortar to set up fully.

Once the curing time has passed, you can apply your grout. If you're using powdered grout, mix according to package instructions and sweep it across the tiles with a squeegee. This lets the grout settle into the lines you have left for it and keeps the squeegee from digging into those lines. Do one section, again about 2 × 3 feet, at a time (Fig. 7-8).

Once the grout is applied on a section, swing your sponge out in a pail of clean water and wipe the excess off the area. Continue this on through. At the job's end you'll note some haze on the tile from grout still on the surface in a very thin layer. This is where the lemon oil comes in. Soak in cloth in lemon oil and rub the tile surface (Fig. 7-9).

Fig. 7-2. Tile is a permanent addition to your bath (Courtesy of Tile Council of America).

Fig. 7-3. Unique bath tile design (Courtesy of Tile Council of America).

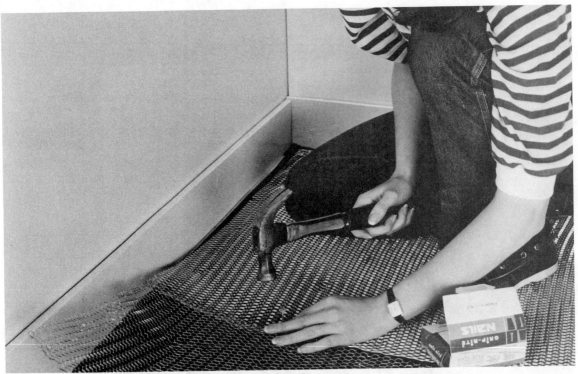

Fig. 7-4. Laying galvanized wire lath (Courtesy of Italian Tile Center).

Fig. 7-5. Spread mortar over about a 2- × -3-foot area (Courtesy of Italian Tile Center).

192

Fig. 7-6. Comb a ripple effect in the mortar (Courtesy of Italian Tile Center).

Fig. 7-7. Laying tile (Courtesy of Italian Tile Center).

193

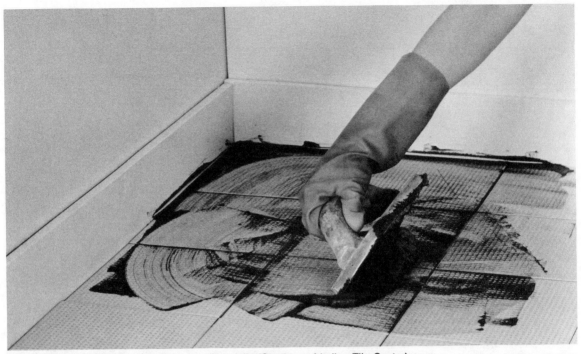

Fig. 7-8. After the tile sets, spread grout diagonally (Courtesy of Italian Tile Center).

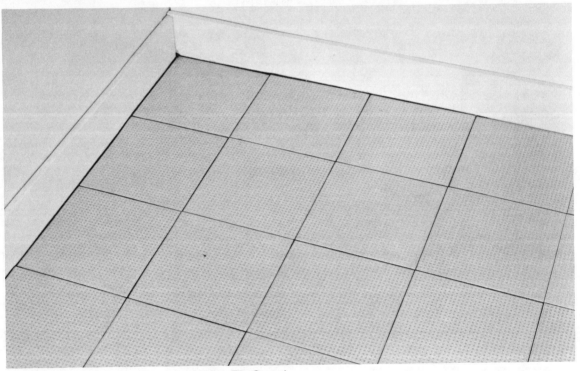

Fig. 7-9. The final tile floor (Courtesy of Italian Tile Center).

Because of the mortar used, Italian tile cannot be walked on while the mortar is damp; you must plan to finish at an exit so you don't need to walk across the floor to get out of the room. Any tile cutting is done with special tile tools, including nippers and a guillotine. These are usually available as rental tool kits and will include just about any tools you'll need to do the floor but that might not otherwise be around the house (Figs. 7-10 — 7-12).

Tiling floors using American tile is a simpler process. Here is a list of the materials:

—Subfloor materials (only if needed).
—A trowel with small notches, 1/16 to 1/8 inch square.
—Adhesive.
—Grout.
—Tile nippers.
—A Carborundum stone.
—A hammer.
—A flat piece of board.
—Cloths.
—A squeegee.
—A toothbrush.

Thin set adhesive of a different type is used here. The tile is snapped into it and stays there, probably for longer than if actual masonry is used. Tiles come in pre-grouted sheets or singly, and the job is faster due to the sheets and the easily spreadable adhesive. The adhesive is similar to that used with resilient tiles. The adhesive can be used on both walls and floors and is a latex formula that allows easy clean-up with water, though it is strongly water-resistant when dry. It is also non-toxic and non-flammable and trowels nicely. The trowel you will use has smaller notches than the one used for thin set mortars.

American made tiles offer a choice of setting methods, but the latex adhesive method is a good choice. Latex adhesives are easily cleaned, easily spread, offer decent working times, and make the

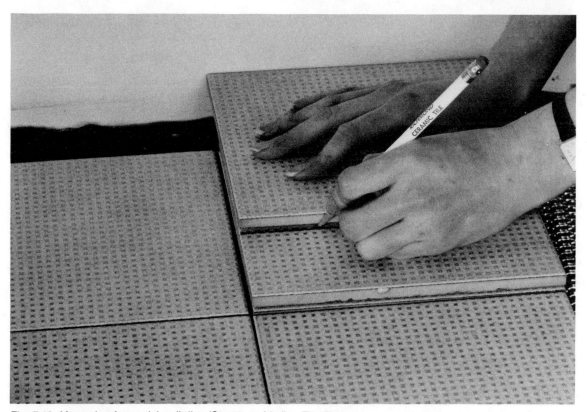

Fig. 7-10. Measuring for partial wall tiles (Courtesy of Italian Tile Center.

Fig. 7-11. Make cuts with a tile cutter (Courtesy of Italian Tile Center).

entire job easier and less messy. Even thin set mortars must be at least 1/4 inch thick, requiring a lot of material (Fig. 7-13).

Ceramic tile can be used in places other than walls and floors. It makes good-looking countertop, even though any basin set in such a top will require a bit more work. Actual tile setting is a basic process so it makes no difference where it's going to go—on a floor, wall, or countertop.

American tiles can go over practically any subsurface (also called substrate). The floor must be clean, dry, and level, and can include any exterior plywood, sheet flooring, vinyl tiles, and so on. In some cases a primer might be needed to assure adhesion, but your dealer can tell you if that's the case. Any glossy or painted surface needs sanding before you lay tile over it, and no springy floor will hold ceramic tile. Any loose flooring must be nailed securely, and if that doesn't work you must consider a subfloor over the present floor. Use at least

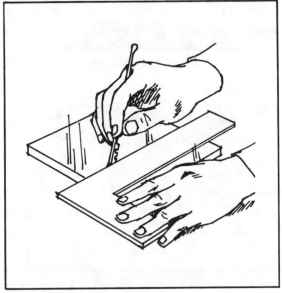

Fig. 7-12. Cutting tile with a glass cutter and square (Courtesy of Hyde Mfg. Co.).

196

Fig. 7-13. Adhesive spreading trowel (Courtesy of Hyde Mfg. Co.).

Begin tiling near the center of the floor (Fig. 7-14). The center is almost always the most visible area so it must consist of full tiles and it's best if patterns start there as well. Snap your chalk lines to determine the room center and lay out the tile loosely before beginning. Try to avoid any tile smaller than half-tile size at edges. This won't always be possible, but checking while tiles are loose will allow you to arrange things so that you have the best chance at the larger sizes. When you begin to install the tiles, work along the chalk lines. Work from the middle to the edges and use a straight edge or square to check trueness after every six or eight tiles are in place. Use a flat board across the tile surfaces and tap it with a hammer to assure adhesion (Fig. 7-15).

American tiles are made to hold a particular joint size in many styles, so that eases the job. In other cases spacers are available for the size joint you wish to hold. Use them; it's easier (Figs. 7-16 and 7-17).

3/8-inch-thick plywood in such cases, nailing at 6- or 8-inch intervals with ring shank nails. Use a primer with plywood subfloors and use minimum 6-penny nails, allowing 1/4-inch expansion joints at the ends and sides of plywood sheets. Fill those joints with adhesive.

From this point, tile setting becomes a simple process of primarily four steps. Adhesive is applied using a trowel with small notches, covering only a small area at a time (thin set adhesives are much faster setting than are mortars, so lay out only as much as you feel you can cover with tile in 15 to

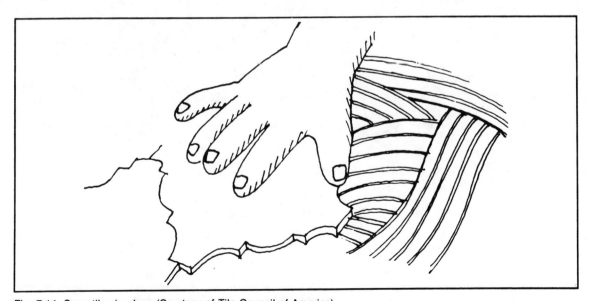

Fig. 7-14. Snap tiles in place (Courtesy of Tile Council of America).

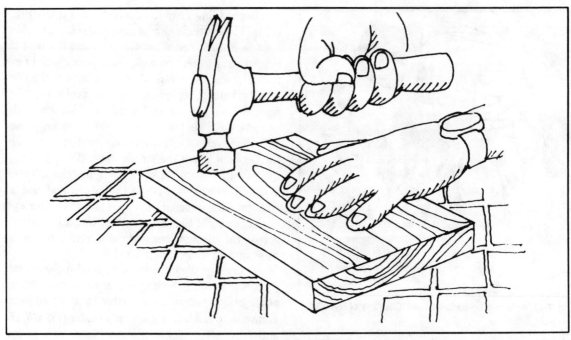

Fig. 7-15. Tap tiles with board and hammer (Courtesy of Tile Council of America).

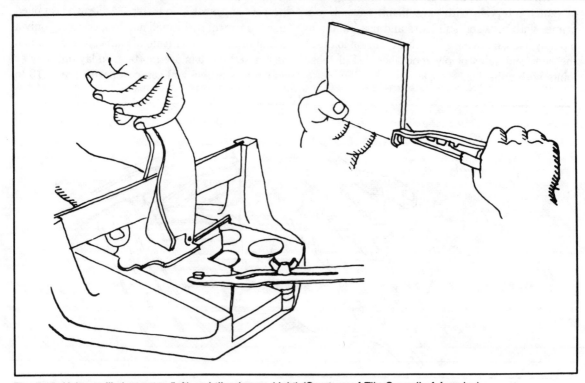

Fig. 7-16. Using guillotine cutter (left) and tile nippers (right) (Courtesy of Tile Council of America).

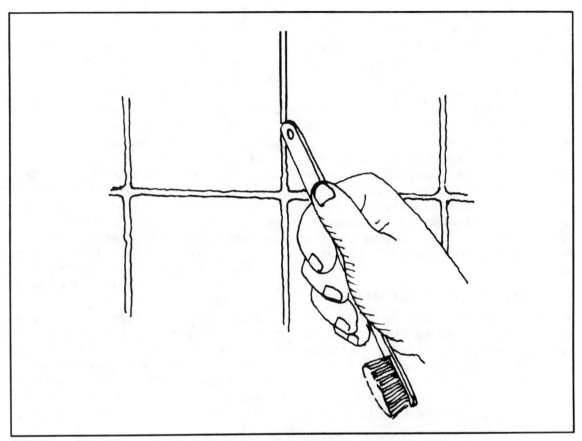

Fig. 7-17. Smooth grout lines with an old toothbrush handle (Courtesy of Tile Council of America).

20 minutes). You want enough time left in each section to make any necessary corrections before the adhesive sets up and makes changes nearly impossible. If you are using very thick tile with a lot of pattern in its surface, coat the back of the tile with adhesive before you set it.

Set each tile with a slight twist and press it firmly into place. Keep the alignment as you go, with all joints the same size and even. Many tiles come with built-in spacers, which are handy. If joints don't line up you've got time to wiggle things around and make adjustments. Clean any excess adhesive off tile faces immediately with water. It is almost impossible to get off once it dries.

Edge tile will almost always require cutting, so the tile must be marked for cutting. Score or mark a line by placing a loose full tile over the last full tile before the one surface meets the other. Now lay a tile over this and butt the top tile on the wall or other surface. Mark the loose center tile and cut along that line. Don't mark and cut a whole row of tiles in this manner because few corners are dead true and you'll have a variation as you go along. Mark each tile as it's needed.

Tile nippers are used to shape tiles where not enough is to be removed to allow the cutter to work. You nibble off a bit at a time with the nippers and use the Carborundum stone to smooth edges after nipping to size. If the edge is to be hidden don't bother with the smoothing (Fig. 7-16).

You will need to wait about 24 hours before grouting so that the adhesive will have its full cure. You can often walk on ceramic tile, or use it otherwise, before the full time has elapsed, but it's best to follow the directions from the manufacturer of the adhesive.

Grout is spread with a rubber squeegee, or trowel, at a diagonal across the joints. The excess is wiped from the face of the tiles and the joints are shaped with the end of a toothbrush handle (Figs. 7-17, 7-18).

Once the grout sets up firmly, wash down the tile face and polish the whole works with a clean, dry cloth to get a finish shine. That's it. You've done a job a pro tile setter would envy.

You'll note as you go along that different adhesives and grouts require slightly different considerations. Some will clean up easily with water while others require paint or lacquer thinner, and some grouts will need a wipe-down with alcohol after drying so that the haze is removed from the face of the finished tile job. Always follow the directions of the manufacturer.

TILE FOR OTHER SURFACES

Wall tiling begins with a check to see that the surface is structurally sound, and a removal of all fixtures, baseboards, and so forth. The wall must be free of paint and grease, and newly plastered walls need a sealer. Also size or shellac gypsum wallboard walls that have yet to be finished.) Lay out the job before you start the actual tiling. Use a plumb line or the plumb vial in your level to drop vertical lines at the center of each wall to be tiled. Cross these with horizontal lines, set with your level. These are your starting points (Figs. 7-19 and 7-20).

Plan the room so that horizontal starting points form a continuous line all around the area to be tiled. Start by laying out a loose course of tile, making sure that fit is good and that where tiles must be cut to meet walls or floors, you can get a half-tile in. This won't always be possible, but is best when it is possible because the tile holds better. If the horizontal line runs above a bath or countertop, the horizontal line should be drawn a full tile's distance above the low point of the tub edge, or the low point of the countertop edge (this is far more important for tubs than countertops). Now follow the basic tile setting directions as described for tiling floors (Figs. 7-21, 7-22).

Tiling countertops is often a good idea in bathrooms with a lot of vanity top area, for even with the greatest span it doesn't add hugely to the cost and the finished tops are extremely durable, as well as attractive. The tile will go over most countertop materials, including Formica and other laminates, as well as old ceramic tile. For new in-

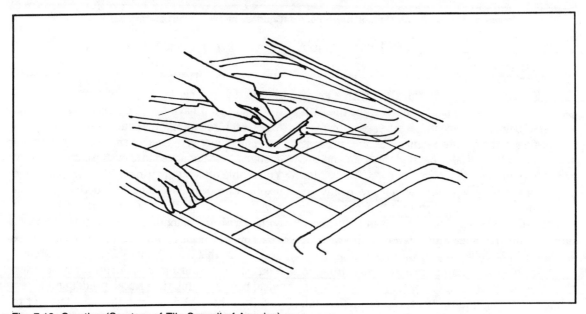

Fig. 7-18. Grouting (Courtesy of Tile Council of America).

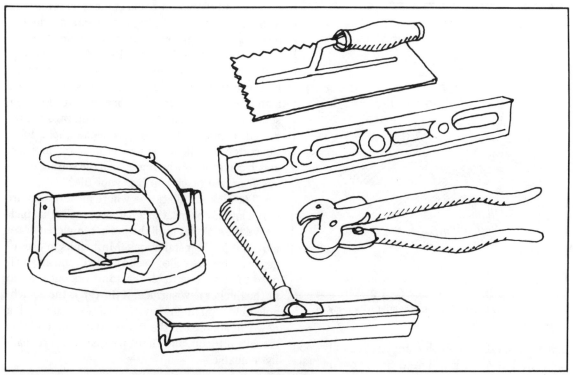

Fig. 7-19. Tile setting tools (Courtesy of Tile Council of America).

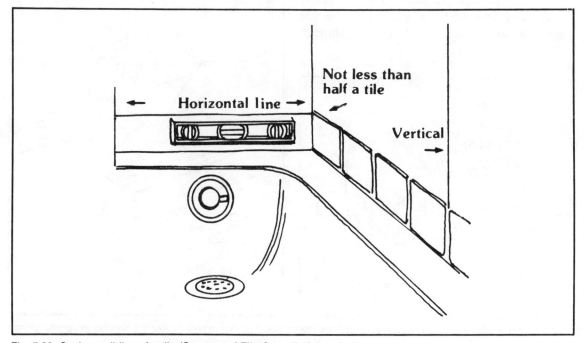

Fig. 7-20. Setting wall lines for tile (Courtesy of Tile Council of America).

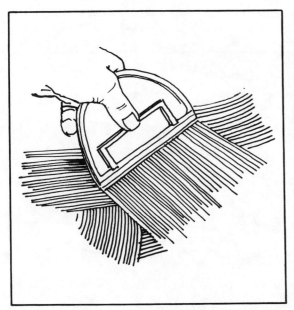

Fig. 7-21. Countertop adhesive spreader (Courtesy of Tile Council of America).

As always, make a graph of the countertop area to be done and get the right amounts of tile and molding, and then you can think of finding the correct tools. These differ a bit depending on the surface to be done, but generally a straight edge, a tape measure or folding rule, a 2-foot carpenter's level, a square, a Carborundum stone, a putty knife or scraper, a sponge, and some clean-up rags are required. If major tile cutting is needed, look for a tile cutter. You'll almost always need tile nippers, which can probably be rented in a tile setting package from the place you buy your tile.

The sink installation is where most of us start to run into problems, though it's not really that bad. Leave the sink out until the job is completed or removed it in old installations. Most sinks in use today are what are called "self-rimmed" and all you'll need to do will be to let the adjusters out a bit to fit the thicker new surface. If the rim is the detachable kind, you might have to look for and install a new rim adapted to the thicker tiles. None of this is really difficult, and all the needed parts are readily available.

stallations, use a 3/4-inch exterior grade plywood and check to see if it will need cross bracing. The top, as with any surface to receive tile, must be clean and smooth but not glossy. Sand any glossy areas. Trim pieces for the edges are available and should be used in most jobs (Figs. 7-23 through 7-25).

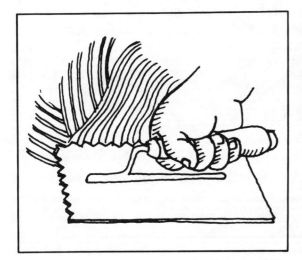

Fig. 7-22. Large area adhesive spreader (Courtesy of Tile Council of America).

Fig. 7-23. Make sure plywood is sanded smooth (Courtesy of Tile Council of America).

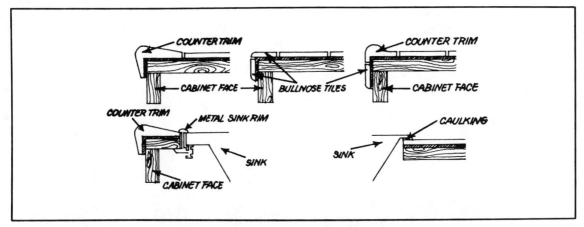

Fig. 7-24. Ceramic tile edge trim shapes (Courtesy of Tile Council of America).

If you're remodeling a bath, you won't be putting the final plumbing in until the countertop is installed, but you might want to make sure of measurements so that things end up the right length. Usually there's only about a 1/2-inch or so difference and this requires almost no change in the supply pipes or the DWV, because there is enough slack to make up for any extra distance. (The tailpiece on the sink will take up DWV slack, while the risers from the supply probably have slight bends in them anyway, so you can get the extra length just by straightening them.)

Lay out tiles loosely before installing with adhesive. You're unlikely to be starting at the center of the countertop, so you'll need to work out your design carefully. If the countertop doesn't have a basin to be installed, you might wish to start at the center. Otherwise it's usually best to begin with a full tile at the front edge of the countertop, leaving space for any molding needed. Check with a piece of molding to see how the fit works. As you move to the back of the countertop you'll note any needed cuts, again trying to get tiles that are at least half-size. Take your time in working out the arrange-

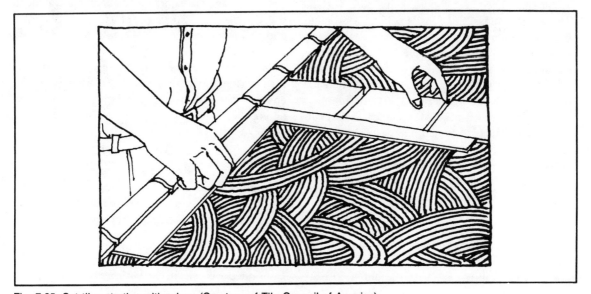

Fig. 7-25. Set tiles starting with edges (Courtesy of Tile Council of America).

ment; it's a small area and won't take a great deal of time to finish (Fig. 7-26).

Once you're satisfied with the loose tile layout you can start the job of tiling. Begin on the countertop by installing the trip pieces on the front edge, with sink edging tiles going on next, and then corners and any other special pieces needed. After that you begin the basic tiling, making sure as you go to keep a running check for trueness and squareness overall. From here complete as you would a tile floor or wall.

RESILIENT TILE FLOORING

Resilient tile flooring comes in a wide variety of styles, colors, and types. Three types are of interest in bathroom work. They are single tiles, self-stick single tiles, and sheet flooring.

Resilient sheet flooring works well for some bathrooms. It's not so easy to install in small bathrooms with a lot of floor clutter around, and in which the flooring must be fitted. It must fit around the vanity base and the toilet, and must fit tightly against the bathtub. While this can sometimes be a problem, it is easily handled if enough of the sheet lays flat to allow accurate trimming.

Sheet flooring is commonly made in three layers: The wear surface, a softer core, and a plastic backing. The sheet should be installed with as few seams as possible. This is seldom a problem in bathrooms because the flooring is available at widths up to 12 feet, and in many lengths. Measure and cut the flooring slightly oversize at first and then trim to fit using the sharpest utility knife blade you have on hand. If there's a lot of trimming, change blades frequently. After 8 or 10 feet of cutting, reverse the blade, and after 20 feet change it. Most sheet flooring is installed with only edge fastening, if that, but a few dabs of adhesive around the edges of the bathtub and toilet will help hold things in place longer and help prevent leaks.

Resilient tiles are easy to install. The tiles simply snap in place. You should work out your pattern ahead of time. Once you have a single row of tiles down, butt the next row against that first row, snapping them into place with the unbutted edge held about an inch off your chosen adhesive. With

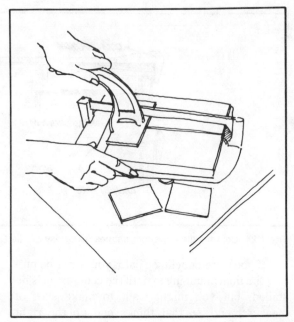

Fig. 7-26. Cutting tile (Courtesy of Tile Council of America).

your other hand hold the tile tightly against the already laid tile.

Border tiles are cut by placing a loose tile over the last already laid full tile near the wall. Make sure the alignment is exact with the under-tile. Take a second tile, butt it against the wall, and draw a line with a pencil or scribe along the loose tile. Cut the tile with scissors or a sharp utility knife and fit into place.

Self-adhesive tiles are also easy to install with their peel and stick method. Again, have your pattern worked out beforehand. Then simply peel the cover off the adhesive back and place the tile in position.

WOOD FLOORING

Wood flooring, either in strips or parquet, is not usually considered suitable for bathroom use. Give careful consideration to likelihoods of continued wetness before flooring a bathroom in wood.

CARPETING

Continued wetness in the bathroom is a danger to carpeting also. While it might not be suitable in the bathroom of a home with small children because of splashing, carpeting can be attractive and warm in an adult bathroom. Choose a carpeting that will resist moisture. Some are treated with mildew, stain, and odor-resistant substances. Use washable carpeting and do not install it permanently.

The floor underneath the carpeting should be in good enough condition to protect the subflooring in case of moisture. Make a paper pattern of the bathroom floor by taping pieces of paper together. Cut out spaces for any fixtures, taking care to be accurate so that your carpet will fit snugly. Tape the pattern face down on the back of the carpet and secure it with tape. Cut out openings for fixtures. If the carpet requires seams they can be made with a pressure sensitive tape.

MOLDINGS AND THRESHOLDS

Base molding serves as a finish between the finished wall and the floor. Vinyl cove base, molded as a single concave strip, is a good choice with many bathroom floors. It comes in a variety of widths and lengths, as well as in many colors.

With the floor protected by dropcloths, apply vinyl adhesive evenly to the wide vertical surface of an inside corner piece. A 3-inch trowel with 1/16 notches works well. Fit a premolded corner into the space. Extreme caution is necessary when working with vinyl adhesive as it is toxic. Follow all cautions on the container carefully. The adhesive will dry in about 10 minutes and excess can be cleaned with soap and water.

Continue by applying adhesive to the back of a straight 4-foot section, then lay that section (adjoining the corner piece) along the wall. Roll it carefully with a steel handroller. Continue along the wall in this manner until you are less than 4 feet from the next corner. Apply the corner piece and measure to determine the size of the piece needed to finish the wall. A utility knife can be used to cut the vinyl cove to the correct length. Allow about 1/8 inch more than the measured amount to insure a snug fit.

Thresholds at bathroom doors are usually wood, metal, rubber, or marble, with marble the traditional favorite. Marble is difficult to cut and

must be purchased in the correct length to fit your doorway. Measure between the doorjambs for correct installation. Place the threshold in place on the floor and mark its height on the doorstops. Cut the doorstops at those marks and remove the pieces. With ceramic/tile adhesive spread between the jambs and along the underside of the threshold, fit the threshold under the doorstops until it rests against the floor tiles. Clean excess adhesive.

Metal edging also installs easily. Cut the binder bar to fit the door opening and place it over the seam where the two flooring materials meet. Screw it into the subfloor. Tuck-in edging that screws to the subfloor is available, so that one side covers the edge of the vinyl and the other edge offers a slot where carpeting can be tucked.

DRYWALL CONSTRUCTION

Drywall finish is a material that requires little, if any, water for application. Drywall finish includes gypsum board, plywood, fiberboard, or similar sheet material, as well as wood paneling in various thicknesses and forms. Gypsum wallboard is most commonly used. Most local codes require at least 1/2-inch-thick gypsum wallboard. You must decide on wall materials and find their thicknesses before any doors are hung and windows installed, for the window and door framing must extend far enough in past the studs to allow you to install molding on them without requiring a great many shims to get a level surface.

If you're going to install ceramic tile, make sure of the tile design and the type of wallboard it will be installed over, and get a total thickness for the installation. If you're using a thin set cement such as Elmer's, you don't really need to figure the depth of cement in your final finish figures because it will probably be 1/16 inch or so. If you decide to use mortar set tiles, you'll have to decide on the set thickness and add that to wall thickness calculations.

Various wood paneling types have differing thicknesses and these need to be taken into consideration as either finish walls over gypsum wallboard, or finish walls by themselves. Solid wood paneling is available in many materials, with redwood predominating, but cedar shingles are also available. If you decide to install redwood as an interior finish panel, first decide on the design and thickness. Generally redwood as a solid material is available as 3/8-, 1/2-, 5/8-, and 3/4-inch material, depending on the style of panel you select.

Gypsum wallboard is not needed as an underwall for solid wood paneling, but it is recommended for underwall for all other types because it helps cut noise and provides a solid base for other, lighter materials. Check codes, but as an underwall, 3/8-inch thickness should suffice for most any code.

After a few years the nail heads show through gypsum wallboard because of normal flexing of the house. That flexing also cracks things along the seams. You can get around this by using a larger number of screw shank nails, or drywall screws, than is recommended. At every third nailing point double up on the nails. That means you'd place two nails about 1 1/2 inches apart on every third nailing point along the edges to be taped. When using gypsum wallboard on ceilings double up the nails at every other nailing point. Such extra nailing adds very little to final finish work, only a few extra nail dimples to fill. The dimples at the edges will be covered by either molding or joint compound anyway.

Use tapeless joint compound, leaving off the tape on the tapered joints and using seams with plastic tape on the untapered joints. A properly taped joint can make a great difference. Using the proper knife to apply the compound also makes a difference. Ten-inch-wide knives work well for spreading compound.

Taping knives narrower than 10 inches are good for filling nail dimples, but not for taping. You need a wide band of joint compound to set the tape in and to fill the tapers, so a wide knife is best. Use the narrow knife to get the compound out of the bucket if you're using 1-gallon buckets, and the wide knife to apply it. Do not scrape the knife on the bucket lip. Keep a special scraper nearby, but don't load the bucket with rejects from the wall. Sooner or later there will be a chunk of gypsum or other debris that will raise a lump and scratch along in the path of your knife. It's best that residue not be returned to contaminate the pail.

Nailing gypsum wallboard can be done either horizontally, which is preferred for long walls because the seams are easier to finish properly, or vertically while cuts are made, using a utility knife and a wallboard square.

Drive your nails at intervals of 6 inches after the board has been cut to size and any required openings cut or drilled. Cutting openings for wall receptacle boxes and switch boxes is easily done by reversing an extra box and using it as a template after getting the location marked. Outline the empty box and cut out, using a compass saw, a wallboard saw, or a utility knife.

The utility knife is used to make long, uninterrupted cuts by scoring through the paper backing along the mark or along a straight edge. Snap that across a sawhorse and then draw the knife across the backing paper to complete the cut. When angle cuts must be made and the angle is not an uninterrupted line across the wallboard, one cut must be made with a knife and one with a saw. Saws are used when cutting wallboard as little as possible to keep down the dust (Fig. 7-27).

Use at least 1 3/8-inch wallboard nails for 3/8-inch thick wallboard and 1 1/2-inch nails for 1/2-inch wallboard. If you're doubling 3/8-inch wallboard, use 1 3/8-inch nails for the first layer and then glue/nail the second layer using 1 3/4- or 2-inch nails. Use nothing but screw shank nails or wallboard screws that go on with a number 2 Phillips fitting for your variable speed electric drill, and have specially designed heads to countersink themselves and let you have the needed dimple to fill with joint compound.

The nail dimple is necessary. All nails must have their heads sunk below the surface of the wallboard so that you can hide them with a dollop of joint compound. Therefore you work at getting a slight depression in the facing paper of the wallboard. The idea is to get the dimple, or depression, without breaking the surface of the paper. It can be achieved consistently with practice. If the dimple breaks the paper, filling well is harder. If the dimple isn't deep enough for the joint compound to cover the nail or screw head, it will show and break the smooth wall pattern.

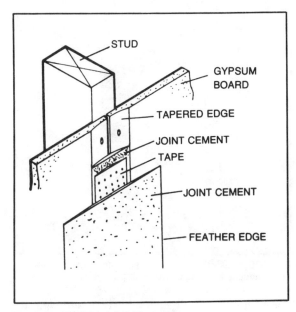

Fig. 7-27. Wallboard finishing steps.

Joint compound application at taped joints is simpler than it seems. Start with a generous layer of compound about as wide as your knife. Into that press the perforated tape joint. Use a 1 1/4- or 1 1/2-inch flexible putty knife to press this in gently but firmly. Then come back with another generous layer of joint compound, covering the entire width of the taper on the boards. This will be about double the width of a knife blade, minus a 1-inch overlap. Accuracy isn't as important as smoothness at this point. Go on from the joint taping to apply the first layer of filling around nail or screwheads. After this layer has dried for about 1 1/2 hours, come back with a wet sponge and a large bucket of warm water to take off the excess joint compounds. Do the taped joints and the wall dimples and get everything as smooth as possible (Fig. 7-28).

After a 12- to 24-hour wait, you can apply the final thinner coating of joint compound to the taped joints and the second layer to the nail dimples. This final compound layer on the joints goes on with a hard knife grip so you get down just as much as is needed to fill any depressions left after the sponging up. Nail dimples might require a third layer of compound later in the day. Once this has dried it should need only a light sanding.

When the joint compound has dried you can prepare the wallboard for its covering. Begin with at least one coat of good sizing, or a very thin shellac, especially if you're considering any kind of wallcovering other than paint (Figs. 7-29 through 7-34). The sizing or shellac will protect the surface while leaving a good base for the wall covering, and will not interfere with other materials, such as paint, you might wish to use later.

PAINTING

If paint is to be your choice for the bathroom, choose good quality gloss and semi-gloss paints where moisture could be a problem or on walls that need frequent scrubbing. Flat paints should only be used on ceilings and in areas that don't get heavily soiled or frequently moistened. Use a top quality roller or brush and keep it clean. Water soluble paints are excellent for use in bathrooms if they get at least 24 hours to dry. Paint is an inexpensive wallcovering and a good choice if you plan to change your color scheme often.

WALLPAPERING

Wallpapers are no longer as difficult to install as they once were, and the newest versions come in a wide variety of styles, colors, and materials.

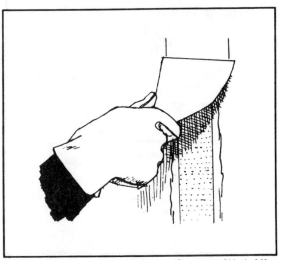

Fig. 7-28. Finishing tips for wallboard (Courtesy of Hyde Mfg. Co.).

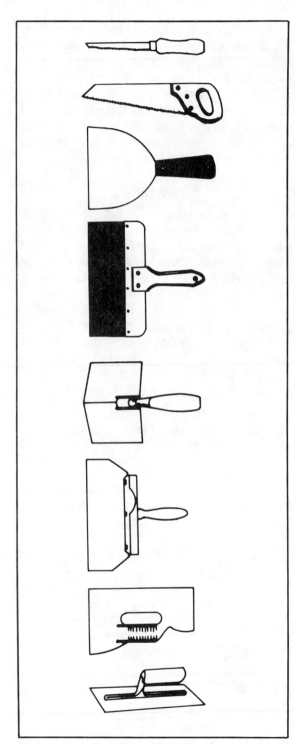

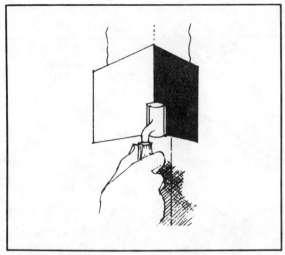

Fig. 7-30. Finish the inside corners with a special tool for best results (Courtesy of Hyde Mfg. Co.).

Avoid foil type wallpapers the first time you attempt wallpapering. They are harder to work with and must be applied precisely to be attractive. Hanging wallpaper is easier if you have a helper.

Start with room measurements. Check the width and length of the type material you wish to use and then use these to figure how much you'll need in your room, minus doors and windows and

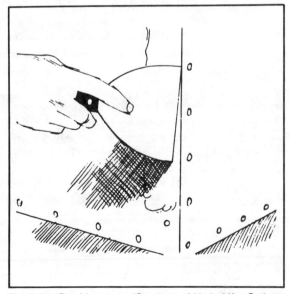

Fig. 7-29. Tools for wallboard installation (Courtesy of Hyde Mfg. Co.).

Fig. 7-31. Outside corner (Courtesy of Hyde Mfg. Co.).

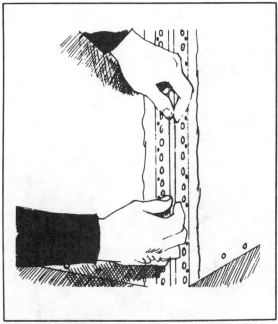

Fig. 7-32. Press metal bead strip into joint compound (Courtesy of Hyde Mfg. Co.).

areas to be covered with other materials. Strippable wallpaper is much easier to remove at a later date for redecorating.

Select your pattern. Pattern matches are of

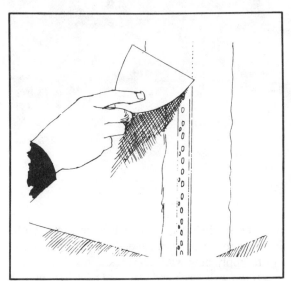

Fig. 7-33. Applying compound to cover metal bead (Courtesy of Hyde Mfg. Co.).

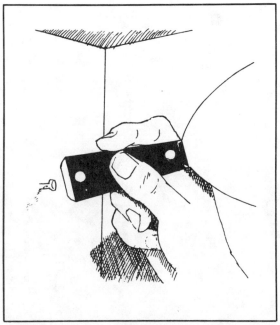

Fig. 7-34. Popped nails can be tapped in with the trowel end cap (Courtesy of Hyde Mfg. Co.).

great importance to the overall impression. There are three basic types of pattern matches to consider. The straight across pattern match has a design that can be matched on a horizontal line, all across the wall, from strip to strip (Fig. 7-35). The drop match lines up on a diagonal from strip to strip. The random match is a design that requires no matching on your part. To wallpaper you will need:

—Large size scissors.
—A 10- or 12-inch-wide glue brush.
—A water trough.
—Wide putty knives.

Most paint supply stores will have just about all you're likely to need, including kits that have layout tables to make glue application simpler. The paper trough is for pre-pasted wallcoverings. Glue or paste for wallcoverings come in both powder and premix forms, with the weight and type of the adhesive used depending on the weight and style of the wallcovering you choose.

Wall preparation is necessary for good adhesion and is generally the hardest part of hanging wallcoverings of most types. This is especially true if the old wall is covered with an old wallcovering

Fig. 7-35. Horizontal match (Courtesy of Thomas Strahan).

that will not come off easily. The wall must be clean and smooth before any new wallcovering is applied and the best undersurface is flat paint. The walls need to be free of grease and any glossy surfaces must be sanded to give the adhesive some tooth. It's best to wash down sanded walls before starting to apply new wallcoverings.

If the walls are new, you need to size them, but

make sure the taped joints are completely dry before sizing. On old walls, old wallpaper is first removed, whether with a wide flexible putty knife and water (add a bit of vinegar to encourage penetration), or a rented wallpaper steamer. Then wash the walls down well and coat with shellac when they're completely dry. Have your tools ready (Fig. 7-36).

Starting the actual wallcovering job is best done in a fairly well hidden corner of the room so you don't have to worry too much about the last sheet matching up with the first. Set up the stepladder and mark off a vertical strip 1 inch narrower than your wallcovering. Use a chalk line set as a plumb line to drop the line to the floor, from ceiling mark, and snap a chalk line. You will need to snap such a line for each strip (Figs. 7-37 through 7-39).

Find the wall height measurement and add about 8 inches to that. Cut a strip to the extra length. Brush or roll adhesive on the back and wait 5 minutes or so before you fold wet sides together towards the middle of the strip. Carry the strip to the wall and hang it, lining the right hand edge up with the chalk line. If you're using pre-pasted wallcovering, place the water tray close to the wall and fill it to the level mark with lukewarm water. Roll

each strip in the tray loosely, soaking it for about 30 seconds. Make sure both sides are wet when you lift it from the tray to the work table (Figs. 7-40 through 7-44).

The strips should overlay the ceiling by about 2 inches as they go up, and you can slide the wet material as needed to get it aligned with your mark. Smooth the strip using the wide brush, and work from the center down and out to the edges, making sure you get out wrinkles and bubbles as you go. If you work from a corner, let the excess material wrap onto the adjoining wall. Roll the edges with a seam roller. Find the pattern match before cutting the next strip, which is then readied for hanging, and hang it with its edge butting the first strip edge. Don't overlap (Figs. 7-45 through 7-47).

Use a very sharp utility knife to trim the first strip at the ceiling and baseboard. This works best if you use a guide or a wide putty knife, and cut along its edge as it is forced to the ceiling and baseboard lines (Fig. 7-48). Wash any excess adhesive off the woodwork and ceiling, and sponge the entire strip if you are working with pre-pasted materials. Work on this way until you reach the corner.

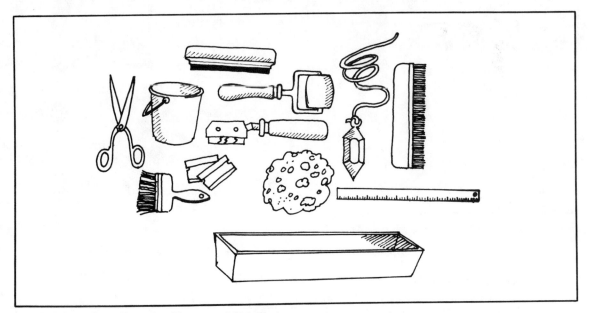

Fig. 7-36. Tools for wallcovering (Courtesy of Style-Tex).

corner. Now measure the width of the excess strip and mark it on the next wall. Drop a plumb line at that spot and hang the strip lined up with the chalked line, sliding the trimmed edge into the corner, using an overlap.

At windows and doors don't look for an exact fit. It's simpler, faster, and neater to paper right up to and over the edges, with diagonal cuts at case molding corners to allow the neat fit required. Trim off the excess here just as you do at the ceiling and baseboard lines.

Wallpaper over removed switch plates, thermostat covers and other such obstacles. Be sure to cut the power to the circuit when working with switch and receptacle covers. Trim around the switch, receptacle, or other item and then reinstall the cover for a neat look (Fig. 7-49).

Fig. 7-37. Easy steps to hanging wallpaper (Courtesy of Hyde Mfg. Co.).

The last strip at the corner will seldom be a full width from the roll. Measure the distance from the edge of the last full strip and the corner, add 1 inch, and trim along that line. Hang on to the excess strip. Hang the strip as always, wrapping it around the

Fig. 7-38. Getting your plumb line (Courtesy of Style-Tex).

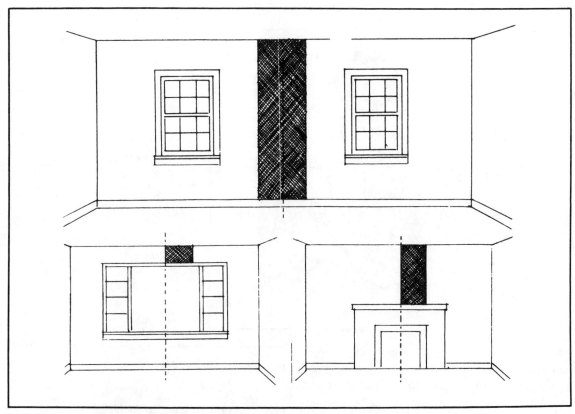

Fig. 7-39. Estimating wallpapering (Courtesy of Hyde Mfg. Co.).

Fig. 7-40. Layout the wallpaper (Courtesy of Style-Tex).

Fig. 7-41. Applying adhesive with a roller (Courtesy of Style-Tex).

Fig. 7-42. Keep the water tray close to the wall (Courtesy of Style-Tex).

The job is nearly done. Let everything dry and check for loose spots. If there are any, simply peel the paper back to a distance that allows you to slip some household white glue under it, press back into place, and all should be well. Wipe off excess glue after holding the repair in place for a few minutes.

If dry bubbles develop in the middle of a strip, you need to slit the bubbles with a razor blade, put

Fig. 7-43. Fold paper to the center for easier carrying (Courtesy of Style-Tex).

Fig. 7-44. Line up the first strip very carefully with the plumb line (Courtesy of Style-Tex).

214

Fig. 7-45. Brush and wipe to remove bubbles (Courtesy of Style-Tex).

Fig. 7-46. Hang corners as shown (Courtesy of Style-Tex).

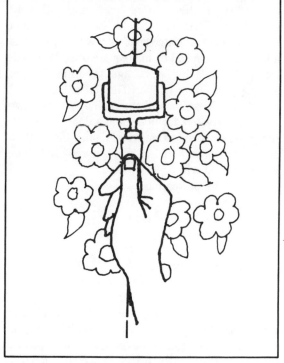

Fig. 7-47. Use a seam roller (Courtesy of Style-Tex).

glue under them, and press them down with a wet sponge.

Estimating room needs, if you don't wish the salesman to do it for you, is simple. If the ceiling is 8 feet high, then a room with a perimeter of 28 feet will require eight rolls, assuming a standard 36-square-foot roll, and allowing 30 square feet of actual coverage which makes allowance for trimming and pattern matching.

Knock off half a roll for each window or door on a wall to be papered. An increase of room size to 36 feet along the perimeter, still with an 8-foot ceiling, will require 10 rolls, while a room 40 to 48 feet around will need 12 rolls.

Fig. 7-48. Trim carefully (Courtesy of Style-Tex).

REPAIRING PLASTER WALLS

Many older homes have walls of plaster. If there are cracks or breaks in the bathroom walls, you will need to repair them before continuing with your remodeling. Structural cracks are large, distinct cracks through all three coats of a wall's plaster in a large area, caused by inadequate of settled footing, lack of bracing, shrinkage, green lumber, or small, poorly placed lumber. They are usually found along joints between wall and ceiling, between two walls, or between a window and a door. Never attempt repair of structural cracks until the settling causing them has ended or been repaired. The materials you will need:

—A knife or spatula.
—A brush.
—A putty knife or trowel.
—A hammer.
—A chisel.
—Water spray.
—Patching plaster, or plaster of paris.
—Glue.

With knife or spatula, open the crack to the lath and widen it to at least 1/4 inch. With chisel and hammer, bevel edges of the crack so that it is wider at the lath than at the surface. This will allow the new plaster to lock firmly behind the old plaster when it dries. Brush loose particles of sand and plaster from the opening. Dampen the old plaster with a brush and cold water so that it will not draw moisture from the new plaster and cause it to set improperly. In a small mixing box, prepare plaster of paris or patching plaster, following package directions. If crack is large, do not use plaster of paris without mixing it in glue or other substances to retard its setting time. Apply plaster with putty knife or small trowel, filling the crack until the new plaster's face comes within 1/8 inch of the surface of the old plaster. Let dry. Dampen this plaster and add more new plaster until its face is flush with old surface. Spray water on this new plaster and keep the entire area damp for 24 hours to assure a slow, hard, strong set.

Map cracks are groups of small cracks running at various angles over a limited area. They are caused by a poor bond between plaster and its base, but while they go through all three layers of plaster, map cracks do not extend across a large surface. Large map cracks are repaired in the same

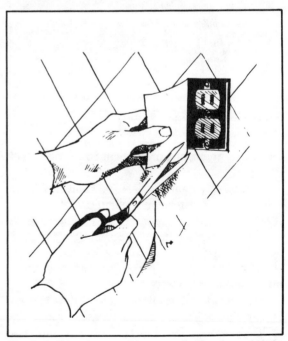

Fig. 7-49. Trimming around receptacle (Courtesy of Hyde Mfg. Co.).

manner as structural cracks, with the same tools and materials. If small, they can be filled with a paste of white lead thinned with turpentine, rubbed into the crack with a cloth, and later sanded.

Shrinkage cracks, smaller than map cracks, usually occur only in the finish layer of a plastered wall. They are caused by poor workmanship, in which the surface was improperly troweled or allowed to dry too rapidly. Usually very numerous, shrinkage cracks must be repaired very carefully in the manner described for small map cracks, or the entire area might need replastering.

Corner cracks are generally caused by shrinking plaster or settling houses. To repair, cut plaster on either side of corner to expose a 6-inch strip of lath or structural member of the wall from the ceiling to the floor. Install metal lath or corner beads in the corner. The area will have to be replastered with three coats of plaster.

Loose or bulging plaster results from the breaking off or loosening of the keys holding the plaster to the lath. It is necessary to remove all the plaster around the break or bulge before replacing it. Large areas of broken plaster require resurfacing with three coats of plaster or the use of the plaster board explained below. Smaller areas of broken plaster, however, can easily be repaired as follows: Bevel the edges of the sound, old plaster as described for structural cracks. Dampen the sound plaster and all exposed lath. Apply the new plaster with a trowel or pointed putty knife, depending upon the size of the opening. Force the plaster hard against the lath so it will ooze behind it and form keys. Apply enough plaster to ring the face of the new plaster even with the surface of the old. Smooth the joint with a trowel. Keep the new plaster damp for 24 hours.

Wall repair with plaster board is the simplest way to repair a large section of smooth finished plaster wall. Furring strips and patching plaster are used in addition to plaster board.

Locate and mark vertical center line of stud on each side of broken plaster. With a square, mark horizontal lines on sound plaster above and below breaks. Cut along line with chisel and remove old plaster within the rectangle. Undercut the edges of

sound plaster. This provides a base for new plaster used later to seal the joint. Measure depth from finish face of plaster to face of lath. If this is greater than the thickness of plaster board, add furring strips to make up this difference. Measure opening and cut plaster board to fit. Mix patching plaster to stiff paste. Wet edges of old plaster thoroughly. Nail board in place, spacing nails at least 1/2 inch in from edge and 6 inches between nails, and countersink slightly. Treat cracks in the same fashion as structural cracks. Cover nail heads with plaster. When dry, size new plaster.

If your plaster walls are in good shape you might simply wish to clean them and repaint. To wash a painted plaster wall, mix 2 tablespoons of trisodium phosphate to 1 gallon of clean, lukewarm water. A paint cleaning compound mixed with water may be used instead. Beginning at baseboard, work up the wall using a circular motion with a sponge to clean a small area at a time. Rinse each area immediately after washing it.

VINYL WALLCOVERING

A relatively new wallcovering has been designed to counteract the need for removing old plastic or ceramic tile before remodeling the room. This vinyl wallcovering is designed to allow replacement or recovering of walls in an average sized bathroom at little expense. The system can even be used in the tub and shower, and time for application is about 4 hours.

The surface is vinyl and the three-layer construction allows this wall material to bridge the gaps in old tile and cracks in the wall. The surface is clear and non-porous vinyl with three-level embossing under that, and a cushion core to mask the wall ridges and gaps (within reason, of course). The foam cushion also serves as something of a sound barrier. The back is a non-woven fiber backing to allow direct installation over just about any surface that is clean and dry, including cinderblock. Special adhesive is needed: a roll-on, mildew-resistant glue to withstand high moisture.

Wall preparation is first. The covering comes in rolls and it takes about 1 quart of adhesive to put up two rolls. Eight rolls of material will cover about 200 square feet. Tools needed:

- A short napped paint roller cover and roller.
- Roller tray.
- A tape or measuring tool.
- A sharp utility knife.
- Scissors.
- A smoothing brush.
- A chalk line and plumb bob.
- A trim guide.
- A stepladder.
- A papering table would be handy.

Prepare the wall by making sure it is clean and dry, free of grease and dirt. Make sure large gaps

Fig. 7-50. Unroll and trim to fit first section (Courtesy of Paris-Wall).

Fig. 7-51. Apply adhesive to wall, not the wallcovering (Courtesy of Paris-Wall).

are spackled and loose tiles or panels repaired.

Use the chalk line and plumb bob as if you were getting a line to install regular wallcovering, and snap your starting line. Start the line 30 inches out from a corner. Seams should not be allowed to fall in corners. Break the fiberglass backing on the wall-covering to make the fold around the corner. Do this by bending out and in a couple of times. Line the piece against your plumb line and butt it directly on the baseboard, leaving 1 inch or so at the top for trimming. Trim (Fig. 7-50).

Apply the adhesive using a short nap roller, in as even a coating as you can. Work just the section to your line. The adhesive now needs to set

Fig. 7-52. Position the first sheet and rub wall (Courtesy of Paris-Wall).

up until it becomes tacky, which will vary depending on what the under-wall is, but you can figure on 15 or 20 minutes for most materials and close to 30 minutes for nonporous materials such as ceramic tile (Fig. 7-51).

Once the adhesive has set up, position the trimmed section carefully and press it in place.

Once the section is perfectly positioned, use your hand, starting at the middle of the section, and move up, pressing to remove bubbles. Repeat the process moving to the sides and down. Use a wet, cold sponge to remove extra adhesive (Fig. 7-52).

Check the pattern for a match as you get ready to put up the second section, and leave the stand-

Fig. 7-53. Check alignment (Courtesy of Paris-Wall).

ard excess at the top. Trim. Apply adhesive. Install as above. Overlap is not required on the side seams. The edges are trimmed at the factory so they will butt together smoothly. Smooth the second section, remove excess adhesive, and get ready to work the next section. Use a straight edge and a very sharp knife to trim the top seam, and the job is nearly complete (Fig. 7-53).

Problem areas are the same as they are for standard wallcoverings: light switches, receptacles, etc. Again, shut the power down and remove any fixtures and plates that get in the way. Install the material right over them, and then come back and trim around the switches or other items. If you are

Fig. 7-54. The finished wall (Courtesy of Paris-Wall).

lucky, switch plates will fit right back on, but the material is thick enough that you might need to find slightly longer screws. Most hardware stores carry these, though you may have to search a bit.

Use the same technique as with other wall-coverings when working around windows, door frames, medicine cabinets, and other obstacles.

Work the material right up to the section and make small diagonal cuts so the corners will lie flat, then do the major part of the trimming at the end of the job as you do the wall plate trimming.

For shower stalls and around bathtubs, give the joints a bit of extra adhesive and make sure the edges butt very tightly to create a water-tight seal.

Fig. 7-55. Wiring in the grid frame (Courtesy of Celotex).

Fig. 7-56. Matching fit of frame (Courtesy of Celotex).

Fig. 7-57. Laying in the ceiling (Courtesy of Celotex).

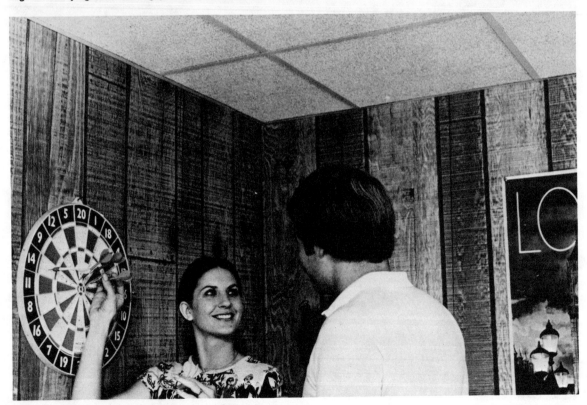

Fig. 7-58. The finished ceiling (Courtesy of Celotex).

If the wall is new, prime or size it before installing this covering, just as with others (Fig. 7-54).

CEILINGS

Ceilings are often done in drywall and the installation is nearly the same as for drywall on walls. If they are to be gypsum wallboard, they should be 1/2 inch thick. As recommended for walls, drywall ceilings should be installed with more than the number of nails normally suggested. Place two nails about 1 1/2 inches apart on every other nailing point along the edges of gypsum wallboard.

Ceilings can also be ceramic tiled, using basically the same method as described earlier for walls and floors. Paint makes an attractive ceiling cover and can be changed often as the mood of the room is changed. Ceiling tile used to be the rec room substitute for the real thing, to save work and cut costs. The cost of ceiling tile is reasonable and its attractiveness has improved greatly in recent years. So has its durability and usefulness under a wide range of conditions, with tile size choices ranging from 1 foot square to 2 feet × 4 feet. Most rooms take less than a day to complete—even for a first-timer—because the materials are all easily worked, to the point where real care is needed only in measurement and cutting.

As an example of ceiling choices, one manufacturer offers 14 different styles in foot-square tiles, as well as a variety of larger panels for suspended ceilings. Finishes vary among tiles; some have a plastic finish, others are rated simply as washable, and some are useful for sound absorption.

Lay-in, or suspended ceiling styles cover an even wider variety of styles, including a reflective surface. You will find perforated, perforated and stippled, unperforated and stippled, mosaic, fissured, colored and textured, reveal edges, square edges with kerfs and back cuts, bevel edges with kerf and back cuts, and trimmed edges.

Installation is simple, starting with a grid layout to give you the correct room size and the design for the metal gridwork to hold the lay-in tiles in place. Install the suspension system, keeping it level by adjusting the wires used to hold the supports. Then simply slip in the full sized panels, as required, and trim and slip in any part sized panels. That's all (Figs. 7-55 through 7-58).

For foot-square ceiling tiles, the job is not much harder. Make sure the present ceiling is sound, and you have two choices in application methods. If the ceiling is sound, you can staple the tiles directly to the present ceiling. This requires two 9/16-inch staples per fastening point, with the second staple driven exactly over the first to spread the second staple's legs in a flare that holds in the gypsum ceiling material. This does not work well on a plaster ceiling.

Instead of staples, you'll probably prefer adhesive. The type of adhesive will depend on the type of tile, but the layout is exactly the same as with stapling. Get your grid, or room center, and work from there out on chalk lines as needed.

For unsound ceilings, or for ceilings where you are ready to install new ceiling tile over no old ceiling, furring strips are best. The furring strips are laid at right angles to the current joists, and nailed at each joist. The staples used then go into the strips, and only one is required at each fastening point. This is the fastening system with the greatest holding power.

Chapter 8
Installing Bathroom Fixtures and Fittings

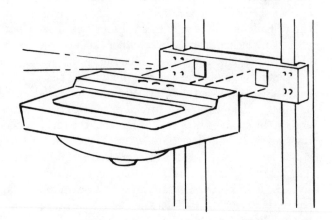

FROM ANALYZING YOUR HOME, YOUR FAMILY needs, and your budget, you should by now have a good idea of the type of fixtures you will install in your new or newly remodeled bathroom. They might be luxurious or simply functional. They might be white, pink, blue, or any one of several other colors. Whatever style you choose, installation will be similar.

CHOOSING AND INSTALLING BATHTUBS

Bathtubs come in enough sizes, shapes, and colors to please most everyone. There are corner tubs, rectangular tubs, round tubs, square tubs, sunken tubs, antique tubs, antique-look tubs, and tubs with whirlpool baths. Most bathtubs are made of molded cast iron with a porcelain enamel finish, formed steel with a porcelain enamel finish, or fiberglass. There are also a few non-traditional bathtub materials being used.

The following instructions refer to the installation of fixtures using plastic pipe. If you are using something other than plastic, please refer back to Chapter 5 which discusses plumbing with various materials. Installation will be nearly the same as with plastic except for connections. Some of the following instructions might be repeats from Chapter 5, but they are important.

The process of installing a new bathtub varies considerably due to the differences in styles available. The following instructions are for a typical job. Be sure to follow the installation instructions included with your new unit.

Bathtub and shower connections differ slightly from other fixtures because the hook-ups are not the same. For a bathtub trap, use a 1 1/2-inch **P** trap that can be solvent welded together at the angle required for proper installation. A metal tub-drain tailpiece comes with the tub-drain hardware and will enter a trap adapter installed in the trap's inlet end (solvent welded again). A polypropylene trap may also be used if it has a special elbow to solvent weld right into the 1 1/2-inch PVC drain pipe (Fig. 8-1).

For a shower, use a two-inch PVC pipe, solvent welded to a trap inlet that reaches up to the shower drain fitting and into it. There, the pipe is either

Fig. 8-1. Tub trap under the floor (Courtesy of Genova, Inc.).

solvent welded to a plastic shower drain or oakum caulked and plastic lead sealed to a conventional metal shower drain.

Where the bottom of a trap is accessible from below, it makes sense to use the type of trap with a cleanout plug. If the trap isn't accessible from the bottom, don't spend the extra money for a unit fitted with a cleanout plug (Figs. 8-2 through 8-7).

Tub and shower water lines are adapted to a 1/2-inch CPVC system with transition adapters, and the shower head is piped from the shower valve to the required height. It is generally considered best, with the tub spout, to hook it into the tub faucet manifold with metal nipples. Use brass. Build air chambers for both hot and cold water supplies to cut down on overpressure when the tub or shower units are turned off quickly.

In many cases bathtubs and showers are installed without line stops because the back of the unit is not readily accessible and there's no point at the front where the units can be placed. Place the line stops under the bathtub, if possible, or in the wall behind the bathtub fixture end, and build a panel that can be easily removed. Then if you ever need to work on the faucets or the shower, you prevent shut down of the entire water supply system. If basement lines are to be left exposed, it's usually easiest to install them there.

With the framing ready, lower the new tub into position. This will probably take two men. Connect the overflow pipe and the drain pipe to the waste pipe connector by tightening the slip joint nuts. Bring water supply lines to faucet height. Secure the pipe to the wall structure. Install the faucet and top plug. Install the elbow and nipple leading to the spout. Install the filler spout and faucets temporarily, and turn water on to check for leaks. Remove the spout and faucets. With waterproof material,

Fig. 8-2. Under-slab fittings must be braced (Courtesy of Genova, Inc.).

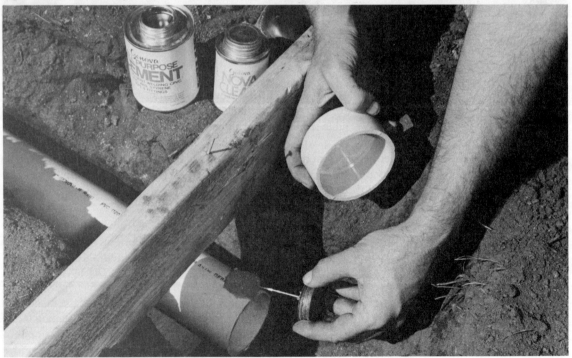

Fig. 8-3. Cementing a joint (Courtesy of Genova, Inc.).

Fig. 8-4. Backfilling by hand (Courtesy of Genova, Inc.).

Fig. 8-5. Build a box around the bath trap waste line (Courtesy of Genova, Inc.).

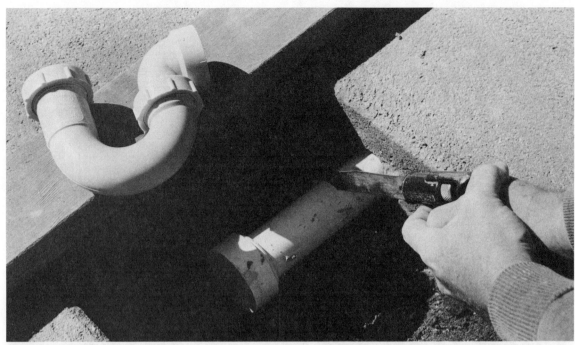

Fig. 8-6. After the concrete cures, cut off the plug and clean up the pipe end (Courtesy of Genova, Inc.).

Fig. 8-7. Solvent weld the trap (Courtesy of Genova, Inc.).

230

line inner walls of tub enclosure, leaving a 2-inch hole for each faucet and a 1 1/2-inch hole for the filler spout. Apply waterproof sealant to all joints between the tub and its enclosure. Permanently install filler spout and faucets.

To install a tub/shower combination, follow the tub installation instructions as far as extending the water supply lines to the correct height. From there, install another pipe to connect a twin L to a shower elbow, 6 feet, 6 inches over the bathroom floor. Anchor the pipe to the wall. Follow the previous instructions with the addition of temporarily installing the shower head along with the filler spout and faucets and checking for leaks. The shower head will be permanently installed at the same time the filler spout and faucets are installed.

SHOWERS

The most popular shower by far is the combination tub/shower. However, you might have an old shower stall to replace or a bathroom too small to hold a bathtub. While you can construct your own shower stall of tile or masonry, you will probably purchase a prefabricated unit of the correct size to fit your room. Installation is simple. The shower is installed directly over a floor drain, with hookup similar to that for tubs. Be sure to follow the manufacturer's instructions carefully.

Personal showers are probably the easiest and least expensive way to add a shower to an existing bathtub. Many people also like a personal shower to replace or add to the permanent shower head so that they can direct water where they like. Again, manufacturer's instructions should be simple and easy to follow for the installation of the personal shower of your choice.

TOILETS

Begin with the waste system fittings, as all drains should be in place before water supply lines are run,

Fig. 8-8. Removing the old DWV is the worst part of most jobs (Courtesy of Genova, Inc.).

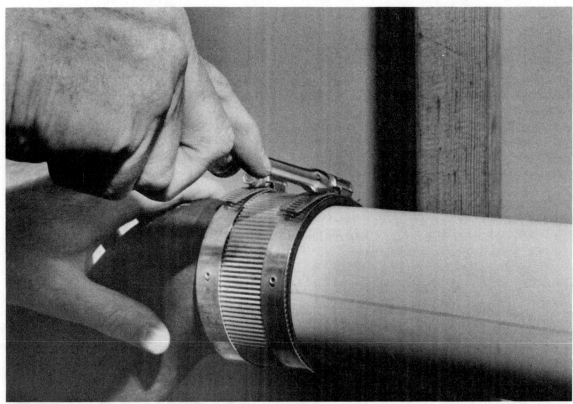

Fig. 8-9. New waste line couples right in (Courtesy of Genova, Inc.).

making testing the system somewhat neater (Fig. 8-8 and 8-9).

The toilet waste fitting is the toilet flange, which is attached to the waste pipe below the floor level. The floor hole needs to be 5 inches in diameter to clear the flange shoulder, after which you clean the DWV pipe and coat its outside with solvent. Clean and coat the inside of the PVC toilet flange fitting, making sure you're getting plenty of cement in place. Push the flange over the pipe, using a slight twist, just as if you were assembling any other pipe-fitting of plastic (Figs. 8-10 through 8-14). Make sure the bolt slots are aligned on either side of the flange (Fig. 8-15). The flange fits flush on the finished floor (or the subfloor, as you choose or your local codes require), so if that's not yet in place, you'll have to have made allowances for its thickness in your measurements. The best method of installing flanges ahead of flooring is to

measure the actual thickness of all flooring layers to be used. Unless you've gotten hold of a very special toilet, the center of the toilet flange should be 1 foot out from the finished bathroom wall surface. Measure the materials to be used to make up the finished wall, as there will be substantial differences between ceramic tiles, tileboard, gypsum wallboard, and various other paneling types. Check the toilet, too. Some makers might not announce on the box that it is not designed to fit the standard 12-inch, rough-in distance. This is more likely to be a problem with toilets made in other countries, especially those using the metric system.

Once the flange is in place, insert special holddown bolts, that are a standard hardware store item, in each of the serrated flange slots. The bolts are inserted so that a line drawn through the bolts would be parallel with the wall behind the toilet. Remove the nuts and washers from the bolts, as

232

Fig. 8-10. Plastic toilet flange (Courtesy of Genova, Inc.).

the flange slots hold them upright.

Unpack the toilet bowl and put it upside down on a thick pad of newspapers. Place a ring of plumber's putty around the bowl's outlet horn to seal it to the toilet flange. Use plenty of putty because any excess will be squeezed out and can be wiped off. If you prefer, use a wax bowl seal (toilet gasket). These are specially made for sealing toilet waste connections and are quite cheap. Make sure you get the type without a plastic flange, and place the flat side against the toilet bowl (Fig. 8-16).

Finally, lay a thin ring of plumber's putty all the way around the base of the bowl where it will touch the floor. This ring seals the floor to bowl joint. Put the ring on firmly so it won't slide off when you tip the bowl into place.

Pop the top on the flange and remove the flashing disc, and discard it. Invert the toilet bowl, holding it right side up over the toilet flange and bolts.

Lower the bowl slowly while keeping an eye on the bolts to make sure that they enter their holes in the bowl base. Square the bowl up with the wall as it touches the floor, and press it down, with a side-to-side wriggle to squeeze out excess wax or putty. A back-and-forth wriggle is also a good idea and the bowl should now be firmly seated on the flange and the floor.

Install both the hold-down washers and nuts on their bolts, snugging them up with a wrench, while being very careful not to over-tighten the nuts. The bowl could crack if you draw the nuts up too tightly, so make sure the hold downs are simply snug (Fig. 8-17).

If your bowl also has front mounting holes, you'll have to run hold-down screws into those. Afterwards the screw and bolt heads are covered with caps to match the toilet. Some caps just snap into place, while others are set with plumber's putty.

Fig. 8-11. Standard installation is similar to slab installation (Courtesy of Genova, Inc.).

Fig. 8-12. The flange is cemented in place (Courtesy of Genova, Inc.).

Fig. 8-13. The flange cements into the slab (Courtesy of Genova, Inc.).

Fig. 8-14. Knocking out the plug (Courtesy of Genova, Inc.).

Fig. 8-15. Special hold-down bolts are set in place (Courtesy of Genova, Inc.).

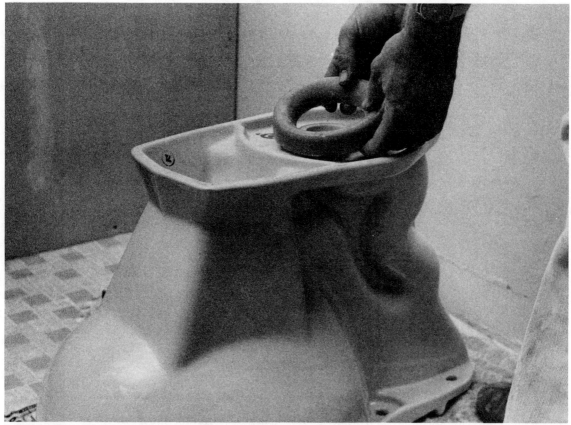

Fig. 8-16. The wax toilet bowl seal is placed (Courtesy of Genova, Inc.).

As you finish the toilet waste installation, clean up any plumber's putty around the caps and toilet bowl where it might have been forced out.

Toilet water supply lines can now be run and installed. Once the toilet bowl is installed, you can mount the toilet tank (some toilets have one piece bowl and tank units and no installation will be necessary). Once that's done, you're ready to bring up the supply riser from the floor or wall stub-out. Water supply lines for toilets and other fixtures should stub-out from the wall or floor and stop valves should be installed for emergency water cut-off and for making repairs. If your stub-out is at the wall, use an angle stop, while from the floor you need a straight stop. The riser then connects rapidly with the tank, making the complete connection a short, quick job.

For most toilets, a 12-inch riser will be long enough, but if not you can use a 20-inch model. Check lengths and cut carefully, making sure to allow for make-up in the fittings. At the stop valve, stab the end of the riser into the fitting and hand tighten it at the connection. The toilet riser will be flat ended to fit the toilet tank inlet. The coupling is a 3/8-inch fixture nut, which might not be furnished with the toilet, but is a standard hardware and plumbing supply store item. The riser can be cut to length with a knife and virtually cannot be kinked. It can be used with standard 3/8-inch compression fittings, or can be flared to work with flare fittings, so it can be adjusted to fit nearly any situation. The riser installation is the same, except for length and end design, no matter what the installation: sink, toilet, or other fixture. Simply cut to length, allowing 1 1/2 inches to stab into the fitting. Make the cut clean and square; it's best to bevel

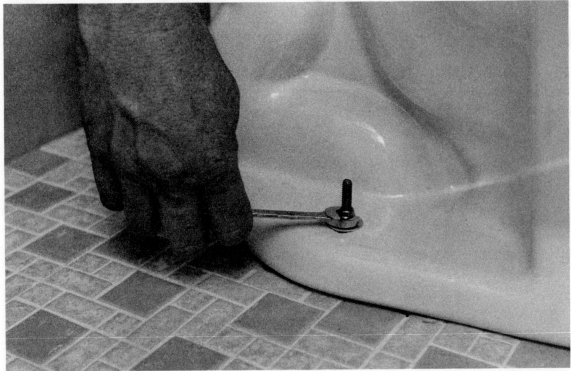

Fig. 8-17. Tighten the hold-down bolts (Courtesy of Genova, Inc.).

the cut end a bit. Slide the fixture flange nut up the molded nosepiece and draw the nut up snug, though not tight. A really tight fitting nut increases the chances of damaging the tank. It isn't needed for a seal so don't over-tighten. If you have a leak, you need a new gasket. Once the tank end is in place, bend a graceful curve into the riser and slide it into the fitting. Then hand tighten the nut. Turn the stop valve on and check for leaks.

SINKS

Basin waste installation should follow the basic instructions that come with each unit, as should the installations of all faucets, pop-up drains, and other drains. Use plumber's putty under both sides of the bowl flanges, around drains and beneath faucets that don't have base gaskets (Figs. 8-18 through 8-23). Once this is done, you're ready to install the waste. Waste stub-outs to sinks can begin inside the finished wall using 1 1/2-inch trap adapters, also called Marvel couplings. You can use the part that

joins—by solvent welding—a 1 1/2 inch-PVC waste pipe. Another choice is a plain 1 1/2-inch PVC pipe with a P trap solvent welded to it. (All PVC trap adapters will accept both metal and plastic traps). Use P traps for wall stub-outs for a sink and S traps for floor stub-outs (Figs. 8-24 through 8-25).

All traps will come with a heavy-duty slip jam nut and a thermoplastic jam nut washer, but if you have a smaller—1-1/4 inch—sink trap and want to use it, get a 1 1/2-inch to 1 1/4-inch reducing jam nut washer, and use it to mount your trap to the 1 1/2-inch trap adapter using the regular slip jam nut (Fig. 8-26).

Assemble the two trap parts, angled or straight as required, so that the long trap arm enters the waste pipe and the trap adapter straight on. When all parts are in alignment, tighten the slip jam nuts at both ends and in the center of the trap.

Use plumber's putty inside all slip nut connections on metal traps to provide a better chance of a leak-free joint. The mineral oils in the putty will

238

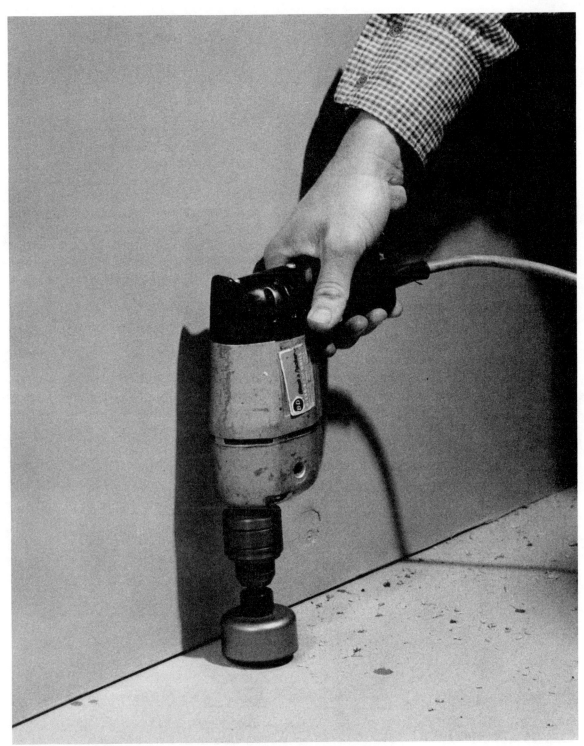

Fig. 8-18. Cutting a hole for the lavatory waste line (Courtesy of Genova, Inc.).

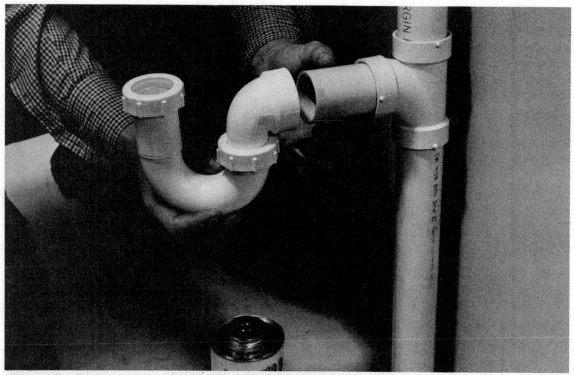

Fig. 8-19. The T is installed, then the trap (Courtesy of Genova, Inc.).

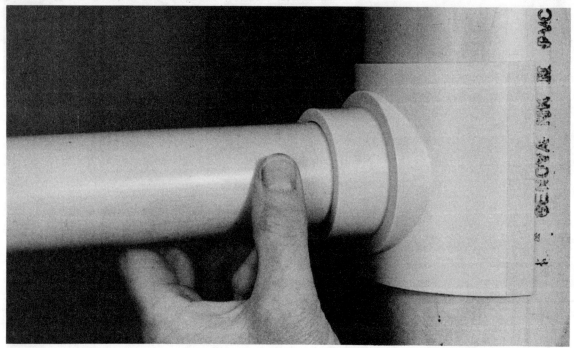

Fig. 8-20. Installing a saddle T (Courtesy of Genova, Inc.).

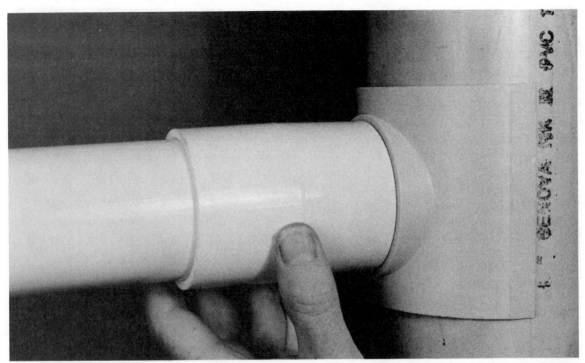

Fig. 8-21. Saddle T for larger pipe (Courtesy of Genova, Inc.).

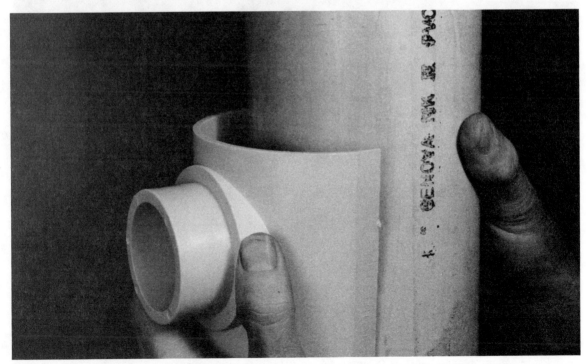

Fig. 8-22. Fitting the T (Courtesy of Genova, Inc.).

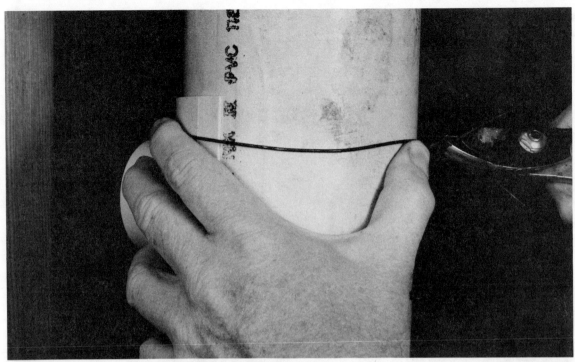

Fig. 8-23. Cement and wire into place (Courtesy of Genova, Inc.).

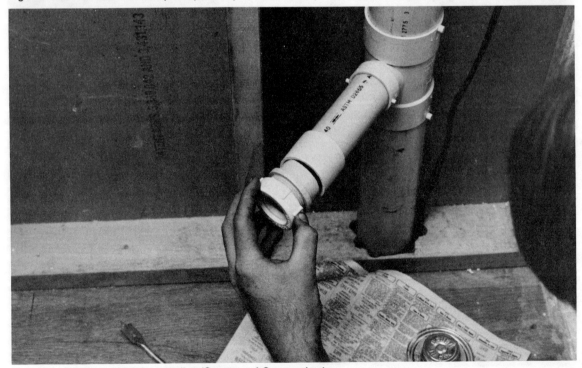

Fig. 8-24. Check the fit of the coupling (Courtesy of Genova, Inc.).

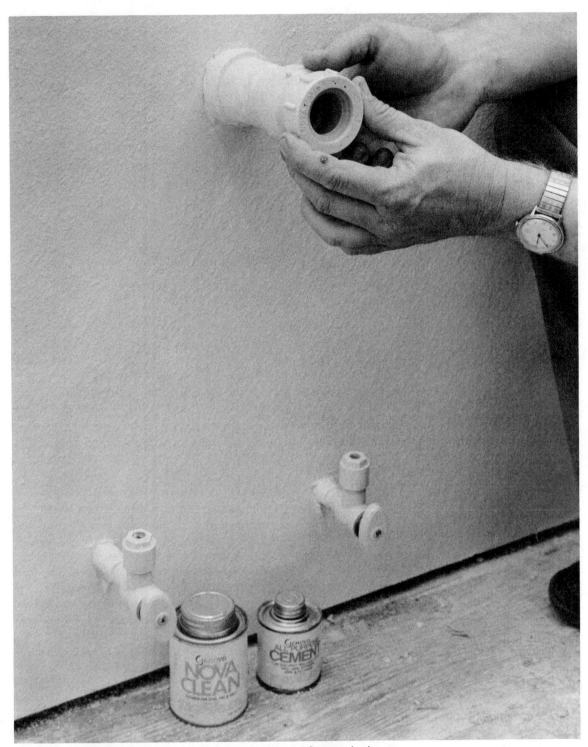

Fig. 8-25. The coupling after drywall is installed (Courtesy of Genova, Inc.).

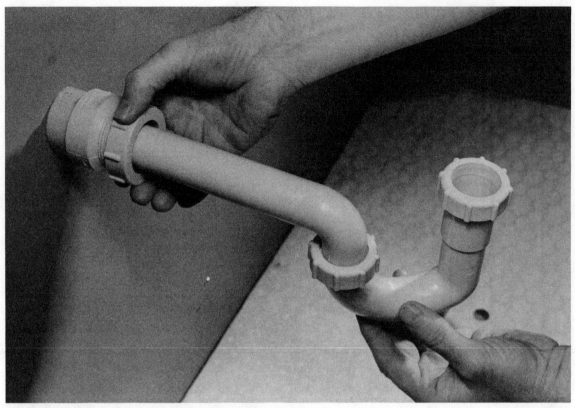
Fig. 8-26. P trap installation (Courtesy of Genova, Inc.).

affect the plastic in some plastic traps. Silicone rubber sealant is another good trap joint sealer. Use the type made for house caulking, bathtub and wall joint sealing, and so on. Again, don't use the material with ABS traps as the silicone attacks the plastic and will damage it over time.

Sink supply line installation is straightforward, from the stub-outs in the wall to the faucet bases. A wall stub-out will use angle stops, while a floor stub-out will require a straight stop, with the adapters for the stops solvent welded to the CPVC supply lines. Select bullet-nosed risers in 12-, 20-, or 36-inch lengths, as needed. The bullet noses will fit most faucets directly, but where they won't, you can cut off the bullet noses and flare the ends to fit the faucets. You must also flare the end of the faucet tube (making sure that the flare nut is installed first), and use a 3/8-inch flare nut to join the ends of the tubes. If you find the faucet supply ends are 1/4 inch, as many are, simply use a 1/4-inch to 3/8-inch flare adapter coupling to make your connection.

Compression fittings can be used instead of flare fittings. With compression fittings, you don't need to buy a flaring tool, and you can use regular brass compression ferrules with the PB risers. Some faucets come with short threaded tailpieces coupled to fixture nuts. With these, it's best to unscrew the tailpieces and connect the risers directly to the faucets, using the same nuts that connected the tailpieces.

Choices of styles and colors of sinks and faucets are as individual as the choices of bathtubs (Figs. 8-27 through 8-30). The only way to determine your own preferences is to shop extensively and know what is available and how prices vary. There are sinks and faucets designed to coordinate with any bathtub and/or shower you have chosen.

Fig. 8-27. Pedestal sink (Courtesy of
American Standard).

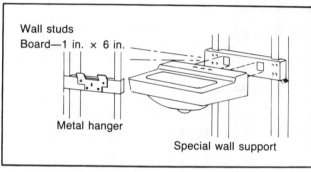

Wall studs
Board—1 in. × 6 in.

Metal hanger

Special wall support

Fig. 8-28. Two ways of mounting
sinks (Courtesy of Sears, Roebuck
& Co.).

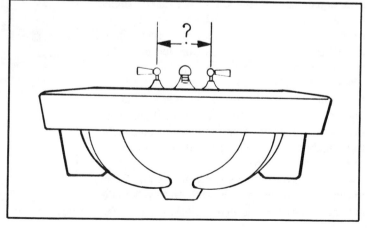

Fig. 8-29. Estimating faucet location
(Courtesy of Sears, Roebuck & Co.).

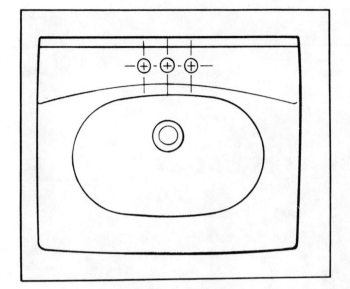

Fig. 8-30. Carefully measure your sink for correctly fitting faucets (Courtesy of Sears, Roebuck & Co.).

BATHROOM STORAGE

Toiletries, such as toothpaste and shaving supplies, can be conveniently stored in a cabinet above or within reach of the sink (Fig. 8-31).

The toiletry cabinet is frequently called the medicine cabinet, but it is not wise to combine the storage of medicine and cosmetics. Medicine should be stored in a special place by itself so there is no danger of confusing it with other supplies. In households with small children, provide, for medicines, a separate cabinet that can be locked. Install it out of reach of the children.

Toiletry cabinets can be wall hung or recessed. Recessed cabinets can be purchased ready for installation or made on the job. Ready-made cabinets usually have mirror doors. Adjustable shelves permit the best use of cabinet space. Shelving should be made of plastic, glass, or enameled metal that is not damaged by moisture or spilled cosmetics.

Place the toiletry cabinet at a convenient height for family needs. The top of the mirror is usually placed 69 to 74 inches from the floor. If you measure from the bottom of the mirror, a distance of 48 to 54 inches from the floor is satisfactory for the person of medium height.

You can save steps by storing some bath linens in the bathroom. Regular sized bath towels folded in thirds lengthwise fit on a shelf that is 12 inches

Fig. 8-31. Bathroom storage space.

246

deep—folded in half, they fit on a shelf 16 inches deep.

The only available space for a towel cabinet in a minimum-sized bath might be above the toilet. If you put a cabinet there, be sure to leave enough space between the top of the tank and the bottom of the cabinet for servicing the tank. The cabinet can be built into the stud space to provide additional depth if the location of the soil stack permits. Pole-supported shelves are easily installed over a toilet and provide some shelf storage at a nominal cost.

If you choose a wall cabinet, it will be one of the last tasks in redoing your bathroom. The main consideration in hanging a wall cabinet is making it level.

To install the wall cabinet, locate and mark two studs at the installation point. With a helper holding the cabinet against the wall, fasten the cabinet to the wall with two nails, driven only partially in. Level the cabinet. Fasten the cabinet to the wall with screws. Remove the nails and fill holes. Now the shelves can be put into the cabinet and it is ready for use.

It is nearly as simple to install a vanity before putting in your sink. Again locate and mark two studs in the position where the cabinet will go. Remove the countertop. Position the vanity into place.

With wood screws, fasten the vanity to the studs through the wall. Check that the top surface is level. The vanity is ready for the installation of the sink.

If you are building your own cabinets into the bathroom, you will follow standard carpentry procedures for the framing and finish of the cabinets. Careful planning and precise work can leave you with custom made cabinets that are tailored to your family's individual needs.

Figures 8-32 through 8-35 present other bathroom fixtures.

CARE OF FIXTURES

You can keep your new fixtures smooth and gleaming if you are careful in your choice of cleansers and do not abuse the fixtures in any way.

Harsh, gritty cleansers soon scratch and mar the surface of a fixture, regardless of the material of which a fixture is made. To test the abrasiveness of a cleanser, put a small amount between two pieces of glass and rub them together. If the glass is scratched, the cleanser is too harsh to use on fixtures. Other precautions to observe in fixture care:

■ Do not use bathtubs or sinks for washing sharp-edged articles. If it is necessary to stand in the bathtub or to place a steplad-

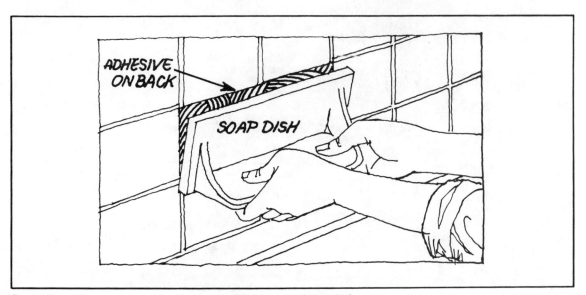

Fig. 8-32. Installing a soap holder (Courtesy of Tile Council of America).

Fig. 8-33. Handles can assist the elderly enter the tub (Courtesy of Kohler Co.).

Fig. 8-34. Shelf and towel bar (Courtesy of NuTone).

248

Fig. 8-35. In-the-wall bathroom scale (Courtesy of NuTone).

der in it when washing walls and windows, cover the bottom of the tub with a rug or mat with a nonskid backing.

■ Do not develop photographic film in sinks or bathtubs. Photo solutions are harmful to enamel surfaces.

■ Do not allow strong solutions, including household and hair bleaches and vinegar to stand in any bathroom fixture, stains may result. Cosmetic lotions, hair preparations and medicines can also stain the sink.

■ Do not allow faucets to drip constantly. The minerals in some water discolor and stain surfaces.

■ Do not leave wet non-slip mats in tub. Some of them make permanent stains. Hang them to dry after each use before replacing in the tub.

Chapter 9

Decorating Your Bathroom and Adding Special Features

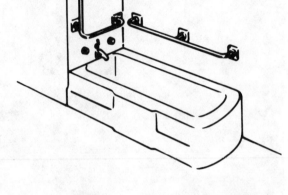

I T'S TIME TO DECORATE YOUR BATHROOM. Your decorations can be sparse and functional, such as plain mirrors, towel racks, and tissue holders. Or they can be elaborate, including special shelves for figurines, dried flower arrangements, live plants, or anything else that catches your fancy.

MIRRORS

While mirrors are necessary and functional in a bathroom, they can also be attractive and add to the overall finished look of the room (Figs. 9-1 through 9-4). Mirrors can be square, round, rectangular, oval, or any one of many unusual shapes. Mirrors come in many qualities and in several forms. You can buy plain mirrors, simply framed mirrors, fancily framed mirrors, and mirror tiles.

Most bathrooms include a mirror over the sink for shaving and applying make-up. This mirror should be well-lighted and placed so that it is easily accessible to all family members. Children might need a step stool in order to see in the mirror. Many

mirrors over sinks are on the front of a toiletry, or medicine, chest.

Many bathrooms also include a full-length mirror for checking clothing and overall appearance before leaving the house. These are often hung on the inside of the bathroom door. If there is sufficient wall space elsewhere, they might be included there. And there are mirrored tub-enclosure doors that provide lots of reflection.

Mirrors can also be used to make a room appear larger. If properly placed, mirrors help eliminate a cramped feeling in a very small bathroom.

Because they are easily breakable and heavy, mirrors require some special care in handling and hanging. Hardboard-backed mirrors are the most convenient because they normally have steel hangers riveted to the backing. The hangers slip over hooks that are screwed into the wall, making installation comparatively easy and quick.

Unbacked mirrors must be hung with J clips and L clips. J clips are steel hooks bent into a J shape and L clips are plastic holders in the shape of an L. The J clips are used at the bottom of the

Fig. 9-1. Mirror is the door for a wall cabinet (Courtesy of NuTone).

Fig. 9-2. Bathroom mirrors reflect the mood of the decorator (Courtesy of NuTone).

mirror and the L clips at the sides. Use small pads behind the mirror to hold it slightly away from the wall.

Construction adhesive is also used to attach mirrors, but it is only a good choice if the mirror is permanent. The adhesive is so permanent that the mirror would probably break if removed from the wall.

To hang any mirror, first be sure that the wall or door surface is flat and smooth. Then mark all attachment points, using a level to assure straight installation. Using your chosen hangers for your particular mirror, carefully install hangers and attach mirror. It might be helpful to have a helper for a larger mirror.

WINDOWS

Bathroom windows often create a problem. You want to let in the natural light without allowing any visibility from outside. Many frosted windows and special bathroom windows are available for just such uses. But if you have a clear-pane window in your bathroom, you might not wish to change the entire window. You can still create the effect you need. Clear window panes can be replaced with opaque glass inexpensively.

Shutters can fit in with the decor of your room and cover your window nicely. The wood accent can add a touch of elegance. If the window is near the shower, the shutters should be protected from the spray.

Fig. 9-3. Mirror accented with lighting (Courtesy of NuTone).

Fig. 9-4. Mirrors are both decorative and functional (Courtesy of NuTone).

If the window is over the tub or tub/shower combination, the window can be inexpensively covered with a second shower curtain, either matching or complementing the first.

Curtains, blinds, and shades are more traditional window coverings that can be used in the bathroom. All allow you the choice of letting in all, partial, or little natural light.

SMALL ACCESSORIES

Towel Rods. Each family member needs rod space for a towel and washcloth. In addition, you will want some extra space for guest use. To hang a bath towel and washcloth folded once lengthwise requires 21 inches. If the washcloth is hung unfolded for quick drying, the washcloth and towel take up 28 inches of rod space. Towel rods on the

254

Fig. 9-5. Towel rods mounted on the basin (Courtesy of American Standard).

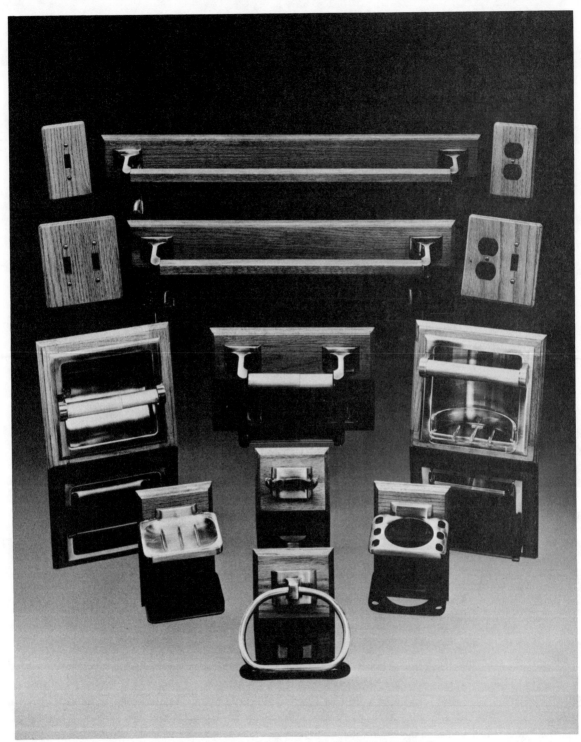

Fig. 9-6. Wood trimmed towel rods and accessories for the bath (Courtesy of NuTone).

Fig. 9-7. Pull-out drying line (Courtesy of Nutone).

sides of the vanity are a convenient height for small children. A towel pole provides for extra towels in a minimum of space.

Towel rods are made of plastic, metal, wood, and ceramic, and they come in many colors, styles, and lengths to provide for all tastes (Figs. 9-5 through 9-8).

Towels and washcloths also come in many colors, patterns and fabrics. If you shop patiently you will find the perfect addition to your new bathroom.

Tissue Holder. Tissue holders of china, metal, wood, or plastic can be recessed in or fastened to the wall (Figs. 9-9 and 9-10). Place the tissue holder so that its bar is about 30 inches from the floor, and if on a sidewall, about 6 or 8 inches beyond the front edge of the toilet.

Soap Holders and Clothes Hooks. Soap holders for the tub and shower are usually recessed. Vitreous china and metal are commonly used materials. For tub use, place the soap holder at about the middle of the wall beside the tub and within easy reach from a sitting position in the tub.

In the shower stall, the soap holder is usually placed about shoulder height and far enough forward so the spray does not reach it. If you prefer, you can install a corner shelf in the shower stall for soaps and shampoos. Wash basin soap holders often come with matching accessories (Fig. 9-11).

Nonrusting hooks for hanging robes and other clothing add convenience. Place the hooks above eye level for safety.

Toothbrush and Tumbler Holder. These accessories are often combined (Fig. 9-12), but can be purchased separately. They can be made of vitreous china, ceramic, metal, plastic, or wood. Some are stationary, others revolve and close flush with the wall. Revolving combination units hold soap, tumblers, and toothbrushes.

Drying Lines and Racks. If clothes are to be dried in the bathroom, it is best to make special provision for the job, rather than depend on towel rods for hanging space. Following are a few ways to provide bathroom drying space: Place hooks in the walls at each end of the built-in tub for attaching clotheslines across the tub when needed. Put

Fig. 9-8. Plastic towel holder (Courtesy of NuTone).

PLANTS IN THE BATHROOM

With its warm, humid atmosphere, the bathroom is often an ideal room for growing many house plants (Figs. 9-13 and 9-15). Plants add color and life to a bathroom. They can be small or large, hung, or set on counters or shelves. They can be near a window or under a grow lamp. Following are just a few of the many house plants that will probably thrive in your bathroom: aglaonema, aspidistra, begonia, callisia elegans, coffea arabica, columnea, dieffenbachia, howeia, philodendron, Easter cactus, and Tradescantia fluminensis (wandering Jew). Check with your local greenhouse or florist for more ideas.

Finally, you can add bath curtains (Fig. 9-15), reading racks (Fig. 9-16) and assist bars (Fig. 9-17 through 9-19) to make your bathroom more functional.

ADDING LUXURY BATHING

Bathrooms in homes have come to be considered a necessity for health and cleanliness. Many

a telescope rod with rubber suction cups over a recessed tub. (This rod may be left in place permanently or stored after each use.) Mount a drying rack on the wall at one end or on the side of the tub. The rack will fold flat against the wall when not in use. Install a clothesline reel with retractable plastic line over the bathtub. Line is hooked to opposite wall for use (Fig. 9-17).

Outlet and Switch Covers. Plastic, wood, and ceramic outlet and switch covers of your choice can add a finishing touch to the scheme of your bathroom. While white or off-white plastic is often used, it can be replaced with a more fashionable color and material.

Laundry Hamper. A laundry hamper might be a necessity for your bathroom. The room can be kept neat and tidy if a large hamper is provided for easy stashing of dirty clothes. Wood, wicker, and plastic are among the common materials. The plastic comes in decorator colors to blend in with any color scheme.

Fig. 9-9. Recessed tissue holder (Courtesy of NuTone).

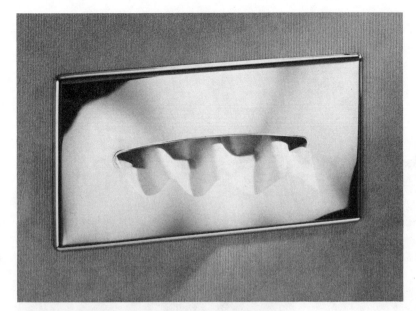

Fig. 9-10. In-wall facial tissue dispenser (Courtesy of NuTone).

homeowners are expanding the uses of the bathroom to include luxury bathing (Fig. 9-20). Any of the following units, sauna, hot tub, whirlpool bath, or steam bath, can be located in or near the bath. They can also be located in separate rooms, basements, and even outdoors.

ADDING A SAUNA

The Finnish sauna is a bathing experience that can

Fig. 9-11. Free-standing soap dish and drawer knob (Courtesy of NuTone).

Fig. 9-12. Toothbrush and tumbler holder (Courtesy of NuTone).

Fig. 9-13. Plants, especially ferns, can be placed near tubs or showers (Courtesy of Kohler Co.).

be experienced individually or as a family activity. Home saunas can accommodate from one to 18 people and some are small enough to fit into the corner of a large bathroom.

The sauna provides dry heat, usually about 8 percent in American models, that allows the body to tolerate heat from 180 to 240 degrees Fahrenheit. About 190 degrees is considered ideal. The lack of humidity combined with high heat encourages rapid perspiration. A session in a sauna is usually followed by a plunge into cold water, so it is best if the sauna be located near a tub, pool, or shower.

Prefabricated saunas are available that can be installed quickly and easily following manufacturer's directions. Styles include both freestanding and built-in units. The packages often include the heater, which can be gas or electric. The smaller electric heaters run on 120 volts while larger ones may require 220 volts.

Inside the sauna will be benches for sitting or lying down while bathing (Fig. 9-21). The number of benches will depend on the size of the unit. The higher the bench the higher the temperature will be.

Woods used for sauna construction include aspen, pine, and redwood because they diffuse heat. The wood must be well-seasoned and free of imperfections. Undried lumber contains pitch and sap that can become extremely hot, causing burns.

Home saunas can be easily built into most any room with common stud-wall construction and simple wiring. The walls can be framed and the ceiling finished on the floor and then erected. Existing room walls can act as outer covering for one or two of the new sauna walls. New outside sauna walls should be covered with wallboard. Use foil-faced mineral batt insulation between the studs in the sauna walls. Windows should be double-glazed. Purchase a special sauna door from a dealer because they must be solid-core wood, or insulated.

The heater for the sauna, if electric, can be placed anywhere in the room. It should, however, be opposite the fresh air vents. Your sauna door might have a vent hole already. If it does not, you can cut a 3-inch hole about 1/2 foot above the floor in the wall, either directly behind or near the heater. You will need to cut a hole through the insulation also. Another vent hole should be cut opposite the heater, about 8 inches below the ceiling. It also should be about 3 inches square. Each vent hole can be covered on the outside with a metal plate.

The entire inside of the sauna must be paneled in the wood of your choice, usually aspen, pine, or redwood. You can build in benches to accommo-date your family. Sauna benches are usually 24 inches wide and 18 inches high. If there is a second bench, it should be 18 inches above the first.

When building a sauna, be sure to only use a heater made especially for a sauna and to follow the manufacturer's installation instructions. Some heaters rely on rocks to help hold the heat and some saunas end with a splash of water on the rocks to create high humidity quickly.

A session in your new sauna will leave you refreshed and feeling good. It is a good idea to take a rest following a sauna. Anyone with a heart condition or high blood pressure should check with a doctor before using a sauna.

Fig. 9-14. Dried flowers and plants are also a decorative addition to baths (Courtesy of NuTone).

Fig. 9-15. Bath curtains are both functional and beautiful (Courtesy of Masonite Corp.).

Fig. 9-16. Wall niche for reading materials (Courtesy of NuTone).

HOT TUBS

Hot tubs have become enormously popular in the last few years. While most are installed as outdoor tubs, they can be placed in a basement and, under certain conditions, directly in the bathroom. If you are lucky enough to have a bathroom that opens into a private garden area, you have the perfect spot to add a hot tub.

Hot tubs, constructed of fiberglass, concrete, or wood, come in many sizes and shapes and can be custom built into any desired design. They are meant for relaxing rather than cleaning. Most people take a cleansing shower before entering the hot tub for a relaxing half hour or so.

Hot tubs require many of the same pieces of equipment that a home swimming pool requires (Fig. 9-22), These include a pump, heater, and filter. The filter will need to be run for at least 2 hours

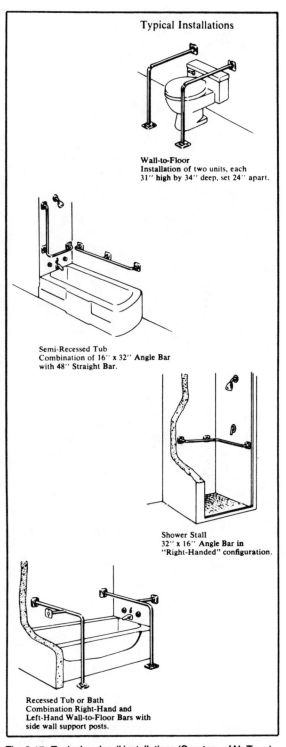

Typical Installations

Wall-to-Floor
Installation of two units, each 31″ high by 34″ deep, set 24″ apart.

Semi-Recessed Tub
Combination of 16″ x 32″ Angle Bar with 48″ Straight Bar.

Shower Stall
32″ x 16″ Angle Bar in "Right-Handed" configuration.

Recessed Tub or Bath
Combination Right-Hand and Left-Hand Wall-to-Floor Bars with side wall support posts.

Fig. 9-17. Typical grab rail installations (Courtesy of NuTone).

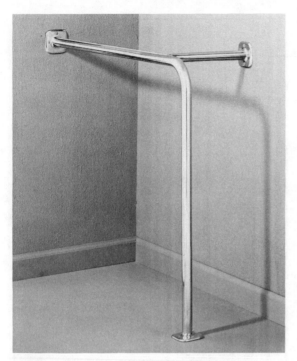

Fig. 9-18. Floor grab rails (Courtesy of NuTone).

each day to keep the water fresh and clean. The heater will keep the water warm and heat it to bathing temperature quickly on demand. A bathing temperature of 110 degrees is a good starting point. You might wish to have the water warmer as you become accustomed to it.

A hydromassage unit located outside the rim of the tub can add extra enjoyment to hot tub bathing.

WHIRLPOOL BATH

When purchasing your bathtub, consider a whirlpool model. A built-in whirlpool is more efficient, comfortable, and relaxing than a portable unit added later. The whirlpool soothes aching muscles and helps relax tired minds.

As all other bathroom equipment, whirlpool baths come in all shapes, sizes, and colors (Figs. 9-23 through 9-25). There will be one to fit your needs. Whirlpool baths, unlike the other luxury bathing units, can be selected to fit into the same space as a conventional bathtub.

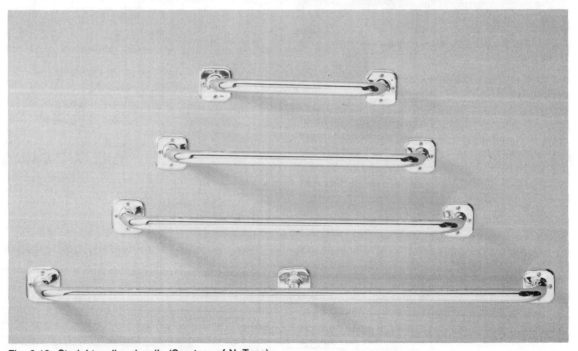

Fig. 9-19. Straight wall grab rails (Courtesy of NuTone).

Fig. 9-20. Luxury bath (Courtesy of Kohler Co.).

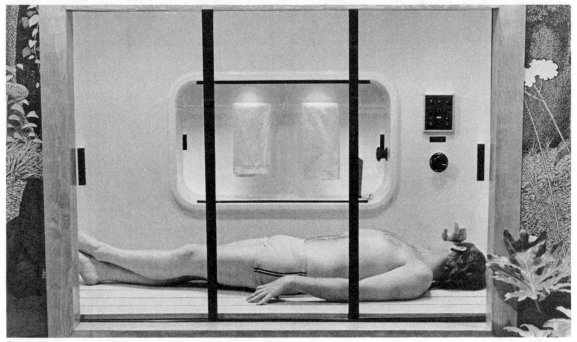
Fig. 9-21. Spa with horizontal bench (Courtesy of Kohler Co.).

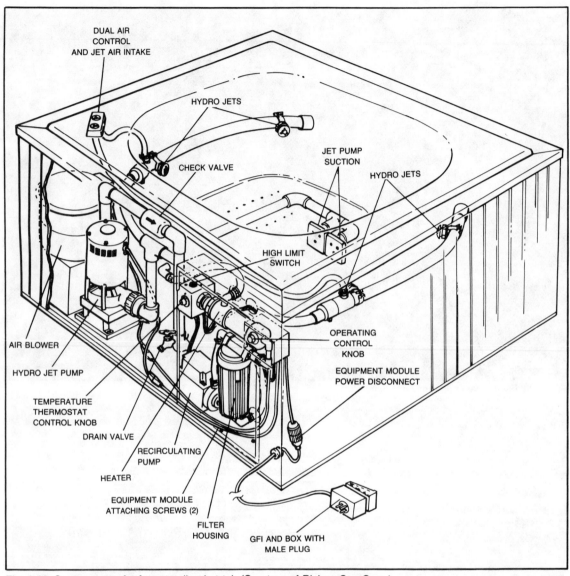

DUAL AIR
CONTROL
AND JET AIR INTAKE

HYDRO JETS

CHECK VALVE

JET PUMP
SUCTION

HYDRO JETS

HIGH LIMIT
SWITCH

AIR BLOWER

HYDRO JET PUMP

TEMPERATURE
THERMOSTAT
CONTROL KNOB

DRAIN VALVE

RECIRCULATING
PUMP

HEATER

EQUIPMENT MODULE
ATTACHING SCREWS (2)

FILTER
HOUSING

GFI AND BOX WITH
MALE PLUG

OPERATING
CONTROL
KNOB

EQUIPMENT MODULE
POWER DISCONNECT

Fig. 9-22. Components of a free-standing hot tub (Courtesy of Riviera Spa Corp.).

STEAM BATH

The steam bath, or Turkish bath, is the opposite of the sauna. The steam bath relies on moist heat. Units are available that will fit into even a moderate sized bathroom. Or you can add a boiler or steam generator to your bath or shower and turn it into a steam bath. Directing jets will be needed to distribute steam evenly throughout the area. Tub or shower steam baths will need a specially-designed glass door to complete the enclosure and confine the steam. The steam unit can be installed in the ceiling or in a vanity and can be located as much as 50 feet from the bathing location.

Steam baths open the skin pores, giving a thorough cleansing, as well as a sense of well being. A 10- or 20-minute steam bath is usually followed by a cold or cool shower. Even though the humidity level during a steam bath is nearly 100 percent,

266

Fig. 9-23. Step-up whirlpool (Courtesy of American Standard).

Fig. 9-24. Garden whirlpool (Courtesy of Kohler Co.).

the steam is easily dissipated by simply turning on the regular shower, condensing the steam to water.

A sunning room with heat lamps can also be installed (Fig. 9-26).

SKYLIGHTS

Many bathrooms could benefit by additional natural light. This can sometimes be obtained by installing a skylight. Skylights are especially beneficial in a bathroom with no windows and no way to add a window, such as a bathroom with no outside walls.

Ready-to-install skylights are on the market that simply require cutting a hole, putting the skylight in position, securing it, and installing roofing over it, using a roof flange. If installed properly, a skylight will add light to the room without leaking (see TAB book No. 1578, *Doors, Windows, and Skylights* for more help).

SOUNDPROOFING

Sound control has become a vital part of house design and construction. It is usually desirable to provide sound insulation between bathrooms and other

Fig. 9-25. Sunken whirlpool (Courtesy of American Standard).

areas of the home.

Sound waves radiate outward from the source through the air until they strike a wall, floor, or ceiling. These surfaces are set in vibration by the fluctuating pressure of the sound wave in the air. Because the wall vibrates, it conducts sound to the other side in varying degrees, depending on the wall construction.

When airborne sound strikes a conventional wall, the studs act as sound conductors unless they are separated in some way from the covering material. Electrical switches or convenience outlets

Fig. 9-26. Sunning room with heat lamps (Courtesy of Kohler Co.).

Fig. 9-27. Bidets are usually located near the toilet (Courtesy of Kohler Co.).

placed back-to-back in a wall readily pass sound. Faulty construction, such as poorly fitted doors, often allows sound to travel through. Thus, good construction practices are important in providing sound-resistant walls, in addition to other measures commonly used to block sounds.

A relatively simple system has been developed using sound-deadening insulating board in conjunction with gypsum board outer covering. This provides good sound-transmission resistance suitable for use in the home, with only slight additional cost.

Good sound deadening can be obtained in a wood-frame wall by using 1/2-inch sound-deadening board nailed to the studs, followed by a lamination of 1/2-inch gypsum wallboard. Slightly better sound deadening can be obtained by using 5/8-inch gypsum wallboard rather than 1/2-inch. Using resilient clips to fasten gypsum backer boards to the studs, followed by adhesive-laminated 1/2-inch fiberboard, also works well. This method further isolates the wall covering from the framing.

Design of the "quiet" house can incorporate another system of sound insulation, called sound absorption. Sound-absorbing materials can minimize the amount of noise by stopping the reflection of sound back into a room. Sound-absorbing materials do not necessarily have resistance to airborne sounds. Perhaps the most commonly used sound-absorbing material is acoustic tile. Wood fiber or similar materials are used in the manufacture of the tile, which is usually processed to provide some fire resistance and is designed with numerous tiny sound traps on the tile surfaces. These may consist of tiny drilled or punched holes, fissured surfaces, or a combination of both.

Acoustic tile is most often used in the ceiling and areas where it is not subjected to excessive mechanical damage. It can be applied by a number of methods: to existing ceilings or any smooth surface with a mastic adhesive designed specifically for this purpose, or to furring strips nailed to the underside of the ceiling joists. Nailing or stapling tile is the normal application method in this system. It is also used with a mechanical suspension system. Manufacturers' recommendations should be followed in application and finishing.

INSTALLING A BIDET

The bidet is a sit-down wash basin that provides both hot and cold water, and sometimes a spray as well (Fig. 9-27). The bidet is designed for cleaning of the perineal area. Its design is similar to that of a sitz bath or a footbath. If your bathroom has the room for one more fixture, you might consider the bidet. Many physicians recommend them for cleanliness.

Because the bidet requires both hot and cold water, as well as a specially designed drain, it will be expensive to install.

TURN YOUR IMAGINATION LOOSE

Now is the time to dream about the luxury bath that would be the ultimate in comfort for you and your family. Once you have all of the necessities provided for, you can design and redesign your bathroom with various fixtures and extras until you arrive at the design that is uniquely yours and that gives your family all of its needs plus some of its dreams.

Your family might need a tub/shower combination and double sinks. The family might want a whirlpool or steam bath. Spend some time on your plans and in shopping. If you consider all angles carefully, you can soon have the bathroom you want and need.

The last chapter of this book will show you how to make simple plumbing repairs. You can do many of them yourself and save money.

Chapter 10

Simple Bathroom Repairs

T HE BEST COURSE OF REPAIR INVOLVES PRE-
ventive maintenance to keep problems from
occurring. Whenever you have to do any maintenance in your bathroom, inspect surrounding fixtures, faucets, pipes, and so on. Replace or repair
worn parts before they fail and you will save
added stress on the system. But there will be times
when a leak springs or a toilet backs up. This chapter will help you to deal with those minor irritations.

SHUTTING OFF WATER

Each member of your household should have some
understanding of the plumbing system and know
the location of the main shut-off valve and the various branch valves. Should a leak occur in any part
of the system, anyone in the house can shut off the
branch in which the leak occurs. In the case of a
leaking pipe, the minutes wasted in trying to locate
the shut-off valve can mean the difference between
slight or extensive damage to decorations, flooring,
and furniture.

All shut-off valves should be tagged to indicate

clearly what part of the system each valve controls.
This will also save a plumber much time, if one is
ever necessary, because he will not have to trace
out the entire system before working on it.

To determine what branch of the system a particular valve controls, close the valve and open the
faucets throughout the house. List all faucets that
are dry when the valve is turned off as part of that
branch of the plumbing. The main shut-off valve,
controlling the water supply for the entire house,
is often located in the basement. Keep it clear. If
the basement is finished with wallboard or other
material, indicate the position of the valve clearly
and make it easily accessible. This might necessi-
tate cutting out a small square of the wallboard and
nailing it back into place with a few short nails that
can be quickly pulled out by hand.

Many failures in the sewage system are due to
the fact that the system is forced to carry away not
only liquids and water soluble waste but all types
of rubbish as well. Caution every member of your
family against throwing solid matter of any kind
into toilets or down sink and fixture drains. A sew-

age system that is properly installed can dispose of liquid matter, but it cannot cope with such items as diapers, metal bottle tops, and other objects. Cleaning out a sewer pipe is expensive and messy.

REPAIRING TOILETS

Clogged Toilet Trap. To clean the trap, first try the plunger. If that fails, work a piece of stiff wire into the trap and attempt to dislodge the obstruction so that it can be pulled or pushed through. A plunger will work best if the lip is first coated with petroleum jelly to help create a seal. With the plunger vertically in the bowl and water above the plunger cup, work the handle up and down to try to dislodge any clog.

The best way to test whether or not the clog has been removed is to pour some water into the bowl. If the clog has been dislodged, the bowl will not fill because some of it will be forced down the drain.

If the clog doesn't dislodge with a plunger, you can try hot water, liquid bleach, and a low-sudsing detergent. Pour two or three large pans full of boiling water into the bowl. Pour 3 cups of liquid bleach and 1 cup of low-sudsing detergent into the toilet and follow with more boiling water. Allow this to sit for about an hour to soften the clog. Use the plunger again to try to dislodge the clog.

If the clog is still not removed, you can try an auger, which is a spring steel coil and made specially for toilet drains. Insert the end of the auger into the drain and slowly turn the handle. Work slowly and carefully, because the auger can crack the toilet bowl.

Leaky Flush Tanks. Before attempting to repair a toilet tank that leaks, it is necessary to understand how the water enters the tank and how it is regulated so that the tank will not overflow.

Water enters the tank through an opening fitted with a valve. The valve has a washer, so that it will completely stop the flow of water when the valve is closed. The opening and closing of this inlet valve is governed by the float that is connected to the valve by a rod. The float is airtight and rests on the surface of the water inside the tank. As the water rises in the tank, the float rises with it until, at

a predetermined point, the inlet valve is closed by the action of the rod attached to the float. The flow of water into the tank is thus stopped.

The handle on the outside of the tank is connected by wire rods to a rubber flush valve that fits over the opening at the bottom of the tank. This opening is connected to the toilet bowl by a section of pipe. When the flush valve is lifted from the valve seat by turning the handle, water rushes out of the tank into the toilet bowl. As the water level in the tank drops, the float drops with it, and this action opens the inlet valve so that water can flow back into the tank. As soon as the handle on the outside of the tank is returned to its normal position, the flush valve drops over the valve seat to prevent any more water from flowing from the tank into the bowl. The tank then fills with water until the inlet valve is closed as the float reaches a set height.

An overflow pipe inside the tank allows water to flow into the bowl, should the inlet valve fail to close at the proper time.

Keep in mind that all the mechanisms inside the tank are delicate and can be thrown out of adjustment rather easily. Make sure that all the rods are working correctly before you begin replacing valves and washers.

There are several places inside the tank where a leak is likely to occur. It is possible to locate the cause of a leaky tank by removing the top and looking at the water level. If the water level is low and water is flowing out of the tank into the toilet bowl, the flush valve is not closing. If the level of the water inside the tank is high and water is flowing out of the tank by way of the overflow pipe, the inlet valve is not closing.

A leak at the flush valve can be due to three conditions. A flush ball that becomes worn, rotten, or distorted in shape will no longer fit tightly over the valve seat. Rust or dirt on the valve seat will also prevent the ball from fitting evenly. When the thin metal rods connecting the flush ball with the tank handle become bent or bind, the ball cannot drop back over the valve seat.

To find which part of the system is at fault and to make the necessary repairs, you will have to shut off the water supply. Most tanks have a small valve located on the pipe running from the bottom of the tank through the floor. This is the supply line to the tank, and when this valve is closed no water will be able to enter the tank. If the tank does not have this valve, shut off the water by closing the right branch valve in the house plumbing system or by lifting the copper float inside the tank, and propping it to hold the inlet valve in a closed position.

Once the water has been shut off, you can remove the flush ball and examine it for wear. This ball is fitted with threads at the top and screwed to the rod linking it to the tank handle. If the ball is worn or out of shape, it should be replaced.

Check the flush valve seat for dirt or rust after the ball is removed. If it appears to be rough, smooth it by rubbing the rim with emery cloth. Remove any sizable pieces of scale or rust with an old knife. After smoothing the valve seat, screw the new flush ball to the connecting rod.

Test the operation of the linkage between the handle and flush ball by turning the handle to the open position and then to the close. The ball should drop on the valve seat when the handle swings closed. If it fails to do this, examine the rods to see if they are bent. The lower rod attached to the flush ball is held in place by a metal guide arm connected to the overflow pipe. This guide arm is adjustable and should be positioned so that it is directly over the valve seat. If it is out of adjustment, the flush ball will not line up properly on the valve seat. If any metal rod is badly rusted it should be replaced, for a corroded rod will not maintain its shape long.

A leak due to failure of the inlet valve to close can also be caused by several factors. It might be due to a worn valve washer or a rough valve seat. If the rod connecting the float to the inlet valve were bent out of shape, it would cause the valve to remain open, as would a leak in the float.

To replace a worn inlet washer, shut off the water from the tank before disassembling the inlet valve. In some tanks this valve is located near the top of the tank, while in others it will be found at the bottom. If the latter, you will have to flush all the water out of the tank to get at the valve. The plunger of the valve is held in place by thumb screws that will probably have to be started with the aid of pliers. The washer is held in place by a nut and a brass ring cap. The ring cap might be so rusted that it will break while it is being removed. If this occurs, you will need a new cap as well as a new washer. While the valve is disassembled, check the valve seat to be sure that it is not rough or nicked.

A copper float containing water will not rise high enough to shut off the inlet valve. You can solder a small leak in the float after draining the water out of it, but replace a float that has a bad leak.

The rod connecting the float to the valve has a great deal to do with how much water flows into the tank before the valve is closed. If the rod is bent upward, the level of water in the tank will be higher. If the rod is bent down, the water level will be lower. When a tank that is otherwise working correctly fails to deliver enough water to the toilet bowl, it is likely that the rod is bent out of shape. This takes only a moment to repair. The water level in the tank should be almost to the top of the overflow pipe. If it is too far under this point, the toilet bowl will not be flushed properly.

Condensation On Tanks. Moisture dripping off the sides of the toilet flush tank and onto the bathroom floor is a source of constant annoyance in many homes. This is usually a year-round affair and can, in time, ruin the flooring and damage a ceiling below if the bathroom is on the second floor. A common cause of the trouble is that the sides of the flush tank are kept at a low temperature by the fresh water entering the tank each time the toilet is flushed. This is especially the case if the fresh water supply comes from a deep well. As the air in every bathroom has a high moisture content, there is bound to be considerable condensation on the tank.

One remedy is to cover the tank with coldwater pipe insulation and to cover this, in turn, with linoleum, sheet plastic, or other material for the sake of appearance.

Sometimes, however, condensation on flush tanks is due to the fact that the valve on the tank is not operating properly and fresh, cold water continues to flow into the tank and out through the overflow line after the tank is filled. This flow of fresh water prevents the water in the tank from reaching room temperature and so the sides of the tank are kept cool. The remedy here is to fix the tank mechanism so that no water enters the tank after it has been filled.

LEAKY FAUCETS

You can probably prevent leaky faucets by changing the washers in all the faucets in your home once a year. If not, repair a leaky faucet as soon as it begins to leak. It won't stop by itself and it can cause additional problems, including stains in the sink or tub. Refer to Figs. 10-1 through 10-13 as you repair leaky faucets and related assemblies.

The first step to repairing a leaky faucet is to turn the water source off to that faucet. If there is a shut-off valve below the fixture, that is all you need to turn off. If there is not, you will need to turn off the main valve or a branch valve, probably located in the basement.

Remove the handle from the faucet and you should be able to see the washer. Turn the screw holding the washer in place counterclockwise to remove both screw and washer. Replace the washer with one of the same size and type, and replace the faucet. The steps for removing the handle and replacing it will vary according to the type of faucet you have. If your faucet no longer drips you are in good shape.

However, there is a chance that your faucet will continue to drip or will now leak around the packing nut, which is located beneath the handle of the faucet. If this is the case, check to be sure you used the correct size washer and tightened all fittings sufficiently. You might have to go through the entire procedure again.

If the faucet still leaks, the seat inside the faucet might be at fault. Water can leak between the washer and the seat if there is not a good contact between the two. If this is happening, you can "dress" the seat. Follow the instructions on a dressing tool to restore the seat to a smooth, round condition.

If the faucet no longer drips but there is now a leak from around the packing nut, try tightening the packing nut with a wrench. If it still leaks, turn off the water supply and proceed as follows. Once more take the handle off and then remove the packing nut. Replace the washer or Teflon-coated packing, whichever you find when you open the faucet up.

CLOGGED DRAINS

A plunger, or "plumber's friend" is used to unstop clogged drains. To use the plunger, partially fill the fixture with water and place the rubber cup over the drain opening. Work the plunger up and down and the resulting alternate compression and suction will generally dislodge any object caught in the drain. If there is no water in the fixture, the plunger will not work because the water must be present to make an airtight seal around the drain. Be sure to give the plunger a fair chance before you resort to some other method of trying to clear a drain. Once the drain is clear, flush hot water through it to clear it completely.

CLEANING THE TRAP

If the drain cannot be cleared with the plunger, it might be possible to get rid of the obstruction by removing the clean-out plug at the bottom of the trap and using a piece of wire to push the obstruction out or pull it back through the opening (Figs. 10-14 through 10-16). Place a pail under the trap to prevent the water that is in the trap from splashing the floor. Remove the plug carefully so that the water will pour into the bucket. You will need an adjustable wrench to loosen the plug. If the plug is plated, put a piece of cloth around it to prevent the wrench from damaging the plating. Once the plug is out, try to dislodge the obstruction in the pipe with a piece of stiff wire. If this fails, you can remove the entire trap by unscrewing the slip nuts located at the top and bottom connections of the trap. When these two nuts have been loosened and moved out of the way, take off the trap and push out the obstruction. While the trap is off, clean it thoroughly inside with a stiff brush and hot water.

If the object blocking the pipe is beyond the

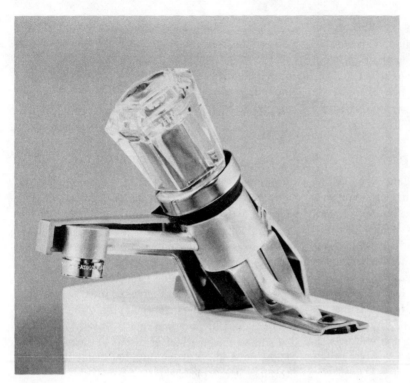

Fig. 10-1. Mixing faucet (Courtesy of Kohler Co.).

Fig. 10-2. Replacement cartridge for faucet (Courtesy of Kohler Co.).

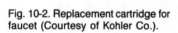

276

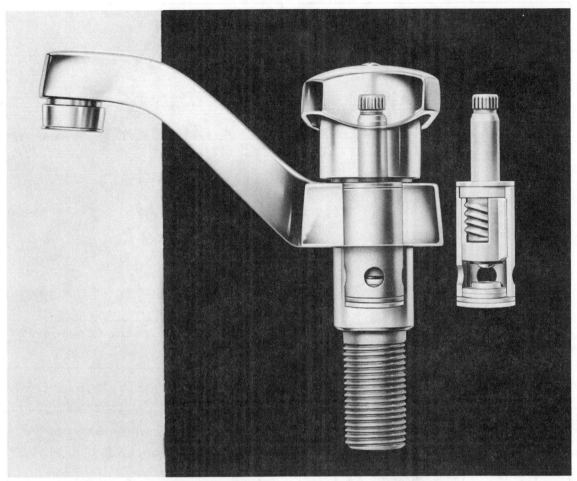

Fig. 10-3. Faucet and cartridge (Courtesy of Kohler Co.).

trap, use a steel spring auger. This resembles a snake in that it is flexible and can be inserted into the pipe. The auger can be rotated and this action will either break up whatever is clogging the pipes, or the auger bit will pierce the obstacle so that it can be pulled out of the pipe.

Before replacing the clean-out plug of the trap, examine the washer to be sure it has not been damaged. Any leakage around this plug will cause the trap to run dry.

Chemical Cleaners. Chemical drain cleaners can be used to clear a pipe when it is impossible to get at the obstruction with a plunger or a steel spring auger. Remove as much water as possible from the fixture and drain so that the chemical will not be diluted. Mix according to the package directions. Be careful not to let any of the solution touch any part of your body. Be sure not to run water through the drain for the recommended length of time, then flush with hot or boiling water.

THE SHOWER DRAIN

Clearing the trap on a shower stall is somewhat different. An often effective treatment is from water pressure from a garden hose. Remove the strainer over the drain and insert the hose as far as possible into the drain. Pack wet rags around the hose to keep it in place and to avoid water splashing back. Have a helper turn the water on while you hold the rags and hose in place. The water pres-

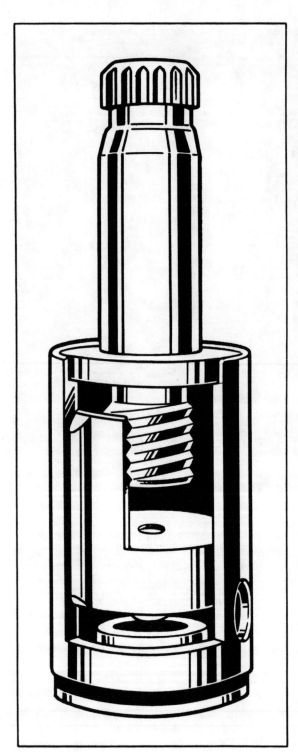

Fig. 10-4. Details of cartridge (Courtesy of Kohler Co.).

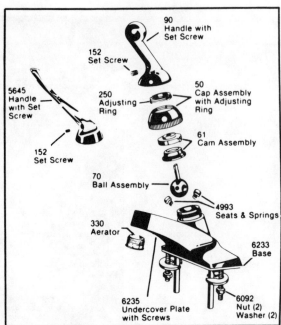

90
Handle with
Set Screw

152
Set Screw

5645
Handle
with Set
Screw

250
Adjusting
Ring

50
Cap Assembly
with Adjusting
Ring

152
Set Screw

61
Cam Assembly

70
Ball Assembly

4993
Seats & Springs

330
Aerator

6233
Base

6235
Undercover Plate
with Screws

6092
Nut (2)
Washer (2)

Fig. 10-5. Details of single level faucet (Courtesy of Delta Faucet Co.).

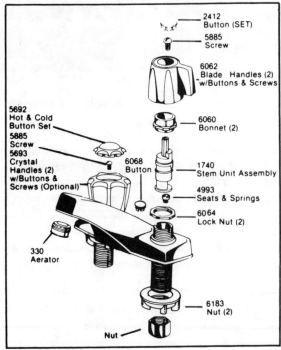

2412
Button (SET)

5885
Screw

6062
Blade Handles (2)
w/Buttons & Screws

5692
Hot & Cold
Button Set

5885
Screw

5693
Crystal
Handles (2)
w/Buttons &
Screws (Optional)

6068
Button

6060
Bonnet (2)

1740
Stem Unit Assembly

4993
Seats & Springs

6064
Lock Nut (2)

330
Aerator

6183
Nut (2)

Nut

Fig. 10-6. Detail of two handle faucet (Courtesy of Delta Faucet Co.).

278

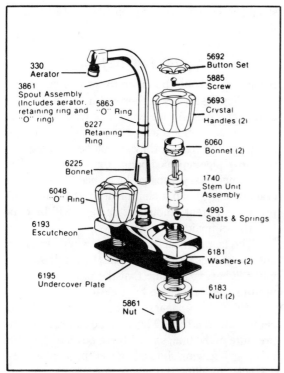

330
Aerator

5692
Button Set

3861
Spout Assembly
(Includes aerator.
retaining ring and   5863
"O" ring)   "O" Ring

5885
Screw

6227
Retaining
Ring

5693
Crystal
Handles (2)

6060
Bonnet (2)

6225
Bonnet

1740
Stem Unit
Assembly

6048
"O" Ring

4993
Seats & Springs

6193
Escutcheon

6181
Washers (2)

6195
Undercover Plate

6183
Nut (2)

5861
Nut

Fig. 10-7. Detail of two handle waterfall faucet (Courtesy of Delta Faucet Co.).

sure may be sufficient to dislodge the obstruction. If not, a plunger may be able to work the clog loose. If that fails, try the chemical cleaner.

NOISY PLUMBING

Many plumbing systems rumble and pound when in use. It can be harmful to the system as well as annoying to the family. Many causes of noisy plumbing can be repaired by the do-it-yourself home mechanic.

A faucet that pounds when it is opened usually does so because of a loose part inside. This can be easily repaired by replacing the washer with a new one or by tightening the loose screw or nut inside the faucet.

Chattering in the pipes can be caused by overhead pipes not secured to the ceiling. When a faucet is opened, water flows through the entire branch of the system of which the faucet is a part. When the faucet is closed, the momentum of the water will cause a loose section of pipe to vibrate. This vibration soon can cause joints to leak. Make certain that all pipes are held securely in place. If they are not, purchase some metal brackets made for

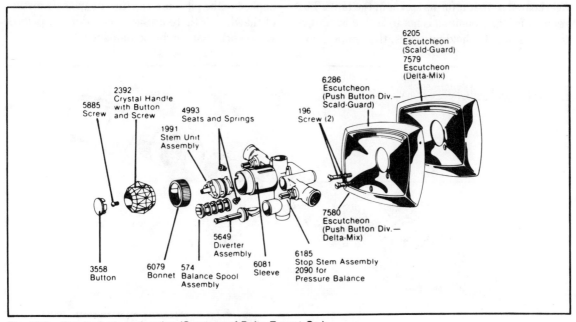

6205
Escutcheon
(Scald-Guard)

7579
Escutcheon
(Delta-Mix)

6.286
Escutcheon
(Push Button Div.—
Scald-Guard)

2392
Crystal Handle
with Button
and Screw

5885
Screw

4993
Seats and Springs

196
Screw (2)

1991
Stem Unit
Assembly

5649
Diverter
Assembly

7580
Escutcheon
(Push Button Div.—
Delta-Mix)

3558
Button

6079
Bonnet

574
Balance Spool
Assembly

6081
Sleeve

6185
Stop Stem Assembly
2090 for
Pressure Balance

Fig. 10-8.   Detail of mix bath valve (Courtesy of Delta Faucet Co.).

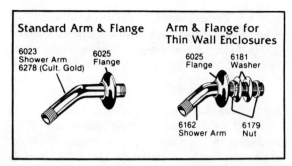

Standard Arm & Flange

6023
Shower Arm
6278 (Cult. Gold)
6025
Flange

Arm & Flange for
Thin Wall Enclosures

6025
Flange
6181
Washer

6162
Shower Arm
6179
Nut

Fig. 10-9. Detail of shower arm (Courtesy of Delta Faucet Co.).

this purpose and use them in sufficient quantity to make all piping secure.

The momentum of water flowing through a pipe is the cause of a condition known as "water hammer." This will cause a chattering and pounding in the system when a faucet is closed. It can be corrected by inserting a short section of pipe in the system, beyond the faucet, that will act as a shock absorber.

Noises in the hot water system are more frequent than in the cold water lines, and they can be due to several factors. A rumble in the hot water tank is generally caused by the water's having been overheated so that it forms steam in the tank. The remedy for this condition is not to let the water get too hot. For household purposes, the temperature should be somewhere between 120 and 140 degrees Fahrenheit.

THAWING FROZEN PIPES

No attempt should be made to thaw frozen pipes until they have been thoroughly inspected for cracks or splits. A pipe will crack when the water inside freezes—not during the thawing process. If there are any cracks, they should be repaired or a section of pipe replaced before thawing begins. Until the necessary repairs have been made on a cracked pipe, keep it shut off from the water supply and no great amount of damage will be done if it thaws unaided.

The fact that the water inside a pipe is frozen does not necessarily mean that the pipe has split, but it is best to assume that the pipe is defective until proven otherwise by a close inspection.

If the pipe appears to be sound, open all faucets connected to it. This is done to decrease the pressure in the line, should there be an undetected opening. Thawing should begin at the point nearest a faucet, to allow the water to run out.

There are various ways of applying heat to the frozen pipe. Bath towels, dipped in hot water and applied to the pipe, are an efficient and safe method of thawing, if there are no decorations or painted woodwork that might be damaged.

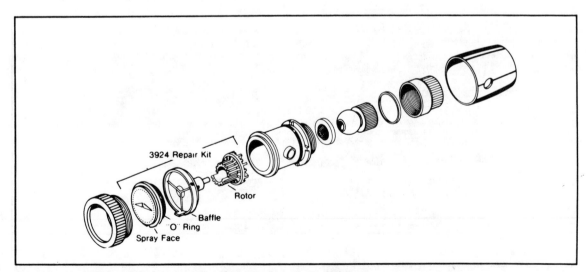

3924 Repair Kit

Rotor

Baffle

"O" Ring

Spray Face

Fig. 10-10. Detail of pulsating showerhead (Courtesy of Delta Faucet Co.).

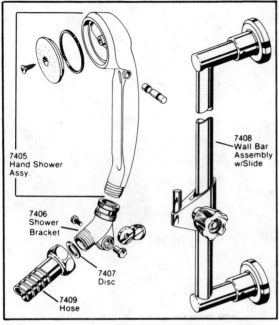

Fig. 10-11. Detail of shower set (Courtesy of Delta Faucet Co.).

A blowtorch can also be used, provided there are no flammable objects about. Play the blow torch back and forth along the length of the pipe and avoid concentrating too much heat at one point. Frozen drain pipes can be thawed by pouring hot water down the drain or by using chemicals that generate heat inside the pipe. Pour the chemicals down a drain in the same manner as chemical drain cleaners.

A very good method of thawing drain lines is to insert a length of small-diameter rubber tubing into the pipe until the end comes in contact with the ice. Attach the other end of the tubing to the spout of a tea kettle containing boiling water. The steam from the kettle will flow through the tubing and soon melt the ice.

Thawing Plastic Pipe. When plastic pipe freezes, do not apply heat directly from a propane or MAPP torch. Do the thawing gently, using hot, wet towels wrapped around the spot you feel is frozen, keeping the towels hot by pouring more hot water on them until the pipes thaw. This may take

Fig. 10-12. Detail of lavatory drain assembly (Courtesy of Delta Faucet Co.).

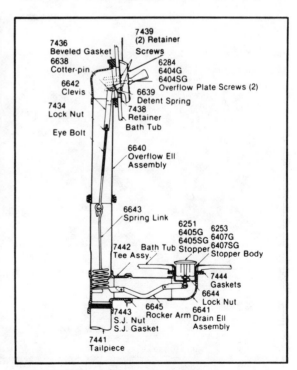

Fig. 10-13. Detail of pop-up bath waste assembly (Courtesy of Delta Faucet Co.).

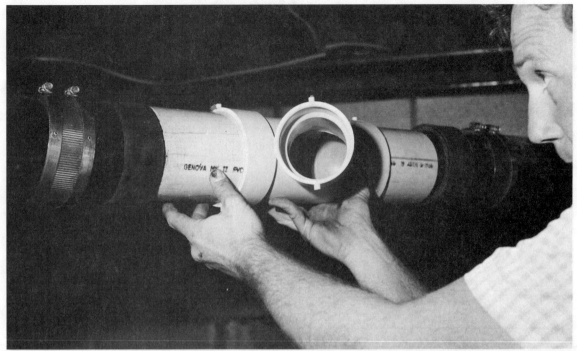

Fig. 10-14. Clean-out plug opening (Courtesy of Genova, Inc.).

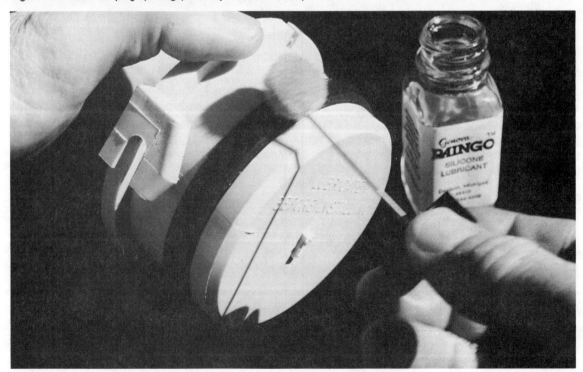

Fig. 10-15. Lubricate the clean-out plug before reinstalling (Courtesy of Genova, Inc.).

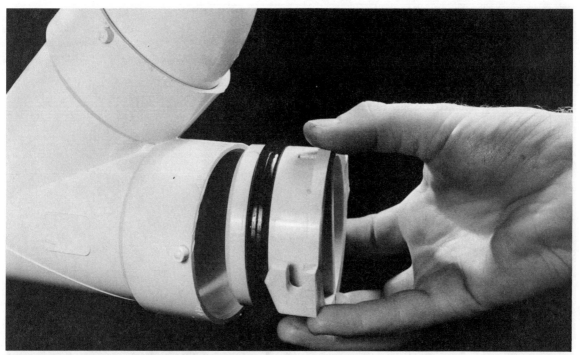

Fig. 10-16. Reinstalling the clean-out plug (Courtesy of Genova, Inc.).

Fig. 10-17. Lead can be poured hot to seal cast iron/PVC joints (Courtesy of Genova, Inc.).

Fig. 10-18. Use oakum to fill (Courtesy of Genova, Inc.).

Fig. 10-19. Plastic lead can also be used (Courtesy of Genova, Inc.).

some time, but it's more sensible than replacing pipe runs when too much heat ruins them.

If the end of a frozen plastic pipe is accessible at a fitting, you might wish to pour hot water from a kettle directly into the detached fitting end. You can use a smaller diameter plastic hose, slipped inside the pipe, to reach faraway frozen areas, feeding the hot water to the smaller line via a funnel.

In general, it is never safe to use open flame on thawing jobs for plastic pipe. Heat tape is not recommended either. If the thermostat doesn't work well it could damage the pipe. Hair dryers can be used, but a check must be kept if they are. If the surface becomes too hot to hold your thumb on, it's too hot and the pipe is going to be damaged if the temperature is held.

Proper installation is the cure for pipe freeze-up, so if yours do freeze, once they're thawed and you're back to using water again, give more than a bit of consideration to locating and changing the problem areas so they'll no longer be problem areas.

SHOWER HEAD REPAIR

When your shower head drips, it is the fault of the handles, just as in a sink faucet. The same method of repair is used. The washer must be replaced, and if the leak is not controlled, replace the packing nut and packing. Other than being mounted on the wall, the shower handles are essentially the same as those at the sink.

LOW WATER PRESSURE

Getting a trickle of water instead of a steady stream can be an annoyance as well as a symptom of a plumbing difficulty. If you have a private water source and the pressure is low in all outlets, you might need to check your source.

If your water is supplied from a city source and your neighbors have plenty of pressure, you might have a problem within the house. First check all shut-off valves to be sure that they are open completely to let a sufficient supply of water through. When the handle is turned all the way clockwise, the valve is completely open.

If just one faucet has low pressure, the prob-

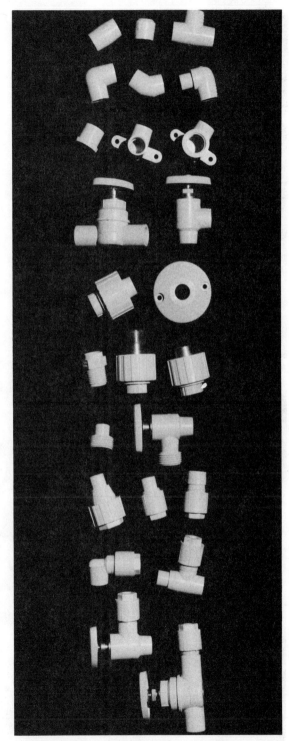

Fig. 10-20. Water supply fittings (Courtesy of Genova, Inc.).

lem is most likely within that faucet. Replacing the washer and cleaning out the inside of the faucet might cure the problem. Be sure to also clean out the mesh screening at the faucet opening that acts as an aerator.

If you still have low pressure, compare the pressure of the hot water supply to that of the cold water supply. If only the hot water pressure is low, the problem could be a clog in the water heater. With the water heater turned off and cool, open the drain valve. This should remove any clog in the pipe. If no clog comes out or your hot water pressure continues to be low, the water heater could be badly corroded and need replacing.

CLEARING THE MAIN DRAIN

Occasionally, the sewer pipe from the house to the septic tank or sewer will become clogged so that the waste water cannot flow out of the system. More often than not, this stoppage is due to some bulky object being forced down a fixture drain. The pipe must be cleared as soon as possible, because a stopped-up sewer pipe will put the entire drainage system out of order. Do not allow any water to go down a drain until the pipe is cleared, or the waste will very likely back up in the pipes and come through the drains at low points in the system.

Most home sewer systems are equipped with a special clean-out plug for just such stoppages. The clean-out plug is usually located in the basement at a point where the sewer line runs through the wall. A brass clean-out plug can be removed with a stilson or a monkey wrench. If the plug is made of iron, it might be necessary to use a cold chisel to start it. If the plug is damaged in this process, you can replace it with a special tapered plug.

Once the plug is out, a "snake" is inserted into the pipe to remove the obstruction. The snake is a long, thin steel band with a heavy point at one end. The steel band is very flexible and can be worked around bends until the point comes in contact with the obstruction in the pipe. By working

Fig. 10-21. Installing a shutoff (Courtesy of Genova, Inc.).

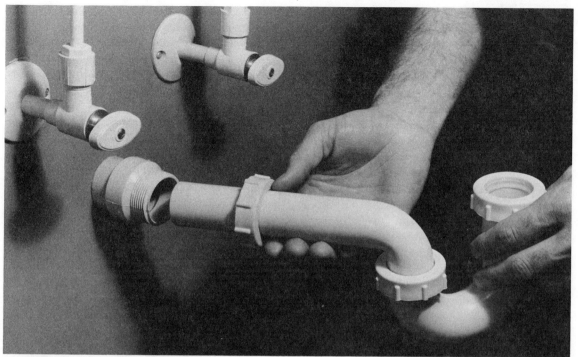

Fig. 10-22. Installing a new trap (Courtesy of Genova, Inc.).

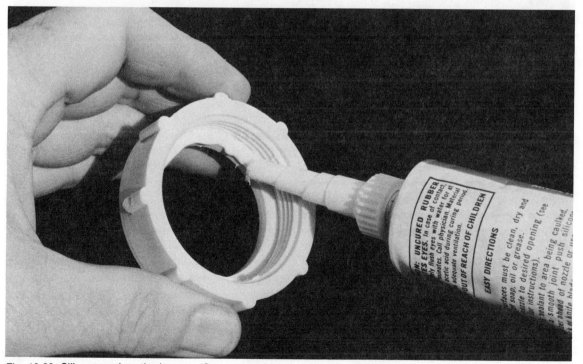

Fig. 10-23. Silicone seal on the jam nut (Courtesy of Genova, Inc.).

the snake back and forth, the object in the pipe is either pushed through the pipe or is broken up into pieces small enough to be carried away by the water. A plumber's snake can be rented from rental outlets. In a poorly installed sewer line, a plugged-up pipe is not uncommon and it may be well to purchase a snake to keep handy.

Cleaning a sewer pipe is an unpleasant task, and if the system continues to clog for no apparent reason, it should be dug up and put down properly.

Underground sewer pipes are subject to attack by tree roots. The small roots work their way through the pipe connections and, if given sufficient time, they will clog the system.

Commercially available products, poured down the fixture drains, will kill the roots but not necessarily remove them completely. A plumber's snake can be used to clear the roots out of the pipe, but this requires considerable effort, especially when the roots are large and densely packed in the pipe.

Plumbers use a powered rotor with a flexible shaft inserted into the pipe, and this will clear the pipe effectively. These are temporary measures, however, for the roots will come back into the pipe. Special sewer pipes are available, constructed so that roots cannot penetrate the pipe joints. When a sewer line is repeatedly attacked by tree roots, the only lasting remedy is to dig it up and have this type of pipe installed.

Outside sewer pipes will fail to operate properly if there is too much or too little pitch to the pipes. While the complete drainage of a pipe depends upon a full charge of water to carry the solid matter through, too much pitch will cause an accumulation of solids at the pipe joints, eventually forming a blockage. To rectify this condition, the pipes should be removed and put down at the right pitch.

Figures 10-17 through 10-19 illustrate how to install and seal a PVC pipe into a cast iron pipe.

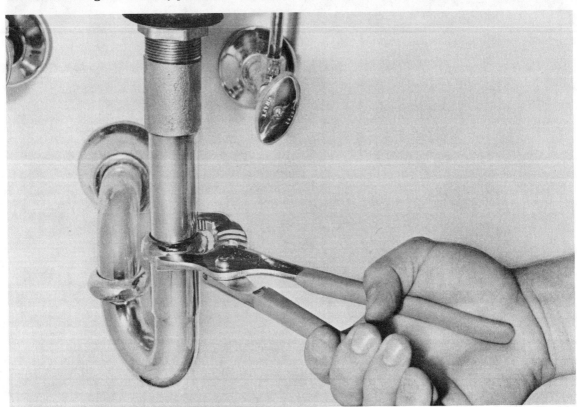

Fig. 10-24. Hand-tightening the sink trap (Courtesy of Crescent).

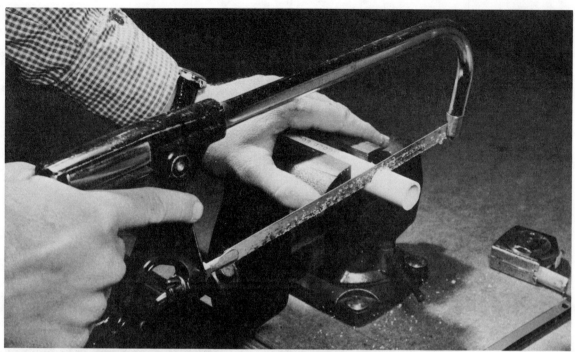

Fig. 10-25. Cutting CPVC pipe for a repair (Courtesy of Genova, Inc.).

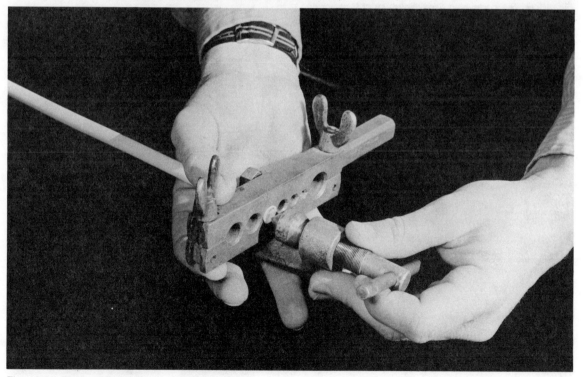

Fig. 10-26. Flaring PB (Courtesy of Genova, Inc.)

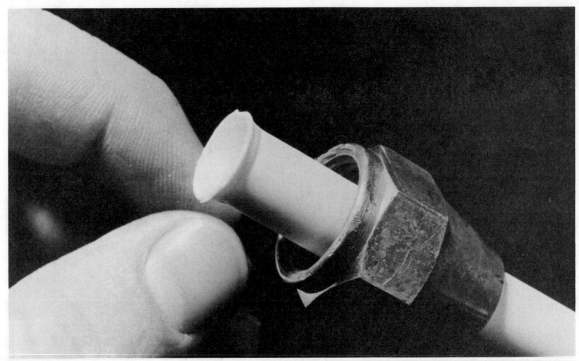

Fig. 10-27. The completed flare (Courtesy of Genova, Inc.).

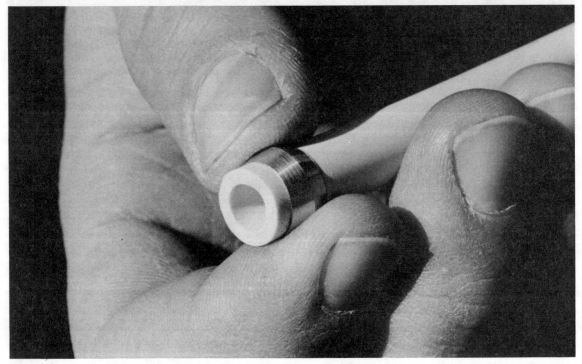

Fig. 10-28. Compression ring on a PB riser (Courtesy of Genova, Inc.).

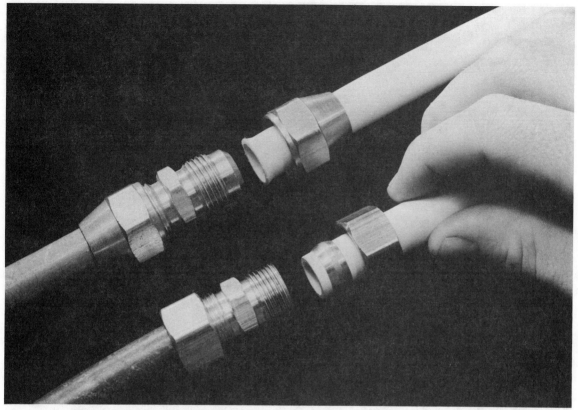

Fig. 10-29. Flare and compression ring side by side (Courtesy of Genova, Inc.).

Figures 10-20 through 10-30 illustrate how to repair and replace bathroom fittings quickly and easily. Refer to installation procedures in earlier chapters for more detailed information.

REPAIRING CRACKS AROUND TUBS AND SHOWERS

As a home settles, cracks can appear in many places, including around the bathtub or shower. Cracks around these areas must be repaired promptly to avoid added damage by water entering the cracks.

Waterproof grout or plastic sealer can be used to repair such cracks. Grout is less expensive, but more difficult to use than plastic sealer. While the sealer comes ready to use in a tube, the grout is in powder form and must be mixed.

Old grouting must be removed before repair can begin. A putty knife will work well. Have newspapers spread over the tub or shower floor while working. Once the grout is removed, use a commercial cleaner to wash the area well. Dry this entire area well and wait about an hour before continuing.

If you are using plastic sealer, apply a line of sealer directly from the tube along the crack. Using a putty knife, push the sealer into the crack and smooth the surface. Plastic sealer dries in just a few minutes.

If you are using grout, mix according to the package directions, until you have a thick paste. Force the grout into the crack with a putty knife and smooth.

REPLACING TILE

If one or a few tiles are missing from the bathroom you can replace them easily if you can match the pattern. The old adhesive must be entirely removed

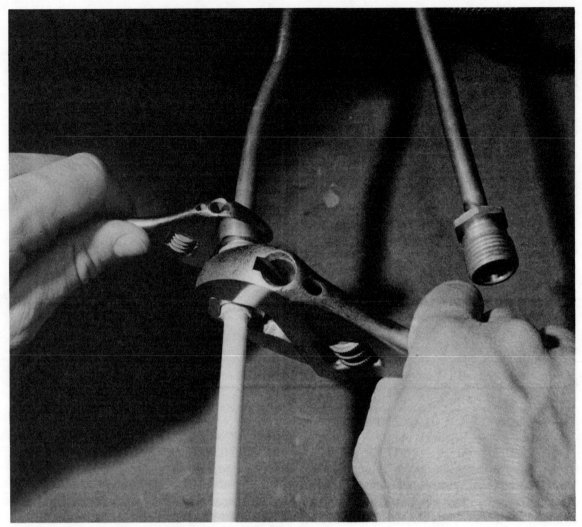

Fig. 10-30. Tightening the fitting (Courtesy of Genova, Inc.).

with a scraper or sandpaper. Check the fit of the new tile. Plastic can be cut with a saw, but if ceramic tile needs cutting you will have to use a cutting tool from a store that sells tiles. Once the fit is correct, spread adhesive on the wall or floor and on the back of the tile and press the tile into place. Wipe off any excess adhesive. If you are working with ceramic tile, you will need to mix a small amount of grout and press it into the tile joints.

YOUR NEW BATH

Congratulations! The bathroom of your dreams can now be yours. Either with all do-it-yourself work or with your efforts plus those of a few experts, you can design and build the bathroom that will meet the needs of your household for many years.

Glossary

aerator—A sievelike device located on a spigot that mixes air with water flow.

air chamber—A chamber placed at the top of a pipe run above a faucet or other fitting to help eliminate the noise of water hammer and the wear caused by water hammer.

air gap—In a water supply system, air gap is the distance between the faucet outlet and the flood line of the basin into which it discharges. Air gap is used to prevent contamination of the water supply by back-siphonage.

anti-siphon—A term applied to valves or other devices designed to eliminate back-siphonage in a system.

backflow—A reverse flow of water or other liquids into water supply pipes carrying potable water. Back-siphonage is a type of backflow.

backflow preventer—A device to prevent backflow.

back-siphonage—A backflow of contaminated water caused by negative pressure in a potable water supply system.

backwater valve—A one-way valve installed in the house drain or sewer that prevents flooding of low-level fixtures when the sewer backs up.

ball-cock—Toilet tank water supply valve, which is controlled by a float ball. The valve is usually of the anti-siphon type.

baseboard—A board placed against the wall around a room next to the floor to make the proper finish between floor and wall.

bidet—A bathroom fixture fitted with both hot and cold water, used for washing the perineal area.

branch—Any part of a piping system other than a riser, a main, or a stack.

branch vent—See revent.

building drain—The lowest house piping receiving discharge from the stack, waste, or other drainage pipes, that then carries that waste to the building sewer outside the house wall.

building sewer—Normally, a line beginning 5 feet outside the building wall (foundation wall). Carries the house sewage underground to the sewer or private disposal system. Need not always be a separate line if a private disposal system is used.

building trap—A device installed in the building drain to prevent gases from the sewer from circulating inside the house drain-waste-vent system.

caulking—Material used to create a water-tight seal.

ceramic—An article made of baked clay. Used to designate a tile made of compressed clay and silica, which is rather glassy or vitreous in nature and will not absorb water.

cesspool—A lined or covered excavation in the ground that receives domestic wastes from the drainage system. Retains organic wastes and solids while allowing liquids to seep through its porous sides and bottom. Seldom legal with current codes.

chlorination—Application of chlorine to water or treated sewage to disinfect or accomplish other biological or chemical results. The process is most often carried out on urban water supply systems, but is sometimes needed to decontaminate rural wells.

cistern—A small covered tank, mainly used to store rainwater for domestic uses other than drinking. Usually placed underground or on a roof.

cleanout—An accessible opening, usually sealed with a screw-threaded male plug (though other forms are available), in the drainage system. Used for cleanout and removal of obstructions.

code—Regulations adopted by local administrative agencies having jurisdiction in residential and other building matters.

CPVC—Chlorinated polyvinyl chlorine. A plastic used to form rigid water supply pipe for residential and other plumbing systems. It withstands heat, cold, and moderately high pressure, and is easily worked and solvent welded, making it a nearly ideal material for water supply lines in the modern residence.

cross-connection—A physical connection between a potable water supply and any non-potable water supply. Such a connection must not exist if the system is to pass inspection.

DWV—Drain-waste-vent. The system that carries away waste water and solid waste.

distribution box—A concrete or other receptacle in the ground with one inlet located above two or more outlets. Used to equally divide the quantity of septic tank effluent among the various branches of a seepage field or bed.

doorjamb—The surrounding case into which and out of which a door closes and opens. It consists of two upright pieces, called side jambs, and a horizontal head jamb.

drain—Part of the drain-waste-vent system, and any pipe that carries waste water or water-borne waste in a building drainage system.

drainage—All the piping that carries sewage, rainwater, and other liquid wastes to their point of disposal or the sewer.

drywall—Interior covering material, such as gypsum board or plywood, that is applied in large sheets or panels.

dry well—An underground excavation used for the leaching of liquids other than sewage into the ground. Usually filled with gravel or small rock.

effluent—The liquid discharge from a septic tank, or any partially treated sewage or other liquid waste.

elbow—A fitting used for making turns in pipe runs.

escutcheon—A wall plate for stub-out to cut-off valve, often used as a partial mechanical support for the water supply system line to a single fixture (Fig. G-1).

fixture supply—Water supply pipe that connects a fixture to a branch water supply pipe or directly to a main water supply pipe.

fixture unit, drainage (dfu)—A measure of the probable discharge into a drainage system for various plumbing fixtures. In small systems such as those in residences, one dfu generally approximates 1 cubic foot of water per minute.

fixture unit, water supply (sfu)—A measure

of the probable demand for water from various plumbing fixtures.

flange—The flat fitting with holes to permit bolting together or fastening to another surface.

float ball—The large copper or plastic ball that floats on the surface of the water in a toilet tank.

flood level rim—The edge of a receptacle, such as a basin, from which water overflows.

flush valve—The device at the bottom of a toilet tank that allows passage of water for flushing the toilet.

galvanizing—Any of several methods of coating a metal, usually steel, with zinc to prevent, or slow, rusting.

grade—The fall or slope of a line or pipes in reference to the true horizontal. Grade is usually expressed as drop in fractions of an inch per foot of pipe length.

hub—Cast iron pipe with one bell-shaped end called a hub and one lipped end called a spigot.

hubless—Cast iron pipe that is without hubs and is joined with neoprene gaskets and clamps.

lath—A building material of wood, metal, gypsum, or insulating board that is fastened to the frame of a building to act as a plaster base.

leaching pit—See seepage pit.

liquid waste—Discharge from any fixture that does not contain fecal matter.

main—Principal pipe to which branches are attached.

main vent—Also known as the stack. Principal vent to which branch vents may be connected.

mechanical fastener—A device not using chemical means or heat to provide support, or keep a joint from separating. Screw threads and nails are prime examples.

mosaic—Small bits of tile, stone, glass, etc., that form a surface design of intricate pattern. Often laid over mortar or metal.

oakum—A fibrous material used to fill large gaps when caulking (Fig. G-2).

pipe joint compound—A sealing compound used on threaded fittings.

pitch—See grade.

plumbing—The practice, materials, and fixtures used in the installation, maintenance, extension, and alteration of all piping, fixtures, and plumbing appliances in connection with any of the following: sanitary drainage, storm drainage and venting systems, and public or private water supply systems within any structure, building, or conveyance. The term covers the extensions of those lines to no more than 5 feet beyond foundation walls of the structure. Not included are gas piping, heating or cooling piping, and pipe for fire sprinklers and stand pipes.

plumbing fixture—A receptacle or other device either permanently or temporarily connected to the water supply system, and which demands a supply of water from that system (Fig. G-3). Discharges used water or other wastes directly or indirectly to the drainage system.

plumbing system—Includes water supply and distribution pipes; plumbing fixtures and traps; drain, waste, and vent pipes; building drains; and includes also their respective connections and devices within a building or structure to a point no more than 5 feet beyond the foundation walls.

potable water—Water free from impurities in amounts sufficient to cause disease or harmful psychological effects; water conforming to the U.S. Public Health Service Drinking Water Standards, or the authority having jurisdiction.

PVC—Polyvinyl chloride. A rigid pipe of plastic, used currently mostly for DWV systems. Somewhat less strong and heat resistant than CPVC, but will meet all requirements for DWV systems and for cold water supply systems.

revent—A pipe installed specifically to vent a fixture trap. Connects with the vent system above the fixture being vented.

riser—A short, vertical pipe in the water supply system, leading from the main, or from a branch to a fixture.

riser tube—A short, flexible tube that connects a fixture to the water supply system.

Fig. G-1. Wall escutcheon (Courtesy of Genova, Inc.).

rough-in—The installation of parts of the plumbing system that can be done before the installation of the fixtures. Rough-in includes drainage, water supply, and vent piping, and any necessary fixture supports, and works with the house framing members.

run—A horizontal or vertical series of pipes.

sanitary sewer—A sewer that carries sewage but not storm, surface, or ground water.

seepage field—An arrangement of perforated or open-joint piping underground to allow septic

296

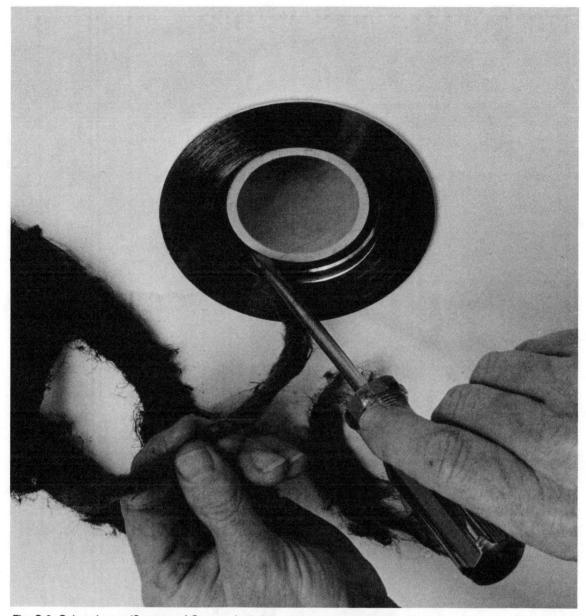

Fig. G-2. Oakum in use (Courtesy of Genova, Inc.).

tank effluent to leach into the surrounding porous soil.

seepage well or pit—Has the same purpose as a seepage field, but is confined to a hole in the ground. Not usually capable of meeting modern codes.

septic tank—A water-tight receptacle that receives raw sewage from the house sewer, digests organic matter retained in it, and allows liquid effluent to discharge into a seepage field or pit.

sewage—Any liquid waste containing animal or

Fig. G-3. Ceramic tile tub fixture (Courtesy of Tile Council of America).

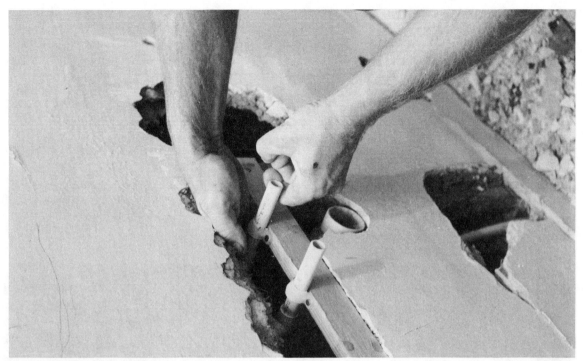

Fig. G-4. Stub-outs (Courtesy of Genova, Inc.).

vegetable matter in suspension or solution. Can also include liquids containing chemicals in solution.

sewage ejector—A device for lifting sewage with a high-velocity stream of air or water.

sewer gas—A family of gases, produced by sewage and in sewage systems, including methane. Some are poisonous, some merely smell bad, and some are explosive, some suffocating. Methane is among the worst because it is heavier than air and settles at the bottom of holes, and is very explosive. Traps are used to keep sewer gas out of the house interior.

slip-joint—A joint used primarily on the fixture side of a trap, made tight with a rubber or plastic washer and a slip-nut.

snake—A coiled tool forced into waste lines to break up obstructions.

soil stack—Main vertical waste pipe. Toilet and branch drains are connected here. The lower end connects into the main house sewage line, the upper end goes through the roof as a vent.

solvent welding—The process by which much plastic pipe is joined to form a plumbing system. The solvent-weld material melts and recombines the plastics it is brushed on, causing fusion of the materials, just as with fusion-welded metals. Materials must be nearly identical for solvent welding.

stack—Any vertical line of drain waste or vent pipes that vents above the roof.

stack venting—A method of venting a fixture through the stack.

storm sewer—A sewer used to carry rain or surface water, cooling water, and similar liquid wastes.

street fitting—A fitting designed to mate directly to another fitting without the need for a length of pipe between the two.

stub-out—The short section of pipe run out, usually capped from the branch or main to the point where a riser tube, or a trap discharge pipe, will meet that main or branch (Fig. G-4). These serve to allow rough-in work to be completed and the walls closed up before the fixtures are installed. The caps remain until the fixture is installed.

subfloor—Boards or plywood laid on joists over which a finish floor is to be laid.

subsoil drain—A drain that collects subsurface water and carries it to a place of disposal.

sweat soldering—The process normally used to join copper pipe and tubing in a system. It requires a good fit at pipe and fittings, and controlled heat applied to a chemically and mechanically clean area that is then fluxed and bonded with tin-lead solder.

temperature-pressure relief valve—Also called a **T & P** valve, or simply a relief valve, this must be installed on top of a water heater to keep the hot water tank from building dangerous pressures inside if the heating system should fail to turn off automatically.

threshold—A strip of wood or metal with beveled edges used over the finish floor to join the floors of two rooms in a doorway.

transition fitting—A fitting specifically designed to join pipe of two different materials, such as copper to plastic, steel to plastic, etc. The transition fitting is designed to accept the different rates of expansion and contraction while still holding a leak-free water seal (Fig. G-5).

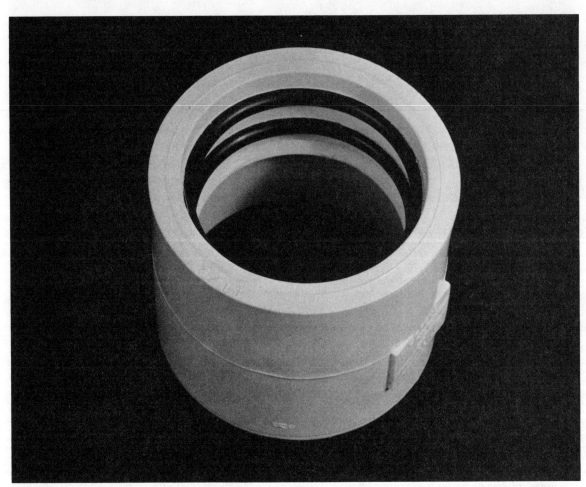

Fig. G-5. Transition adapter, copper to PVC (Courtesy of Genova, Inc.).

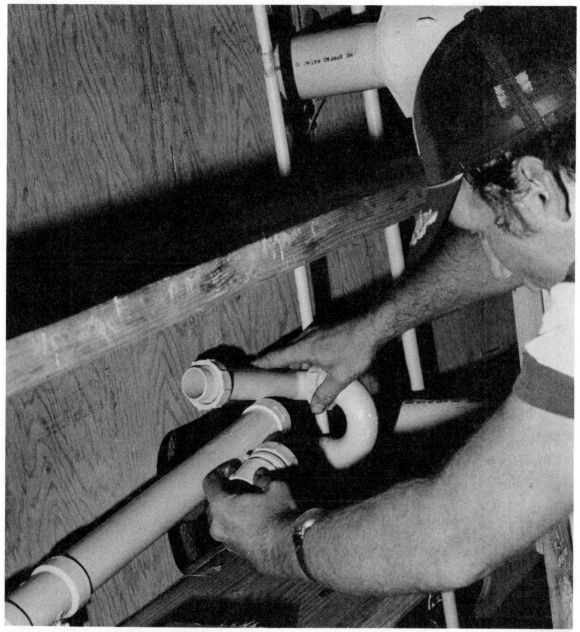

Fig. G-6. Trap being fitted (Courtesy of Genova, Inc.).

trap—A device used to provide a liquid seal to keep sewer gases out of the house without affecting the outflow of sewage or waste water through it (Fig. G-6).

trap seal—The vertical distance between the crown weir (in this case water dam against the passage of air) and the top dip of the cap.

vacuum—For plumbing purposes, any pressure less than that of the atmosphere.

vacuum breaker—A device used in a water supply line to allow air in and prevent back-siphonage from low pressure.

valve—A device that controls the flow of water.

vent stack—A vertical vent pipe installed to provide circulation of air to and from the drainage system.

vent system—A pipe or pipes installed to provide a flow of air to or from a drainage system, or to provide a circulation of air within such a system to protect trap seals from siphonage and back pressure.

waste—Liquid-borne waste free of fecal matter.

water hammer—The noise produced as a system is suddenly shut down, for instance at a shower valve. It causes pounding and overpressure in the system and is eliminated by the installation of properly sized air chambers.

water main—The water supply pipe for public use.

water supply system—The water service entrance pipe, water distribution pipes, and the necessary connecting pipes and fittings, control valves, and devices in or adjacent to the building or premises.

well—Driven, dug or bored hole in the ground from which water is pumped. Dug wells are seldom used any more.

wet-vent—A vent that also receives the discharge of wastes other than from toilets.

Index

Index

Edited by Cherie R. Blazer

Other Bestsellers From TAB

☐ HOME ELECTRICAL WIRING AND MAINTENANCE MADE EASY

With this exceptional sourcebook as your guide, you'll be amazed at how simple it is to learn professional wiring techniques that are in compliance with the most recent National Electrical Code requirements—whether you want to install a light dimmer, inspect your home's wiring system or install a complete wiring system from scratch! 272 pp., 550 illus., 4-color throughout, packed with color illustrations, 8 1/2 " × 11".

Paper $19.95　　　　　　　　　　　**Hard $28.95**
Book No. 2673

☐ ALL ABOUT LAMPS: CONSTRUCTION, REPAIR AND RESTORATION—Coggins

You'll find step-by-step directions for making a wall lamp or a hanging lamp from wood, novelty lamps from PVC plumbing pipe, and designer lamps from acrylic or polyester resins. Shade projects range from needlepoint and fabric models to globes, balls, and tubular forms. There are suggestions for advanced projects, using salvaged and low-cost materials, and more! 192 pp., 196 illus., 7" × 10".

Paper $16.95　　　　　　　　　　　**Hard $24.95**
Book No. 2658

☐ UPHOLSTERY TECHNIQUES ILLUSTRATED—Gheen

Here's an easy-to-follow, step-by-step guide to modern upholstery techniques that covers everything from stripping off old covers and padding to restoring and installing new foundations, stuffing, cushions, and covers. All the most up-to-date pro techniques are included along with lots of time- and money-saving "tricks-of-the-trade" not usually shared by professional upholsters. 352 pp., 549 illus., 7" × 10".

Paper $16.95　　　　　　　　　　　**Hard $27.95**
Book No. 2602

☐ CABINETS AND VANITIES—A BUILDER'S HANDBOOK—Godley

Here in easy-to-follow, step-by-step detail is everything you need to know to design, build, and install your own customized kitchen cabinets and bathroom vanities and cabinets for a fraction of the price charged by professional cabinetmakers or kitchen remodelers . . . and for less than a third of what you'd spend for the most cheaply made ready-made cabinets and vanities! 142 pp., 126 illus., 7" × 10".

Paper $12.95　　　　　　　　　　　**Hard $19.95**
Book No. 1982

☐ HOW TO REPAIR HOME LAUNDRY APPLIANCES—2nd Edition—Gaddis

Covering both electric and gas versions of today's washers, dryers, and hot water heaters—as well as water softening and purifying units—Gaddis shows you, step-by-step, how the machines work and how to get to the root of your problem as quickly and easily as possible. Important tips on needed tools, professional troubleshooting tricks, and proper installation and repair procedures as well as specific repair procedures for both electrical and mechanical systems are all covered in clear, nontechnical language with plenty of show-how diagrams and illustrations to reinforce each step. 230 pp., 137 illus., 7" × 10"

Paper $14.95　　　　　　　　　　　**Hard $21.95**
Book No. 2662

☐ 66 FAMILY HANDYMAN® WOOD PROJECTS

Here are 66 practical, imaginative, and decorative projects . . . literally something for every home and every woodworking skill level from novice to advanced cabinetmaker: room dividers, a free-standing corner bench, china/book cabinet, coffee table, desk and storage units, a built-in sewing center, even your own Shaker furniture reproductions! 210 pp., 306 illus., 7" × 10".

Paper $14.95　　　　　　　　　　　**Hard $21.95**
Book No. 2632

☐ TILE FLOORS—INSTALLING, MAINTAINING AND REPAIRING—Ramsey

Now you can easily install resilient or traditional hard tiles on both walls and floors. Find out how to buy quality resilient floor products at reasonable cost . . . and discover the types and sizes of hard tiles available. Get step-by-step instructions for laying out the floor, selecting needed tools and adhesives, cutting tiles, applying adhesives, and more. 192 pp., 200 illus., 4 pages in full color, 7" × 10".

Paper $12.95　　　　　　　　　　　**Hard $22.95**
Book No. 1998

☐ HARDWOOD FLOORS—INSTALLING, MAINTAINING AND REPAIRING—Ramsey

Do-it-yourself expert Dan Ramsey gives you all the guidance you need to install, restore, maintain, or repair all types of hardwood flooring at costs far below those charged by professional builders and maintenance services. From details on how to select the type of wood floors best suited to your home, to time- and money-saving ways to keep your floors in top-top condition . . . nothing has been left out. 160 pp., 230 illus., 4 pages in full color , 7" × 10".

Paper $10.95　　　　　　　　　　　**Hard $18.95**
Book No. 1928

Other Bestsellers From TAB